Equity and Trusts

YOU'VE GOT IT
CRACKED

Nutshells – your essential revision and starter guides

- Presents you with the essentials of law in clear and straightforward language, explaining the basic principles

- Incorporates colour to help distinguish cases and legislation and aid ease of use

- Breaks the text down into bite-size chunks and includes bullets where appropriate to aid navigation, assimilation and retention of information

- Opens each chapter with a short introduction to outline the key concepts covered and condense complex and important information

- Closes each chapter with a checklist to enable you to check that all your learning needs have been met

- Provides a model question with answer plan at the end of each chapter to enable you to fully prepare for both exam and essay questions

- Includes diagrams throughout to illustrate difficult concepts

- Places important key definitions and statutory provisions in boxes to help highlight the key points to remember

- Contains a host of useful tools including tables of cases and statutes, a list of examination tips, and a list of useful web resources

Available from all good booksellers

NUT**CASES**

Equity and Trusts

SIXTH EDITION

by
CHRIS CHANG
LLB, Barrister (UK)
Advocate and Solicitor (Malaysia)

SWEET & MAXWELL

THOMSON REUTERS

First edition – 1997
Second edition – 2000
Third Edition – 2003
Fourth Edition – 2007
Fifth Edition – 2010

Published in 2013 by Sweet & Maxwell
part of Thomson Reuters (Professional) UK Limited
(Registered in England and Wales, Company No. 1679046. Registered Office and address
for service: Aldgate House, 33 Aldgate High Street, London EC3N 1DL)

For further information on our products and services, visit
www.sweetandmaxwell.co.uk

Typeset by YHT Ltd
Printed in Great Britain by
Ashford Colour Press, Gosport, Hants

No natural forests were destroyed to make this product;
only farmed timber was used and re-planted

A CIP catalogue record for this book is available from the British Library.

ISBN: 978-0-414-02569-1

Contents

Using this Book

DETAILED TABLE OF CONTENTS
for easy navigation.

TABLES OF CASES AND LEGISLATION
for easy reference.

CHAPTER INTRODUCTIONS to outline
the key concepts covered and condense
complex and important information.

Protection of
in Land

INTRODUCTION

The estates and interests cap
Law of Property Act 1925. W'
law depends on its requi
on the Formal and In'
Upon th

BOXED "THINK POINT"
throughout with further case
analysis and questions
to encourage critical thinking.

THINK POINT

Although an owner of land owns t.
to the heavens, there are statutory
the land. Think about what these ar
use of the land.

In addition, other third party ri
owner's use of the land. Consid
be.

ⅈ tests for whethe.
ⅈe two tests set out in *Hollan*ⅈ
ⅈords in Elitestone Ltd v Morris [1997]
ⅈecided that a bungalow erected on pillars
  These cases were also approved in *Ch*ⅈ
(2000) 22 E.G. 147, where it was held that a hⅈ
ropes and connected to utilities was a chatteⅈ
nature of the tenancy of a houseboat was
annexation. In *Cinderella Rockerfellas Ltd v Ru*ⅈ
decided that a vessel which was moored perⅈ
ⅈf the land for the purpose of assessing its ⅈ
  ⅈt it was nonetheless a chattel rather thⅈ
    ⅈ for rating purposes.
      *ⅈssex Reserve Forces & Cad*ⅈ

COLOUR CODING throughout
to help distinguish cases and
legislation from the narrative.
At the first mention, cases are
highlighted in colour and italicised
and legislation is highlighted in
colour and emboldened.

Table of Cases

Table of Statutes

Introduction to Equity and Trusts

1

WHAT IS EQUITY?

Essentially, equity is the law that prior to the Supreme Court of Judicature Acts 1873 and 1875, was applied by the Chancellor and subsequently by the Court of Chancery. Maitland has said that equity is a jurisdiction that is supplementary to, or, a gloss on the common law designed to mitigate its severity. The nature and development of the law is such that it is not possible to give a definitive explanation of what equity is.

> "Equity is no part of the law, but a moral virtue, which qualifies, moderates and reforms the rigour, hardness and edge of the law, and is a universal truth; it does also assist the law where it is defective and weak ... and defends the law from crafty evasions, delusions, and new subtleties, invented and contrived to evade and delude the common law ... . Equity therefore does not destroy the law nor create it but assist it."

Per Sir Nathan Wright in *Lord Dudley v Lady Dudley* (1705) Pr. Ch. 241.

However, whilst the basis of equity are the principles of fairness and equity, the distinction with the common law is not one based on strict rules in the case of the common law and discretion in the case of equity. Harman L.J. in *Campbell Discount Co Ltd v Bridge* [1961] 1 Q.B. 445 (at p.459), stated that "equitable jurisdiction is exercised only on well-known principles".

FUSION OF COMMON LAW AND EQUITY

The Supreme Court of Judicature Acts 1873 and 1875 fused the administration of common law and equity.

Key Principle

There is some suggestion that the **Supreme Court of Judicature Acts 1873 and 1875** have fused the substantive systems of common law and equity.

1

UNITED SCIENTIFIC HOLDINGS LTD V BURNLEY BOROUGH COUNCIL 1977
The issue was whether the timetable specified in a rent review clause in a lease for the completion of various steps for the determination of the new rent payable, in the absence of a contrary intention, was of essence to the contract.

Held

❖ (HL) In the absence of a contrary intention, the timetable specified in a rent review clause was not of the essence to the contract. [1978] A.C. 904.

Commentary

The traditional view is that only the jurisdiction for dispensing common law and equity have fused with the two systems remaining separate. As Professor Ashburner (*Principle of Equity* 1st edn, 1902) suggested, "the two streams of jurisdiction though they run in the same channel; run side by side, and do not mingle their waters". Thus, legal and equitable rights and interests remain separate and distinct but administered in the same court.

However, there are other views that support the contention that the two systems of common law and equity have fused. Lord Diplock in *United Scientific Holdings Ltd v Burnley Borough Council* [1978] A.C. 904 (pp. 924–925) stated that

> "... [t]he innate conservatism of English lawyers may have made them slow to recognise that by the **Judicature Act 1873** the two systems of substantive and adjectival law formerly administered by Courts of Law and Courts of Chancery were fused".

This dictum has been widely criticised as suggesting that the two systems of law and equity are fused and is incorrect.

The better view appears to be that the two systems of common law and equity are not fused but there has been an influence of one system on the other in their development. Somers J. in *Elders Pastoral Ltd v Bank of New Zealand* [1989] 2 N.Z.L.R. 180 (p.193) supports this when he says that

> "...the fact that both are administered by one Court has inevitably meant that each has borrowed from the other in furthering the harmonious development of the law".

The two systems of common law and equity may be coming closer together but they are not yet fused. Indeed, many academics such as Hayton have argued that the common law and equity cannot be fused because legal and equitable rights, interests and remedies are different, and therefore it is wrong to say that the two are fused. This is demonstrated in *Westdeutsche Landesbank Girozentrale v Islington Borough Council* [1996] 2 All E.R. 961, where the House of Lords decided that whilst in equity the court could grant compound interest, at common law the court could only award simple interest, thereby recognizing that the two systems are still separate and distinct. However, this was distinguished in *Sempra Metals Ltd (formerly Metallgesellschaft Ltd) v IRC* [2007] 4 All E.R. 657 where the House of Lords ordered compound interest in the case of a common law claim of restitution. If this is correct then this would support the argument that the common law and equity are coming closer together as the court did not maintain the theoretical distinction between common law and equity.

Further, in *MCC Proceeds Inc v Lehman Brothers International (Europe)* [1998] 4 All E.R. 675 Mummery L.J. was of the view that under the **Judicature Acts** the substantive law was not changed.

TRUSTS DISTINGUISHED FROM OTHER CONCEPTS

[a] Trusts compared with contracts

Key Principle

The presence of a contract does not prevent a trust from arising.

> BARCLAYS BANK LTD V QUISTCLOSE INVESTMENTS LTD 1970
> (See Ch.6.)

Held

❖ (HL) Where the money had been given for a specific purpose that couldn't be carried out, the money was to be held on a resulting trust for the party providing the money. [1970] A.C. 567.

Commentary

Notwithstanding the presence of the contract for the loan, a resulting trust arose where the purpose for which the money was given had failed. This makes it clear that the presence of a contract does not prevent a trust from arising if the circumstances support the existence of a trust.

As regards the definition of a trust, Millett L.J. in *Armitage v Nurse* [1998] Ch. 241 at 253, suggested that a trust created an "...irreducible core of obligations owed by the trustees to the beneficiaries and enforceable by them which is fundamental to the concept of a trust".

[b] Trusts compared with Debt

Key Principle

The restriction on a party's freedom to use an asset does not necessarily mean that a trust exists.

BLUE SKY ONE LTD v MAHAN AIR 2009

One of the claimants was the legal owner of a number of aircraft and the claimants had entered into a series of complicated transactions with regards to the purchase and funding of aircraft. The first defendant airline leased one of these aircraft which was chartered to the second defendant which also controlled the finance company that lent money to the claimant to fund the original purchase. The claimant sought a number of remedies including the delivery of the aircraft which the second defendant had retained. The second defendant alleged that the aircraft had been held on trust for the second defendant or the finance company on the basis that there were restrictions in how they could deal with the aircraft.

Held

❖ (QBD) Where a dispute arose as to whether a trust existed, the claimant had to prove that there was a common intention between the parties as to the existence of a trust. Even though a legal owner was restricted in his ability to use property as he wished as a result of the contract it had entered into, this did not give rise to a trust. [2009] EWHC 3314.

Commentary

In this case the restrictions flowed from the contract and could not form the basis of a trust. However the court did stress that the mere fact that a transaction was a loan did not mean that a trust could not exist (*Barclays Bank Ltd v Quistclose Investments Ltd* [1970], see above). However evidence that the transaction was of a loan would sometimes make it inconsistent with an inference of a resulting trust and the implication would be that the transaction was a debt as opposed to a trust. On the evidence the relationship between the parties appears to be of a debtor and creditor relationship and as a trustee and beneficiary. In *Re Kayford Ltd (in Liquidation)* [1975] 1 W.L.R. 279, the court decided that circumstances which appear to be a debt in fact supported the inference of a trust.

[c] Trusts compared with gifts

Key Principle

Where an intended gift fails, equity will not presume that a trust was intended.

> JONES V LOCK 1865
>
> A father handed a cheque to his nine-month old son stating that "I give this to baby for himself". He then immediately removed the cheque for safekeeping. Although steps were taken to see his solicitor, the father died before he could set up a trust for his son. The cheque was found amongst the father's personal effects.

Held

❖ (CA in Ch) Although there was an intention to make an outright gift, the attempt to make such a gift failed. In the absence of an intention to set up a trust, a trust could not be implied. (1865) L.R. 1 Ch. App. 25.

Commentary

Equity is reluctant to find the existence of a trust where an intended gift fails. However, there may be situations where an intention to create a trust could be inferred, in which case, the court may be prepared to find the existence of a trust. In the case itself, the court was reluctant to find that loose talk by the father could give rise to a trust. A similar conclusion was reached in *Pappadakis v Pappadakis*, *The Times*, January 19, 2000, where the court refused to find that an invalid assignment of a life insurance policy could be regarded as a valid declaration of trust.

Key Principle

There must be a serious intention to create a trust.

> LAMBE V EAMES 1871
>
> (See Ch.2.)

Held

❖ (CA in Ch) The words used by the testator were insufficient to give rise to a trust. The gift to the widow was an absolute gift. [1871] 6 Ch. App. 597.

Commentary

If the court found that a trust existed, the gift to the illegitimate son would have been invalid. However, the court decided the use of precatory words, such as that used in the case, imposed merely a moral as opposed to a legal obligation on the donee.

[d] Trusts and powers

Key Principle

One of the essential differences between a trust and a mere power is that a trust is mandatory (i.e. it imposes a duty on the trustee) whereas a power is discretionary.

> **BURROUGHS V PHILCOX 1840**
> In his will, a testator left property for his two children for life and gave the survivor the power to dispose of the property amongst the testator's nephews and nieces or their children, either all to one of them, or, to as many as the surviving child should think proper.

Held

❖ (Ch) This gave rise to a trust with a power of selection. Upon the failure of the survivor of the two children to exercise the power, the estate was distributed to the nephews and nieces in equal shares. (1840) 5 My. & Cr. 72.

Commentary

Lord Cottenham decided that a trust rather than a power arose on the facts. His Lordship went on to say that the intention will be implemented by fastening a trust on the property.

Key Principle

It is a question of intention whether a trust or a power is intended.

> **RE WEEKES' SETTLEMENT 1897**
> A testatrix gave her husband a life interest in some property with the power to dispose of all such property by will amongst their children. The will did not contain any gift over in default of appointment by the husband. The husband died without exercising the power.

Held

❖ (Ch) The testatrix intended to give her husband a mere power rather than impose a trust. Accordingly, the children were not entitled to the property. [1897] 1 Ch. 289.

Commentary

If a trust existed, then the children would have been entitled to an interest in the property. However, as there was no trust but a mere power, the property went back to her estate on a resulting trust.

[e] Trusts compared with conditional gifts

Key Principle

It is a matter of construction whether a conditional gift or a trust is intended.

> RE FRAME 1939
> A testator gave all his money and insurance policies to a donee on condition that she adopted the testator's daughter and also gave his son and two other daughters £5 each. The donee was unable to obtain an adoption order.

Held

❖ (Ch) The word "condition" used by the testator was not in its strict legal sense. The bequest to the donee was one on trust that the court could enforce. [1939] 2 All E.R. 865.

Commentary

It is clear that the words used to create what is allegedly a conditional gift, are not necessarily conclusive. It is a matter of construction as to whether what was intended was a trust or a conditional gift. As Simonds J. stated (at 867),

> "... [a] devise or bequest, on condition that the devisee or legatee makes certain payments does not import a condition in the strict sense of the word, but a trust".

EQUITABLE DOCTRINES AND MAXIMS

In exercising its equitable discretion, the court relies on various principles and precepts. The common equitable doctrines of satisfaction, performance, conversion and election are one set of the precepts used by the court. The general basis of the equitable doctrines is the equitable maxim "equity imputes an intention to fulfil an obligation" i.e. that there is a presumed intention that a person who has an obligation to perform will carry out that obligation. The doctrines are inter-linked with the equitable maxims and were evolved in the Court of Chancery. Although the maxims and doctrines are still used by the courts, the view is that they are now used by the courts to achieve a particular outcome as the equitable doctrines and maxims are more flexible than rules.

However, over time the equitable doctrines have become less significant. In reality, the doctrines were not necessarily compatible with equity itself given that it is a branch of the law that operates on conscience rather than doctrines. The focus here will be on some of the equitable maxims which are supported by the equitable remedies. These can be said to be the general principles of equity applied by the courts. However, some equitable maxims have been regarded as being equivalent to a rule especially those in respect to title and property.

Key Principle

The application of the equitable maxim "equity deems that as done what ought to be done" means that in some situations an interest in land is deemed to be personalty or vice versa.

FLETCHER v ASHBURNER 1779

The testator left his house and his personal estate to trustees on trust to sell so much of it as shall be necessary to pay his debts and then for his wife for life and thereafter to sell the property and divide it between his son and daughter. In the event that either of the children predeceased the testator's wife, the survivor was entitled to the estate absolutely. The daughter and then the son predeceased the testator's wife. The son's heir at law applied for a conveyance of the real property devised by the will. The next of kin claimed to be entitled to the house because the direction to sell the real property converted it into personalty.

Held

The next of kin were entitled to the property as the direction to sell had converted the real property into personalty. (1779) 1 Bro. C.C. 497.

Commentary

The application of this maxim is the basis for the operation of the doctrine of conversion. Since January 1, 1997, the doctrine of conversion in respect of trusts of land has been abolished: s.3 of the Trusts of Land and Appointment of Trustees Act 1996 ("TLATA 1996"). However it should be noted that the doctrine still applies in a number of cases including under a court order to sell land and where an option to purchase of land has been granted. The equitable maxim applies in cases where there is an agreement for the sale of land or other property and the remedy of specific performance is available. However the maxim and doctrines do not apply where specific performance is unavailable: *Thomas v Howell* (1886) 34 Ch.D. 166.

Key Principle
Equity acts "in personam".

> PENN V LORD BALTIMORE [1750]
> The plaintiff and defendant entered into an agreement as a compromise to disputes between them as regards the boundaries of their lands, and agreed that a particular line should be the boundary. They also agreed that commissioners should delimit the boundary within a certain limited time. This period of time expired before the commencement of this action and the agreement made provision for the conveyances from the one party to the other accordingly. The plaintiff sought specific performance of the agreement.

Held
❖ (LC) The jurisdiction to decide on the boundaries in this case was with the King in Council. However as a result of the contract between the parties the court had jurisdiction to decide this matter. An order for specific performance of the contract which was executed in England was granted in respect of the boundary dispute between two provinces in America. The conscience of the party was bound by the agreement and as the parties were within the jurisdiction of the court, which acts in personam, the court could decide that it was an agreement. (1750) 1 Ves. Sen. 444.

Commentary
This decision is a landmark decision in equity because it laid down the principle that the Court of Chancery could have jurisdiction to decide on the ownership of land outside the court's jurisdiction. It demonstrated the court's readiness to use equity to intervene in appropriate cases and despite the difficulties inherent in this equity provided the means for the court being able to intervene.

Key Principle
He who comes to equity must come with clean hands.

LEE V HALEY 1869

The Plaintiffs had carried on business under the name "The Guinea Coal Company". This was a large business which operated from No. 22 Pall Mall for a number of years. The defendant who was previously in the plaintiffs' employment set up a rival business under the name Pall Mall Guinea Cola Co at No. 46, Pall Mall. The plaintiffs sought to restrain the defendant from trading under that name or any other form which would mislead customers into believing that the defendant's company was the same as the plaintiffs'. The defendant, inter alia, alleged that the plaintiffs did not have the exclusive right to use the name "Guinea Coal Company" as it was used by other businesses in London. The court granted an injunction which restrained the defendant from using the name "The Pall Mall Guinea Coal Company" in Pall Mall. The defendant appealed.

Held

❖ (CA in Ch) Even though the plaintiffs did not have the exclusive right to use the name, the court had properly granted the injunction. This was on the basis that the defendant was not entitled to use the modified name in order to mislead others to believe that the defendant's company and the plaintiffs were the same. However there was no objection to limit the injunction to prevent the use of the name in a particular location. There was no delay on the part of the plaintiff in applying for the injunction which prevented him in seeking the interlocutory injunction. The plaintiff did not have to come to the Court until he had the evidence that others had been misled by the defendant's use of the name. With regards to the allegation of the plaintiffs having intentionally sold short weight, if the defendant had been able to prove this it would have prevented the plaintiffs from being granted the interlocutory injunction. (1869) 5 Ch. App. 155.

Commentary

The court made it clear that if the plaintiffs did not come to court with clean hands, it would have prevented them from being granted the equitable remedy on the basis of the maxim. On the facts of the case although the defendant made the allegation it was not proven in court. However as will be seen in Chapter 5, the maxim does not necessarily mean that a claimant who does not come with clean hands will be denied a remedy. In *Tinsley v Milligan* [1994] 1 A.C. 340 the House of Lords decided that a claimant to an interest in a property was entitled to succeed if the claim did not rely on pleading an illegality notwithstanding that the title was acquired in the course of an illegal transaction. See also *Tribe v Tribe* [1995] 4 All E.R. 236.

Key Principle

He who seeks equity must do equity.

> **O'SULLIVAN V MANAGEMENT AGENCY AND MUSIC LTD 1985**
>
> In 1970, O'Sullivan who was a young and unknown composer and performer of popular music, entered into a management contract which had unfavourable terms without independent legal advice. O'Sullivan became successful and after the parties fell out he brought an action against the management company claiming that the management contract was void because of undue influence. The company acknowledged the claim but denied that it had to pay all the profits it had made back to O'Sullivan and one of the grounds for their argument was that "he who comes to equity must do equity".

Held

❖ (CA) O'Sullivan was entitled to have the management contract set aside even though restitutio in integrum was not possible as the contract had been performed. Where a contract had been entered into by a person as a result of a breach a fiduciary relationship as in this case, it could be set aside in equity even though the court could not place the parties in the exact position they would have been in before the contract was entered into. However, the court should try and achieve what was just between the parties by asking the wrongdoer to give up his profits whilst at the same time providing remuneration for the work done. In this case as O'Sullivan would not have become famous had it not been for the management company, the latter was entitled to reasonable remuneration including providing a profit element for all their work. [1985] 3 All E.R. 351.

Commentary

The essential basis of this maxim is that the claimant would not be given the equity's support unless he or she had also acted fairly. Therefore the court will not grant a remedy in favour of a claimant who has done an illegal act unless, as noted above, the claimant does not have to rely on the illegal act or purposes in order to support the claim.

Key Principle

Equity looks to intent and not to form.

PAUL V CONSTANCE 1977
(See Ch.2.)

Held

❖ (CA) The repeated statement that the money was "as much yours as mine" was sufficient to constitute a declaration of trust in favour of himself and the plaintiff. [1977] 1 W.L.R. 527.

Commentary

The court in reaching this conclusion applied the maxim "equity looks to intent not to for" and found the existence of an intention to create a trust despite the settlor not using the term trust nor putting this down in writing or in a formal way. So long as the intention to create a trust is clear the court will be prepared to find the existence of a trust. The corollary is that if what was intended was a gift which failed because of the lack of formalities then the court would be reluctant to find the existence of a trust in order to save the gift unless the requisite intent was present: *Jones v Lock* (1865) L.R. 1 Ch. App. 25.

Key Principle

Equity will presume that an act done by a covenantor is in performance of his covenant.

LECHMERE V LADY LECHMERE 1735
The settlor covenanted that he would buy freehold land worth £30,000 within a year of his marriage and settle it on trust for himself for life, with a jointure in remainder for the defendant, thereafter a remainder to their sons in tail male, with a remainder to the settlor, his heirs and assigns forever. At the time of the marriage the settlor owned some plots of lands in fee simple. He later acquired some life interests and reversionary interests in land. More than a year after his marriage, he bought some fee simple estates but did not settle these on trust for the defendant. The issue was whether any of the purchases could be regarded as being in performance of the covenant.

Held

The land, which was owned at the time the covenant was made, would not be covered by it. Likewise, the life interests and the reversionary estates did not fall under the covenant as these were of a different nature from that covenanted. However, the fee simple estates purchased subsequently would be regarded as being in performance of the covenant, even though they were bought more than a year after the marriage. (1735) Cas. t. Talb. 80.

Commentary
This decision is important because it makes it clear that:
- [i]   there can be partial performance of a covenant;
- [ii]   if the property purchased is different in nature from that covenanted there is no performance; and
- [iii] any property owned by the covenantor prior to the covenant being made would not normally be covered by it.

Other equitable maxims and principles which the courts apply include the following:
- Delay defeats equities;
- Where the equities are equal the first in time prevails;
- Equity imputes an intention to fulfil an obligation;
- Equity follows the (common) law;
- Equity will not suffer a wrong without a remedy;
- Equity will not allow a trust to fail for want of a trustee (see Chapter 7);
- Equality is equity;
- Equity imputes an intention to fulfil an obligation;
- Equity will not allow the use of a statute or law as an instrument of fraud (see Chapter 3);
- Equity will not assist a volunteer (see Chapter 2); and
- Equity will not perfect an imperfect gift (see Chapter 2).

THINK POINT

What is the difference between a mere power fiduciary and mere power non fiduciary? How are the obligations of the donee of the power different?

What approach will the court take when two or more of the equitable maxims apply but each leads to a different outcome? How would the court resolve the conflict?

Creation of Express Private Trusts

2

INTRODUCTION

In order for a private express trust to be valid, the trust must satisfy the three certainties, it must comply with the requisite formalities for the creation of a private trust and the title to the property must be properly vested in the hands of the trustees in consequence of a declaration of trust.

In *Knight v Knight* (1840) 3 Beav. 148, the court made it clear that the three certainties for the creation of a private trust are the:

- certainty of intention;
- certainty of subject matter; and
- certainty of objects.

The formalities for the creation of a private trust are contained in ss.53(1)(b) and (c) of the Law of Property Act 1925. The constitution of trust revolves around the vesting of the trust property in the hands of the trustee and this may also involve compliance with the appropriate formalities.

[A] CERTAINTIES

(i) Certainty of intention

Key Principle

There must be certainty of intention to create a binding trust. Precatory words will not be sufficient to evince such an intention.

> LAMBE V EAMES 1871
> A testator left his estate to his widow. The bequest was phrased "to be at her disposal in any way she may think best, for the benefit of herself and her family". The widow by her will gave part of the estate to an illegitimate son of one of the testator's sons.

Held

❖ (CA in Ch) The gift to the illegitimate son was valid as the property was not subject to a trust. (1871) 6 Ch. App. 597.

RE ADAMS AND THE KENSINGTON VESTRY 1884

A testator left all his estate to his widow absolutely. The bequest was phrased to be

> "in full confidence that she would do what was right as to the disposal thereof between the children either in her lifetime or by will after her decease".

Held

❖ (CA) The wife took an absolute interest in the property unfettered by any trust in favour of the children. (1884) 27 Ch. D. 394.

RE B 1999

Upon separating a couple negotiated a settlement. The court approved this and made a consent order. Under the agreement, title to the family home was transferred to the mother who remained there and brought up the child there. She maintained the house and took over the mortgage loan payments on it. The father had a 30 per cent charge on the house to be realised on its sale and was responsible for maintenance payments for the child until she finished full-time education. Subsequently, the child fell out with her mother. She claimed that she was entitled to the 70 per cent of the house held by the mother. The father signed an affidavit that he would not have agreed to the reduction in his share of the house unless he believed the daughter would get the remainder. The consent order had provided that the house was to be held for "the benefit of the said child".

Held

❖ (CA) The child was not entitled to a beneficial interest in the house. The consent order had been badly drafted and the words "for the benefit of the said child" could be ignored for the purpose of creating an express trust in the child's favour. It could not have been intended that the mother would have borne the cost of bringing up the child and making the mortgage loan repayments but then not have a beneficial interest in the house. (1999) 2 F.L.R. 418.

Commentary

In *Lambe v Eames*, the breadth of the wife's discretion was such as to indicate a gift rather than a holding on trust. On the terms of the will the wife could retain or dispose of the property, as she thought best. Similarly, in *Re Adams and the Kensington Vestry*, there was no obligation on the wife and hence no claim by any other party to an interest in the property. In *Re B*, the evidence clearly contradicted the meaning of the words.

Key Principle

Precatory words may set up a future executory gift.

> COMISKEY V BOWRING-HANBURY 1905
>
> A testator left his estate to his widow absolutely. The bequest was phrased to be in full confidence that she would make such use of it as the testator should have made of it and upon her death she would devise it amongst such of her nieces as she thought fit. In default of any disposition by her, during her life or by will, the property was to be equally divided amongst the nieces.

Held

❖ (HL) There was an absolute gift to the widow subject to an executory gift to such, if any, of the nieces she should choose. [1905] A.C. 84.

Commentary

The words used are similar to those in *Re Adams and the Kensington Vestry*, above, where there was held to be no trust. Here, there is a difference. There is no trust binding on the widow during her life because she could dispose of the entire property. There is, however, a potential gift to the nieces whereby they could expect an equal share if the widow made no disposition or, if she did make a disposition, they could expect to be in the class of discretionary beneficiaries. The court stressed that in ascertaining the question of certainty the court had to construe the document as a whole and in this case this gave rise to evidence of a trust. In *Harrison v Gibson* [2006] 1 All E.R. 858, the court stressed that where there is a formal trust document this needs to be construed in its entirety. The court should give the words used their normal meaning but take into account the context in which they are used. See also *Wallbank v Price* [2007] EWHC 3001 on the difficulty in construing a document drafted by a lay person as to the intention of the parties.

Key Principle

Circumstances including a pattern of behaviour or dealing may constitute sufficient evidence of intent to declare a trust.

PAUL V CONSTANCE 1977

The deceased separated from his wife in 1965. In 1967 he set up home with the plaintiff until his death in 1974. In 1969, the deceased received £950 compensation for an industrial injury. This was placed into a deposit account in the deceased's name but money was withdrawn and used for their joint purposes. On several occasions the deceased said "the money is as much yours as mine". The deceased died intestate and the defendant, who was the widow, claimed his estate.

Held

❖ (CA) Dismissing the defendant's appeal, in the circumstances the repeated statement that the money was "as much yours as mine" was sufficient to constitute a declaration of trust in favour of himself and the plaintiff. The judge was correct to award the plaintiff a half share. [1977] 1 W.L.R. 527.

ROWE V PRANCE 1999

The claimant sought a declaration that she was the beneficial owner of a half share of a yacht, which was in the name of the defendant. She claimed that the defendant expressly constituted himself as trustee of the yacht. Although he was married to another woman, the claimant and defendant had lived together on the yacht and she had given up her flat in order to do so.

Held

❖ (Ch D) The claimant was entitled to a half share under an express trust. The defendant had frequently referred to the yacht as "ours" and had spoken in terms of the yacht giving her "security" in the sense that she had an interest in it. He had also explained that the yacht couldn't be in her name as she was not a qualified Ocean Master. The circumstances indicated that she had a substantial interest. The court used the equitable principle that "equality is equity" and gave her a half share in the proceeds of sale. (1999) 2 F.L.R. 787.

Commentary

[1] To create an express trust, the settlor's words and actions must show a clear intention to dispose of the property in such a way that someone else could acquire a beneficial interest. In *Re Steele's Will Trusts* [1948] Ch. 603 it was held that a valid trust was created where previously judicially approved words were used. In the case there was evidence that the settlor relied on the words of the earlier case to create a valid trust. Similarly in *Re Harding (Deceased)* [2007] EWHC 3, the court held that the words "it is my wish that everything I possess be taken over by the Diocese of Westminster to hold in

trust ..." created a valid trust. This was because of the use of the words "in trust" following the prior use of precatory words evidenced an intention to create a trust.

In *Margulies v Margulies*, Lawtel, March 16, 2000, the Court of Appeal found insufficient evidence of an intention to create a trust, where, a father who had excluded a son from his will wrote a number of letters to his solicitor. It was argued that this showed a favourable change in attitude to the son. It was held that the father was well used to instructing solicitors and that if he had intended to make any binding arrangements he would have done so. In *Duggan v Governor of HMP Full Sutton* (2004) 2 All E.R. 966, money which a prisoner was required under prison rules to transfer to the prison governor for safekeeping, was not held on trust as there was no intention to create a trust. The relationship was more akin to that of banker and customer. The claimant's argument that the money should have been held in a separate interest bearing account failed. The same conclusion was reached in *Azam v Iqbal* [2007] EWHC 2025 but in *Re Ahmed & Co* [2006] EWHC 480, the court concluded that the Law Society's obligation to create a fund to hold monies when exercising its regulatory powers over solicitors constituted a trust.

[2] Where the terms of the trust are unclear, this negates an intention to create a trust. In *Re Challoner Club Ltd*, *The Times*, November 4, 1997, the trust failed because there was uncertainty of the terms of the trust. Likewise, in *Pappadakis v Pappadakis* [2000] W.T.L.R. 719, a document entitled "Declaration of Trust" which was intended to take effect as an assignment of a life policy could not be regarded as creating a trust where no trustees had been identified.

Key Principle

In the interpretation of documents the court will look at the objective meaning of the words used as opposed to the subjective intention of the parties.

SHAH V SHAH 2010

The claimant sought to dispose of shares in favour of his brother by signing a letter to that effect. In the letter he stated

> "this letter is to confirm that out of my shareholding of current 12,500 in the above company I am as from today holding 4,000 shares in the above company for you subject to you being responsible for all tax consequences and liabilities [arising] from this declaration and letter ...".

There had been a family feud which gave rise to previous legal proceedings. He delivered the letter with a signed share transfer form but
did not provide the share certificate. The claimant subsequently "argued
that this was not sufficient to vest the legal title in the share in his
brother. He contended that at most the letter was a gift rather than a
declaration of trust and as it was incomplete and not constituted it was
ineffective because of the maxim that equity will not assist a volunteer.
Alternatively, he argued that the disposition was as a result of a misrepresentation by two of his brothers or a mistake. The judge found
against the claimant who appealed.

Held

❖ (CA) When interpreting a document, the court needs to have regard to the
intention of the person making the statement as manifested by the words
used taking into account all the relevant circumstances of the case. It should
not have regard to the subjective intention of the person making the statement. On the facts of the case the claimant had manifested an intention that
the letter was to take effect immediately. From the evidence it was clear that
the parties intended the registration to take place subsequently and the
claimant had used the words "I am ... holding" rather than "assigning" or
"giving". He also referred to the document as a "declaration". As such the
inference was that he was to hold the shares until they were legally transferred to his brother on registration of the shares which accordingly must be
taken to have intended a trust and not a gift. There was no error by the judge
and on the issue of misrepresentation the judge was entitled to reach the
conclusion that there was no misrepresentation on the evidence before him.
[2010] All E.R. (D) 121.

Commentary

It is clear that where the words to be interpreted are in a document the court
is directed to look at the objective meaning of the words used, construed in
the context of the relevant circumstances of the case instead of the subjective intent of the parties. It had to come to a conclusion on the meaning
based on what was said rather than what was intended. A similar approach
was also taken in *Webb v Oldfield* [2010] EWHC 3469. Clause 2 of the will
stated that the executors should protect the claimant's money "by the discretion of [the] executors in view of addiction". However, clause 3 provided
that the residue of the estate was given the beneficiaries absolutely in equal
shares. The court was asked to consider if clause 3 made the gift absolute
despite the provisions of clause 2. The judge stated (at para.21) that

"... I am to discern the intentions of the testatrix from the words used by her in the will itself to express her intention, when considered against the relevant background to the case. It is not open to the court to rewrite the will so as to import into it what the testatrix might have intended to say".

The court decided that clause 2 did not give rise to a discretionary trust in respect of the share given by the clause 3 to the claimant. The claimant was therefore entitled to the one-third share of residue absolutely.

(ii) Certainty of subject matter

Key Principle
The subject matter of a trust must be identified with certainty.

> PALMER V SIMMONDS 1854
> A testatrix bequeathed her residuary estate to A. The bequest was phrased to be for his own use and benefit in full confidence if he should die without children, he would, after providing for his widow, leave the bulk of her residuary estate to B, C, D, and E.

Held
❖ (VCC) The terms of the bequest did not describe the subject of the gift with sufficient certainty to create a trust. (1854) 2 Drew. 221.

Commentary
[1] There was no binding obligation on the inheritor to hold the property on trust during his lifetime. Being for his full use and benefit he could dispose of it as he wished. As in *Comiskey v Bowring-Hanbury*, there could have been an executory gift but unlike that case there was no way of ascertaining the subject matter of the potential gift. Thus B, C, D and E would not be beneficiaries able to enforce the gift.

[2] Difficulties arise where there is a trust of part of a homogenous bulk, for example, "10 per cent of the shares I hold in X company" without having set aside the specific shares for the trust. In *Re London Wine Co (Shippers) Ltd* [1986] P.C.C. 121, the court held that there was no certainty of subject matter where the subject matter had not been separated from the bulk. A similar conclusion was reached in *Re Goldcorp Exchange Ltd* [1994] 3 W.L.R. 199 which concerned the sale of gold which had not been specifically identified and allocated to the plaintiffs. However, in *Hunter v Moss* [1993] 3 All E.R. 215, there was a valid trust where the subject matter was 50 shares out of a

shareholding of 950 shares even though it had not been separated from the rest of the shares. This later decision was followed in *Holland v Newbury* [1997] 2 B.C.L.C. 369 which distinguished *Hunter v Moss* with *Re Goldcorp Exchange* on the basis that shares were different from gold.

Key Principle
The investment powers relating to the subject matter of a trust must be identified with certainty.

RE KOLB'S WILL TRUSTS 1962
A testator bequeathed his estate to trustees on trust to invest in "such stocks, shares and/or convertible debentures in the blue chip category" as his trustees thought fit but not to invest in British or other government securities or trustee securities or fixed interest stock or debentures. The trustees sought a declaration as to the meaning of the instructions as to investment.

Held
❖ (Ch) The term "blue chip" depended on the standards of the testator and was not an objective quality. The testator had not communicated his standard of blue chip to the trustees and thus the investment instructions were void for uncertainty. [1962] Ch. 531.

Commentary
Here, the subject matter was not uncertain but the means of investing it was. The trust was still valid but its investment terms were void for uncertainty. The statutory powers of investment consequently applied.

Key Principle
An uncertain term as to subject matter may be valid if there is a means of ascertaining its value.

RE GOLAY'S WILL TRUSTS 1965
The testator directed that the beneficiary of his will benefit from the use of a flat during her lifetime and "receive a reasonable income from my other properties ...". The trustee sought a declaration that the direction was void for uncertainty.

Held

❖ (Ch) The phrase "reasonable income" was capable of being interpreted. The testator's intention could be given effect. The phrase was not meant to depend on the subjective interpretation of another person. It could be objectively determined by the court. [1965] 1 W.L.R. 969.

Commentary

The court's view was that it could make an assessment as to what this "reasonable income" was as it was familiar with making such assessments in family and succession law cases. The courts appear willing to save a term if it is ascertainable even if it has not been pre-defined with exact certainty. This judgment has been criticized as misunderstanding the function of the certainty of subject matter test in that the test is to ensure that the trustees can administer the trust. Hence, the requirement that trustees must know exactly the subject matter of the trust. In this context "reasonable income" does not seem to provide that certainty.

Key Principle

A residuary sum is not sufficiently certain if it is in the power of the donee to determine its size.

SPRANGE V BARNARD 1789
The testatrix left £300 to her husband. The bequest was phrased: "by which she gives it to her husband; but so much as shall be remaining at his death to her brother and sisters".

Held

❖ (Rolls Court) The £300 vested absolutely in the husband. The property to be left over to the relatives was not sufficiently certain to give rise to a trust. (1789) 2 Bro. C.C. 585.

Commentary

This case could easily have been decided on the point that there was inconclusive intent to create a trust. However, the case is decided on the point that there is no certainty of subject matter. See also *Re Last* [1958] 1 All E.R. 316 and *Ottaway v Norman* [1972] 2 W.L.R. 50.

(iii) Certainty of objects

There must be a beneficiary who can enforce the trust.

> RE ENDACOTT 1960
> The testator left his residuary estate to the Parish Council "for the purpose of providing some useful memorial to myself".

Held

❖ (CA) As a matter of construction, the bequest was not a gift but imposed an obligation in the nature of a trust. The trust could not be charitable because the parish's activities were not solely charitable. The gift could not take effect as a non-charitable trust, because its terms were insufficiently certain. [1960] Ch. 232.

Commentary

Normally, a trust must have human beneficiaries or a charity as its beneficiary in order to be enforceable. There is an anomalous class of gifts to public bodies, which though not charitable can be held to be bound in trust where the bequest is sufficiently precise. This case fell outside the anomalous class. The gift was thus void for lack of a beneficiary. A beneficiary who can enforce, is an essential element of a trust: *Morice v Bishop of Durham* (1805) 10 Ves. 522.

Key Principle

In a discretionary trust it is sufficient that it can be said with certainty whether a given person falls within the class or not.

> McPHAIL V DOULTON 1971
> A settlement was made of shares for the benefit of employees of the company and their relatives and dependants. The trustees had absolute discretion as to how, whether or when they should distribute money from the fund. The executors of the settlor's estate argued that the settlement was void for uncertainty.

Held

❖ (HL) The settlement created a trust not merely a power. The test for certainty of objects in a discretionary trust was whether it could be said with certainty whether any given individual was or was not a member of the class. [1971] A.C. 424.

Commentary

[1] In a fixed trust, all beneficiaries must be ascertained or ascertainable and hence a complete list needs to be capable of being drawn up for there to be certainty of objects: *IRC v Broadway Cottages* [1955] Ch. 20.

[2] In *McPhail v Doulton*, the formulation for the test of certainty for a discretionary trust was in fact taken from the test set out for powers in *Re Gulbenkian's Settlement*, below. The logic behind the new test was that a trustee could discharge his duty within the terms of his discretion without necessarily knowing at any one time whom all the potential beneficiaries were. This is illustrated by the terms of the discretion here, where it was not intended that the trustees should use up the fund's income in any one year but could hold back money, till the need arose. Equally, if a significant need arose then capital could be used from the fund.

[3] In *Schmidt v Rosewood Trust* [2003] 2 All E.R. 76, the question arose as to whether the mere object of a power was entitled to disclosure of trust accounts and information. It was held that such a person was entitled to disclosure in relation to personal matters but that the court had jurisdiction to supervise disclosure to balance the interests of all the parties. In the case of a discretionary trust, it was held in *Breakspear v Ackland* [2008] EWHC 220 that trustees should keep confidential the settlor's wishes as regards the exercise of their discretion contained in a "wish letter" to enable the trustees to make appropriate enquiries. However, Briggs J. suggested that the trustees may relax or abandon the confidentiality of the "wish letters" as they think fit, taking into account the needs and interests of the beneficiaries.

The Privy Council in *Schmidt v Rosewood Trust* also approved the dicta of Lord Wilberforce in *McPhail v Doulton* on the issue of the distinctions and similarities between trusts and powers. It was stressed that the key distinction was that in a discretionary trust of income there was a mandatory trust to pay the income with discretion to select shares and recipients. In the case of a power, there was no necessary obligation to pay out income. Of the similarities between discretionary trusts and powers it was affirmed that both discretionary beneficiaries and objects of powers had the right to be considered by trustees but could not terminate the trust.

In applying the test in *McPhail v Doulton* the court should look to the conceptual certainty of the description of the class.

RE BADEN'S DEED TRUSTS (NO. 2) 1973
The House of Lords in *McPhail v Doulton* remitted the case back to the Chancery Division in order to apply the test as now set out.

Held

❖ (CA) Affirming the application of the test by the Chancery Division the court said it was necessary to distinguish between conceptual certainty and evidential difficulty. The terms "relatives" and "dependants" were not conceptually uncertain. They could each be given the widest meaning attributable, which would avoid uncertainty. Relatives could be interpreted as meaning "all descendants of a common ancestor" which would be sufficiently conceptually certain for a person to be identified as being within that class or not. [1973] Ch. 9.

Commentary

The issue was whether a court could find sufficient conceptual certainty in the terms used, against which a person could be tested as to whether he came within the class or not. In *Re Tuck's Settlement Trusts* [1978] Ch. 49, the phrase "an approved wife" was regarded as conceptually certain as it was qualified by the term "of Jewish blood by one or both of her parents". This latter term could itself be subject to ascertainment by the Chief Rabbi. In *Re Barlow's Will Trusts* [1979] 1 W.L.R. 278, it was held that the terms "family" and "friends" were sufficiently certain. This could be explained on the basis that the case concerned a gift subject to a condition precedent. In these cases the courts have shown a preference for holding a trust or gift valid.

Key Principle

A power of appointment is valid if it can be said with certainty whether a person is within the class or not.

RE GULBENKIAN'S SETTLEMENT 1970
The question arose as to whether powers of appointment were void for uncertainty. The potential appointees were described as

"all or any one or more to the exclusion of the other or others of the following persons, namely ... any wife and his children or remoter issue for the time being in existence whether minors or adults and any person or persons in whose house or apartments or in whose company or under whose care or control or by or with whom ... may from time to time be employed or residing ...".

Held

❖ (HL) Provided there was a valid gift over in default of appointment, a power of appointment was valid if it could be said with certainty whether a person was a member of the class or not. Where the language was ambiguous it was the court's duty to seek to ascertain the settlor's intentions. That the court had to disentangle the language did not of itself mean the power was uncertain. [1970] A.C. 508.

Commentary

[1] The court's emphasis is on giving effect to the settlor's intent to allow the power to be exercised with discretion. In *Re Manisty's Settlement* [1974] 1 Ch. 17, the trustees were empowered at their absolute discretion to add anyone to the class of beneficiaries other than an excepted class. The excepted class was sufficiently certain to make anyone other than part of the excepted class sufficiently certain. The apparent breadth of the class may have been regarded as inconsistent with the nature of a power. The court, however, took the view that the exercise was certain and had been allowed for by the settlor. Similarly, in *Re Hay's Settlement Trusts* [1982] 1 W.L.R. 202, a power to appoint anyone apart from a small number of specified persons was conceptually certain and administratively workable.

[2] It is generally thought that the test of administrative unworkability applies to discretionary trusts but not powers: *R. v District Auditor ex parte West Yorkshire Metropolitan County Council* [1985] 26 R.V.R. 24. Where the power is exercised by a fiduciary, then administrative unworkability may be a way of determining the validity of the power: *Mettoy Pension Trustees Ltd v Evans* [1991] 1 W.L.R. 1587. In *Re Harding (Deceased)* [2007] EWHC 3, the court was of the view that if a trust did exist, it would have failed for being administratively unworkable. In this case the beneficiaries were potentially the black community of four London Boroughs.

[B] FORMALITIES

The formalities applicable to the creation of a private express trust are focussed on s.53(1)(b) of the **Law of Property Act 1925** which requires that a declaration of trust of land or any interest in it must be manifested and proved by some writing signed by some person who is able to declare such trusts of by his will. The other relevant provision is s.53(1)(c) of the **Law of Property Act 1925** which provides that a disposition of an equitable interest or trust subsisting at the time of the disposition must be in writing signed by the person disposing of the same or by his lawfully authorised agent in writing or by will.

Key Principle
It is a fraud for a person to whom land is conveyed as trustee, and who knows it was so conveyed, to deny the trust and claim the land as his own.

> HODGSON V MARKS 1971
> (See Ch.5.)

Held
❖ (CA) The failure to satisfy the requirements in s.53(1) of the **Law of Property Act 1925** to create an express trust of land in favour of the donor does not prevent the existence of a resulting trust back to the donor. [1971] Ch. 892.

Commentary
The requirement of evidence in writing of a declaration of trust does not mean that other evidence of a trust cannot be adduced where the absence of writing is being used to deny the nature of the transaction. The case embodies the equitable maxim that equity will not allow a statute to be used an instrument of fraud.

In *Close Invoice Finance Ltd v Abaowa* [2010] EWHC 1920 the court stated that under s.53 (1)(b) of the **Law of Property Act 1925** the evidence in writing must be produced in order to evidence the existence of a declaration of trust in respect of land. This must be before the matter became a dispute. On the facts of the case the court found there was no compliance with the statutory provision as the written declaration of trust was a sham and produced only after the freezing order had been made. The judge stated (at para.87) that where the parties produced the written declaration of trust after a dispute arose it would be wrong to allow that to be provided as proof of compliance with the statutory provision as

> "...that cannot be what was intended when s.53(1)(b) was enacted. To permit such a practice would defeat the whole object of the statutory requirement, which is after all concerned, even in its own terms, with the manifestation and proof of the trust which is said to have been declared".

Key Principle

A disposition of both the legal and equitable interest of personalty simultaneously need not be in writing but the disposition must be complete, otherwise there may be a resulting trust back to the settlor.

VANDERVELL V INLAND REVENUE COMMISSIONERS 1967

In 1958, Vandervell decided to make a gift of £150,000 to the Royal College of Surgeons. At the time 100,000 shares in Vandervell Products Ltd (VPL), a company which he controlled, were held by a bank on trust.

It was decided that the shares should be transferred to the college and that an option to buy them should be granted to a trustee company and that sufficient dividends to pay for the endowment should be declared on the shares. The trustee company's principal activity was to act as trustee of settlements made in favour of Vandervell's children. On November 19, the transfer deed of the 100,000 shares was executed by the bank, which was sealed by the college the next day along with the option deed. Dividends were declared on the shares. In 1961, the trustee-company exercised its option to buy back the shares for £5,000. Vandervell was assessed for surtax on the dividends paid on the basis that the transaction amounted to a settlement of property of which he had not absolutely divested himself. It was argued that Vandervell had not divested himself of the beneficial interest in the shares because there had been no written disposition within the meaning of s.53(1)(c) of the **Law of Property Act 1925.**

Held

❖ (HL) Section 53(1)(c) was inapplicable as it applied to situations where the beneficial interest was divided from the legal interest and was designed to prevent secret, fraudulent dealings behind the legal owner's back. Where, as here, the beneficial owner directed the bare trustee (the bank) to deal with both the legal and beneficial interest (transferring them to the college) there was no need to satisfy s.53(1)(c). The option, however, was vested in the trustee on trusts not defined. There was a resulting trust back to Vandervell of the benefit of the option. He had not divested himself of the shares and was liable to surtax for them. [1967] 2 A.C. 291.

Commentary

The decision is questionable. As the shares were being moved from being used as security for a trust to Vandervell's wife to a beneficial interest for the college, this would seem to be a disposition of a beneficial interest. Vandervell had set up a clever scheme to transfer shares to the college whereby as owner of the company he could control the amount of dividends payable and as owner of the option at an undervalue he would recover control over the shares. In a commercial sense he had not divested himself of his interest in her shares, but the court's reasoning behind his retention of an interest is not convincing.

Key Principle

An oral declaration of a disposition of an equitable interest is ineffective to transfer the interest for the purposes of s.53(1)(c) of the **Law of Property Act 1925**.

GREY V INLAND REVENUE COMMISSIONERS 1960

In 1949, H made a settlement for each of his five grandchildren and a sixth for existing and after born grandchildren. On February 1, 1955, he transferred 18,000 shares to the trustees of the settlements as nominees. On February 18, 1955, he orally directed the trustees to hold the shares in blocks of 3,000 for each of the settlements with the intent of divesting himself of any interest in the shares. On March 25, 1955, the trustees executed declarations of trust of the shares; H, though not expressed to be a party thereto executed the declarations. The declarations recited H's oral direction of February 18. The transfers of the shares were assessed for stamp duty.

Held

❖ (HL) The directions of February 18 were dispositions of the equitable interest in the shares within the meaning of s.53(1)(c) of the **Law of Property Act 1925**. As these were not in writing, they were not effective for that purpose. However, the declarations of March 25 were effective as dispositions of his equitable interest and were assessable for stamp duty. [1960] 1 A.C. 1.

Commentary

The substance of the arrangement was a transfer of the beneficial interest in shares from the settlor to the children. A direction by a beneficiary to trustees that a benefit should be held for third parties is a disposition of an equitable interest, which had to be in writing. A declaration of oneself as trustee of a beneficial interest under a trust does not amount to a disposition of an equitable interest if as intermediate trustee active duties are retained. If the property is held as a bare trustee then this may be a disposition. See *Grainge v Wilberforce* (1889) 5 T.L.R. 436. In *Nelson v Greening & Sykes (Builders) Ltd*, *The Times*, January 22, 2008, the Court of Appeal considered that where an individual (who had the beneficial interest) was a trustee of the equitable interest for a third person, he is not regarded as having "dropped out" nor ceased to be a trustee. Although it may be more convenient to deal directly with the third person, it did not mean that the trustee had dropped out of the picture. It should be noted that this was not a case on s.53(1)(c) **Law of Property Act 1925** but on a constructive trust.

Key Principle

A specifically enforceable contract could make the transferor a constructive trustee of property to hold for the transferee who thereby acquired an equitable interest.

OUGHTRED V INLAND REVENUE COMMISSIONERS 1960

Under a 1924 settlement, a mother had a life interest in 100,000 pre-ference shares and 100,000 ordinary shares in a company. Her son was the owner of the shares subject to the mother's life interest. By an oral agreement on June 18, 1956, it was agreed that he would transfer his interest in the shares intending to give her absolute title to them. This was in return for her transferring 72,000 shares to him. By a deed on June 26, 1956, the mother and son released the trustees and stated that the shares were held in trust for the mother absolutely. The transfer was expressed to be in consideration for the release. On the same day a deed was made by the trustees and the mother transferring the shares to her for consideration of 10 shillings.

Held

❖ (HL) The transfer was assessable for ad valorem stamp duty, being an instrument whereby the property (the settled shares) was transferred by sale to the mother. By the transfer, the mother acquired the reversionary interest as if it had been transferred direct from the son. [1960] A.C. 206.

NEVILLE V WILSON 1996

JE Ltd was the registered owner of all but 120 of the issued shares in UE Ltd. The 120 shares were in the names of two directors of UE Ltd as nominees for JE Ltd. In 1965 it was resolved to transfer all the registered shares held by JE Ltd to the shareholders of JE Ltd in proportion to their shareholding. This did not extend to the 120 shares. From 1969 onwards, JE Ltd was regarded as having been defunct and was dissolved. The issue arose as to the beneficial ownership of the 120 shares in UE Ltd. The plaintiffs, who were two shareholders of JE Ltd, claimed that the shares were held on a constructive trust for the shareholders in proportions corresponding to their shareholdings in that company. At first instance, the judge ruled that the 1965 resolution did not extend to the 120 shares. The plaintiffs appealed, raising an alternative claim that there was an agreement in 1969 between the shareholders of JE Ltd for the informal liquidation of the company. Under this, the debts and liabilities of the company were to be discharged and the balance of the assets distributed to the shareholders in proportion to their shareholding. This included the beneficial interest in the 120 shares. The issue arose as to whether the requirements of s.53(1)(c) of the **Law of Property Act 1925** would render the agreement ineffective for lack of writing.

Held

❖ (CA) Section 53(1)(c) of the **Law of Property Act 1925** did not render such an agreement ineffective. The effect of the agreement, between the shareholders as to the disposal of the assets of the company, gave rise to a constructive trust between them. In accordance with s.53(2), it did not require compliance with s.53(1)(c). The beneficial interest in the 120 shares was vested in the shareholders JE Ltd in proportion to their shareholding and not in the Crown as bona vacantia. [1996] 3 All E.R. 171.

Commentary

In *Oughtred v IRC*, the oral agreement of June 18 was a specifically enforceable contract. At that point, the son became a constructive trustee of the equitable reversionary interest. It was said that s.53(1)(c) does not apply to constructive trusts (which is true) and thus the transfer to the mother of the interest was complete without writing and that the subsequent deeds of transfer were confirmatory of the transfer rather than the actual transfer itself. The court found that notwithstanding the constructive trust, the transfer in writing did pass some beneficial interest in the shares, which attracted ad valorem stamp duty. The case of *Neville v Wilson* is a good illustration of the application of s.53(2).

Key Principle

A declaration of trusts of personalty does not require compliance with s.53 of the Law of Property Act 1925.

RE VANDERVELL'S TRUSTS (NO. 2) 1974 (SEE VANDERVELL V IRC, ABOVE)
In 1949, Vandervell had set up trusts for his children. Vandervell
Trustees Ltd was the trustee. Vandervell intended that the trustee held
the option on unspecified trusts for the children or his employees. It
was this option in *Vandervell v IRC* which the court held returned to him
on resulting trust because he could not be said to have divested
himself of his interest. Having been held liable to surtax, Vandervell, by
deed of January 19, 1965, transferred all his rights in the option to the
trust company, the shares to be held on the trusts of the children's
settlement. Vandervell died in 1967. The Inland Revenue assessed his
estate to £628,229 in respect of the dividends from 1961 to 1965, i.e.
from the exercise of the option till the deed of divestment. The plaintiffs, who were executors of the estate, brought this action against the
trustees for a declaration that the estate was entitled to all monies
received by the trustee as dividends between 1961 and 1965. This was
on the basis that as Vandervell had not divested himself of all interest
in the shares, he should be entitled to the dividends on them. They
also contended that the option of the beneficial interest in the shares
could not be held on the trusts of the children's settlement because
there had been no disposition within s.53(1)(c) of the **Law of Property
Act 1925.**

Held

❖ (CA) Until 1961, the trustee held the option on such trust as might
thereafter be declared by the trustee or Vandervell. As no clear trusts had
been declared there was a resulting trust to Vandervell. In the exercise of the
option, £5,000 was used from the children's settlement, the trustee held the
100,000 shares on trust for the children as indicated by the trustee's and
Vandervell's intention. Neither the extinction of the option after its exercise,
nor the declaration of trust amounted to disposition of an equitable interest
within s.53(1)(c). [1974] Ch. 269.

Commentary

Having been caught for not ensuring that the declaration of trust of the option
divested him of all interest in the shares, Vandervell's estate was now told
that he had no interest in the value of the dividends on the shares because
the declaration of trust for the children didn't have to be in writing. Whilst
there was sympathy for Vandervell because of the court's reasoning and
because he was paying tax at up to a rate of 95 per cent, he might have been
better off keeping things simple.

In *Drakeford v Cotton* [2012] 3 All E.R. 1138 the court decided that an
informal declaration by two trustees to hold money in the accounts on trust

for themselves was a declaration of trust and did not need to comply with s.53(1)(c).

Key Principle
Section 53(1)(c) of the **Law of Property Act 1925** should not apply to a right of nomination of a beneficiary under a staff pension fund.

> RE DANISH BACON CO LTD STAFF PENSION FUND TRUSTS 1971
> The question arose as to whether the appointment of, or subsequent replacement of, a nominee to receive benefits under a staff pension scheme required compliance with any formalities.

Held
❖ (Ch) Although the appointment had some testamentary characteristics it was not a testamentary paper and there were no special formalities required for nomination of a pension beneficiary. Even if s.53(1)(c) applied, the original form of appointment which complied with the fund's rules and the subsequent letter as acted upon by the trustee would be a sufficient connection of documents to satisfy the requirements of writing. [1971] 1 W.L.R. 248.

[C] CONSTITUTION OF TRUSTS

Key Principle
The appropriate mode of vesting property in a trustee must be used.

> MILROY V LORD 1862
> S attempted to transfer shares to SL by a voluntary deed. Shares can only be transferred fully by registering the new owner of the shares with the company. This was not done.

Held
❖ (CA) The transfer of shares was not effective. Moreover, the court dismissed the claim that a failed transfer could constitute a declaration of trust. (1862) 4 De. G.F. & J. 264.

Commentary
The formalities for the transfer of other kinds of property include:
[a] a transfer of a legal estate in land must by deed: s.52(1) of the **Law of Property Act 1925**;

[b] a disposition of a subsisting equitable interest must be in writing: s.53(1)(c) of the **Law of Property Act 1925;**

[c] a legal assignment of a chose in action should come within s.136 of the **Law of Property Act 1925;**

[d] a transfer of shares must comply with ss.770 to 773 of the Companies Act 2006; and

[e] a transfer of personalty can be done by delivery or deed of gift.

Key Principle

Equity will not perfect an imperfect gift.

> JONES V LOCK 1865
> (See Ch.1.)

Held

❖ (CA) There had not been a transfer of the property, as it had not been delivered. It could not be construed as a declaration of trust. (1865) L.R. 1 Ch. 4.

Commentary

[1] As in *Milroy v Lord*, a failed transfer cannot be treated on default as a declaration of trust because, without clear evidence, the attempt could be inferred as an outright gift as much as a trust. In contrast in *Shah v Shah* [2010] All E.R. (D) 121 the Court of Appeal found the existence of a trust where there was an incomplete transfer of some shares as the evidence was sufficient for the court to find that a trust had been intended rather than an outright attempted gift.

[2] In *Choithram International SA v Lalibai Thakurdas Pagarani* [2001] 1 W.L.R. 1, the Privy Council held that an oral declaration by a donor that assets vested in himself already were now to be held as trustee of a charitable foundation was sufficient to create an immediate and unconditional gift. This was so, even though the assets had not been transferred to the other trustees. The donor had executed a deed setting up a charitable foundation. He then orally declared that he gave the assets to the foundation. The Privy Council found that on the facts the intention to create the gift in favour of the trust was unequivocal. It would be unconscionable for the donor to go back on the gift to the trust. Although the court should not assist a volunteer it should also not officiously defeat a gift.

[3] In *Pennington v Waine* [2002] 1 W.L.R. 2075, the Court of Appeal declared that there was no single policy consideration behind the principle that equity will not perfect an imperfect gift. The court found the key question to be whether it would be unconscionable for the donor to change her mind. In this case the donor had told the donee of the gift of shares, she had signed the transfer form and given it to a partner in the firm. The partner had told the donee that he need take no further action. Moreover, the partner had agreed to become a director of the firm. Without a transfer of shares he could not have become a partner. It is not clear that this case falls under the principle in *Re Rose*, below, as the donor might have taken further action to process the transfer of shares. The case seems to be broader than *Re Rose* and appears to follow the pragmatic approach in Choithram.

[4] In *Shah v Shah*, it was argued that there was a principle of benevolent interpretation applicable to gifts which ought to ensure that the intention to make the gift in this case is effective and avoid the declaration of trust. Arden L.J. referred to *Choithram* and *Pennington* and stated that the principle of benevolent construction was not to be invoked in the present case. The words used in the letter were sufficiently clear and as such the court was able to conclude that there was a declaration of trust. There was no doubt in this case which would require the court to have recourse in other circumstances to the benevolent principle referred to above. It should be noted that although *Choithram* and *Pennington* may indicate a more liberal approach in trying to find the existence of gifts or trusts in cases of uncertainty, the decision in *Shah v Shah* indicates that the court has yet to move away from the traditional approach.

Key Principle

Where the transferor has done all in his power to complete the transfer, the transfer will be given effect in equity.

RE ROSE 1952

The deceased had transferred 10,000 shares in a company to his wife on March 30, 1943. On the same day, he transferred another 10,000 shares in the same company to trustees to hold on trust. The transfers were done in the form required by the company's articles of association. These allowed the directors to reject any transfer. On the date of execution, the transfers and share certificates were handed to the transferees. These were duly stamped and registered on April 12, 1943, and registered in the books of the company on June 30, 1943. On the deceased's death estate duty was claimed on the ground that the gift was not completed by April 10, 1943 (the relevant date for completion of transfer to avoid the tax).

Held

❖ (CA) The deceased had done everything in his power to transfer the legal and beneficial interest in the shares. By the execution the transferees had become beneficial owners of the shares and he had ceded (notwithstanding that he was still registered owner) any claim to a beneficial interest in them. Having regard to the nature of the property and its mode of transfer as well as the directors' ability to hold up registration, the transferor was in a position of trustee. The beneficial interest in the shares passed bona fide on March 30, 1943, and consequently was not assessable for estate duty. [1952] Ch. 499.

ZEITAL V KAYE 2010

There were two disputed gifts of shares in a company called Dalmar Properties Ltd which R had incorporated in 1988. There were two subscriber shares issued in the names of AK and KK, the agents who set up the company. Each of them signed an undated blank share transfer form in relation to the share they each held leaving the name of the transferee blank. These share transfer forms were held by R who died intestate in 2004. His partner, S, whom he had not married, claimed he had given her the shares whilst the administrators of the estate, his wife and daughter who were the defendants argued that as R had not completed the transfer of the shares or its interests to S and as he held the shares beneficially this belonged to the estate.

There were two separate alleged gifts:
- in respect of the first share transfer form R completed the form naming S as the transferee and dated it October 27, 1997 and gave it to S around August 2003; and
- in respect of the second share transfer form R gave S the form in its original state, without adding her name as transferee nor did he put a date to it.

The judge at first instance decided that the defendants had no legal and beneficial interest in the shares. In respect of the first share, this was successfully transferred to S as R by handing over the duly completed share transfer form had done all within his power to transfer the share. Until S was registered as the legal owner of the share R held the legal title to it upon trust for S who thereafter became the beneficial owner of the share. The defendants appealed against the decision in respect of the second share transfer.

Held

❖ (CA) In respect of the second share transfer form, the court would allow the appeal as the judge was wrong to find that R's actions had transferred the beneficial interest to S. He had not purported to declare a trust nor did he seek to assign the share to S or her trustee. His actions were not sufficient to divest the equitable interest from himself to S. The purported gift to S failed as an imperfect gift and the defendants were entitled to that beneficial interest as administrators of the estate. [2010] EWCA Civ 159.

Commentary

In *Re Fry* [1946] Ch. 312, the court took a much stricter view. Fry owned shares in an English company. He made a voluntary transfer of these. He sent the transfer papers to the transferees, which were then sent to the company for registration. Under wartime regulations, the consent of the Treasury had to be obtained. Before it was obtained, he died. It was held that the intended gift failed as it was not complete and that the property should revert to his estate. It was said that he had not done all within his powers to transfer the shares because the Treasury could have requested further details from him before giving consent.

The Court of Appeal decision in *Zeital v Kaye* has clarified the position with regards to the rule in *Re Rose* and the decision in *Pennington v Waine*. Rimer L.J. stressed that the point Arden L.J. was implicitly making in *Pennington v Waine* was that in those particular circumstances no question arose as to the donor's omission to deliver the certificates to the donee as the share certificates were already held by the company. What is interesting in the decision in *Zeital v Kaye* was the absence of the share certificate in respect of the first share transfer form which was presumably lost and the court was prepared to accept that the first transfer was valid. The court suggested that the absence of the share certificate could indicate the absence of an intent to transfer but if there were some other explanation for its absence it would not prevent the gift from being completed.

Key Principle

Where transferees have provided consideration they may seek specific performance to complete the transfer of property.

PULLAN V KOE 1913

By a marriage settlement it was provided that the wife would settle any after-acquired property exceeding £100 in value. She received £3,285 from her mother, which she put in her husband's bank account, which was used by her husband to buy securities. On his death the trustees claimed the securities from the estate.

Held

❖ (Ch) The securities were not part of the estate but were part of the trusts of the marriage settlement, the beneficiaries of which were the children. The children could seek specific performance to ensure that the securities were part of their trust rather than the father's estate because they were deemed to be part of the consideration in the marriage settlement. [1913] 1 Ch. 9.

Commentary

They could proceed in equity notwithstanding that an action in common law was time barred. The requirement of consideration is a straightforward common law principle but was being given effect through equity to enforce a trust.

Key Principle

Equity will not assist a volunteer to enforce a trust.

RE PLUMPTRE'S MARRIAGE SETTLEMENT 1910

Upon marriage, the husband and wife covenanted with the trustees that the wife's after-acquired property would be settled on trust for the husband and wife successively for life thereafter to the children, if any, and thereafter to the next of kin. The husband bought shares in the wife's name, which she sold and bought other shares with the proceeds. In 1909, the shares were worth £1,125. The wife died childless. The trustees sought a ruling as to whether the property was bound to the trusts of the settlement or whether they should seek to secure the transfer of the property given that the next of kin were volunteers.

Held

❖ (Ch) The next of kin were volunteers being strangers to the marriage consideration. They could not enforce the covenant against the husband. [1910] 1 Ch. 609.

Commentary

The question is whether the property should be recovered. Otherwise, it will fall into the hands of undeserving volunteers. If the trustees stay passive its ownership will remain with the individual who can deal with it more freely. The justification for not forcing the trustees to act is the maxim that equity will not assist a volunteer. The courts can use this approach because as the property had not been transferred into the settlement yet, the trust was not fully constituted. The Contracts (Rights of Third Parties) Act 1999 provides that a third party may sue upon a contract if expressly allowed or if the contract purports to confer an enforceable benefit. It can be argued that this provision means that a beneficiary of a covenant to settle could sue upon the covenant personally.

Key Principle

The court will not indirectly assist volunteers to enforce a covenant that they could not enforce by direct means themselves.

RE PRYCE 1917

A marriage settlement contained a covenant to settle the wife's after acquired property on the trusts of the settlement. The husband made a gift of certain reversionary interests to which he would be entitled when his mother died. He predeceased his mother. His wife was entitled to a life interest in the marriage settlement's property, thereafter the property went to the children, if any, and then to the next of kin. The reversionary interest was bound up in another settlement. The question arose as to whether the trustees should seek to enforce the transfer of the property to the settlement.

Held

❖ (Ch) The property should be part of the settlement but the trustees need not enforce it as the next of kin, who were ultimately entitled, were volunteers. The trustees should not take any steps to assist the volunteers. [1917] 1 Ch. 234.

Commentary

[1] Volunteers by not providing consideration could not sue in common law for damages for breach of covenant to settle property. If trustees were to do this, or sue in equity for specific performance of the promise, then the volunteers would be in a better position than they would be on their own.

[2] In *Re Kay's Settlement* [1939] Ch. 329, it was held that the trustees should not pursue specific performance but that they should also not take proceedings at common law for breach of covenant. This approach was also taken in *Re Cook's Settlement Trusts* [1965] Ch. 902. The approach was, however, departed from in *Re Cavendish Browne's Settlement Trust* (1916) W.N. 341 where the court allowed the trustees to sue for and obtain damages for breach of covenant.

Key Principle

The concept of a trust of the benefit of a covenant can be used to enable a beneficiary to sue upon a trust.

FLETCHER V FLETCHER 1844

Fletcher covenanted with trustees, for himself, his heirs, executors and administrators to pay the trustees £60,000 within 12 months of death to be held on trust for his sons, John and Jacob. If both sons were alive at his death and attained the age of 21, the money was to be held on trust for them in equal shares as tenants in common. John survived his father but died before reaching 21. Jacob claimed the full amount. The trustees refused to accept the money or take proceedings to claim it without the direction of the court.

Held

❖ (VCC) Jacob could claim the full amount direct from the executors. The trust was perfect in the sense that the covenantor had incurred liability in law because the covenant by deed could be enforced at law. Equity would allow Jacob to stand in place of the trustees to sue or he could sue in his own name at law. (1844) 4 Hare. 67.

Commentary

[1] The trust was not fully constituted, as the £60,000 had not been transferred to the trust. The trustees would not have sought to force constitution of the trust, as this would assist a volunteer. However, in the present case, it was construed that there was a trust of the benefit of the covenant, which was constituted by the covenant made to the trustees. If this is the case it might seem simpler for the trustee to sue at common law. However, the beneficiary could not compel the trustee to do so unless there was deemed to be a trust of the benefit in which case the beneficiary could sue anyway. The difficulty in most of these cases would be ascertaining the requisite intention to create the trust of the benefit of the covenant.

[2] Where the trust is of future property, it would seem that the volunteer beneficiary could not enforce at all: *Re Ellenborough* [1903] 1 Ch. 697. Conversely, where the beneficiary is party to the deed then he may sue for damages at common law even when a volunteer: *Cannon v Hartley* [1949] 1 All E.R. 50.

[3] In *Don King Productions v Warren* [1999] 2 All E.R. 218, two boxing promoters pooled their resources into a partnership. They agreed that, as well as the existing agreement, new promotions and management agreements would be held for the benefit of the partnership. It transpired that some of the subsequent agreements could not be assigned at law. It was held that notwithstanding that they could not be transferred the partner held the benefit of the agreements on trust for the partnership. Thus there was a trust of the benefit of a contract.

Key Principle
The rule in *Strong v Bird* serves as an exception to the rule that equity will not assist a volunteer.

STRONG V BIRD 1874
Bird borrowed £1,100 from his stepmother who lived in his house paying £212.10 per quarter. It was agreed that the loan should be paid off by her deducting £100 from each quarter's rent. This was done twice but thereafter the stepmother refused to make the deduction and paid the full charge until her death four years later. Bird was appointed sole executor of the estate. The next of kin claimed that Bird owed the estate £900.

Held
❖ (Ch) The appointment as executor relieved him of the debt. [1874] L.R. 17 Eq. 315.

Commentary
Where a person owing a debt is made executor he is released from the debt provided that there was a clear ongoing intention to forgive the debt. If this is the case the volunteer who is forgiven the debt for no consideration will be assisted by equity. This is a convenient result given that it would be difficult for the executor to sue himself. The rule has also been extended to complete the constitution of trusts as seen in *Re Ralli's Will Trusts* [1964] Ch. 288. Even though the constitution was entirely fortuitous in this case it did not matter.

In order for this rule to apply the claimant must be able to satisfy two criteria.

- There must be an intention on the part of the donor to make an immediate inter vivos gift. An intention to make a gift in the future does not suffice and as such the attempted gift of a motor car sometime in the future was held not to be sufficient for the rule to apply: *Re Freeland* [1952] Ch. 110.
- That the intention to give must have continued until death and hence if the donor treated the property as his own to do as he wished during his lifetime, this negates a continuing intention to give: *Re Wale* [1956] 1 W.L.R. 1346.

Key Principle

The principle of *donatio mortis causa* serves as an exception to the rule that equity will not assist a volunteer.

WOODARD V WOODARD 1995

A father, who was dying from leukemia, told the defendant that he could keep the keys to his car, as he (the father) would not be driving it anymore. This was in the plaintiff''s presence. The father died three days later. The plaintiff claimed the proceeds of the sale of the car, which amounted to £3,900. The defendant argued that the father either made an outright gift or a *donatio mortis causa* (DMC) of the car.

Held

❖ (CA) From the evidence, it was clear that the defendant would have to return the car on the father's recovery. There was, therefore, no outright gift of the car. However, the gift had been made in contemplation of death and on condition that the gift was to be made absolute on the father's death. It was irrelevant that the defendant already had possession of the car and the set of keys. There was a valid DMC of the car. [1995] 3 All E.R. 980.

Commentary

[1] A gift made inter vivos can take effect if the three essentials laid down by Lord Russell in *Cain v Moon* [1896] 2 Q.B. 283, are satisfied:

  (a) the gift must have been made in contemplation, though not necessarily in expectation, of death;

  (b) the subject matter of the gift must have been delivered to the donee; · and

  (c) the gift must have been made under such circumstances to show that the property is to revert to the donor if he should recover.

[2] The rule allows a volunteer to take a gift of property that would otherwise go to the deceased's estate. There appear to be two exceptions to the rule that any personal property can be the subject matter of a DMC. The first is with regards to cheques which are issued by the donor in favour of the donee. The cheque is not seen as a delivery of the money represented by the cheque but merely a revocable order to the bank to pay. The second is with regards to company shares. In *Re Weston* [1902] 1 Ch. 680 it was suggested that there cannot be a DMC of shares. Some have argued that the decision is a misunderstanding of the decision in *Ward v Turner* (1752) 2 Ves. Sen 431. However in *Staniland v Willott* [1852] 3 Mac. & G. 664 it was suggested that provided the share certificates, which are the indica of title, are transferred to the donee there is no reason why there cannot be a DMC of shares.
Since the decision in *Sen v Headley* [1991] Ch. 425 it would appear that land can be the subject matter of a DMC.

[3] As regards the requirement of the gift being made in contemplation of death, it has been clarified by the decision in *Wilkes v Allington* [1931] 2 Ch. 104 that it is sufficient that the donor contemplated death in one manner even though he died from a different cause. It should be noted that the court may be able to infer in appropriate cases that the gift was made in contemplation of death where the circumstances are such that such an inference could be made. Obviously if the donor does not die the DMC is ineffective and can be revoked by the donor at any time.

[4] One of the other essential criteria for a DMC is that there must be a delivery of the subject matter of the gift or something representing it which gives control to the property. The nature of the delivery is dependent on the property itself.

- Chattels – there must be delivery of the property itself or some means of control so that the donor cannot access the property. In *Re Lillingston* [1953] 2 All E.R. 184, there was sufficient delivery for the purposes of a DMC although what was delivered did not provide sufficient access to the donee provided the donor was not able to get at the property. In that case the donor gave the donee the only key to a safe deposit box at Harrods saying that "when I am gone, you go and get the jewellery". The donee was not able to access the jewellery without the appropriate authority from the donor or the password. However as the donor was excluded from accessing the property there was sufficient delivery. See also *Re Mustapha* [1891] 8 T.L.R. 160 and *Re Craven's Estate* [1937] 3 All E.R. 33.
- Choses in action – the donor must hand over the documents which provide the evidence or indicia of title possession which entitles the

donee to claim the money or property: *Birch v Treasury Solicitor* [1951] Ch. 298. The delivery of a bank passbook in that case was sufficient as was a Post Office Savings Book in *Re Weston* [1902] 1 Ch. 680.

THINK POINT

It has been argued that the trust of the benefit of the covenant is the way in which the covenant to transfer can be enforced against the settlor. What is the difficulty with being able to establish that the trust of the benefit of the covenant exists? Do you think that in practice the courts will be able to find such a trust exists on the facts of a case?

In the context of formalities, read the cases of *Vandervell v IRC* and *Re Vandervell's Trusts* (No. 2). Do you think the courts made the correct decision in each of the cases? Consider especially whether it was right for the court to conclude that there was no disposition of an equitable interest on the exercise of the option but the creation of a trust in the latter case.

Secret and Protective Trusts

3

Secret Trusts

. . . .

INTRODUCTION

The original basis of the secret trust lies with the maxim "equity will not allow a statute to be used as an instrument of fraud". A secret trust exists outside the will as the testator wishes to avoid the publicity in respect of the trust. The will is a public document and hence the testator may wish, for his own personal reasons, to avoid the disclosure of the existence of the trust in the will. Section 9 of the Wills Act 1837 ("WA 1837") provides the formalities for a testamentary disposition to be effective and valid after death. The original justification for secret trusts is that the secret trustee is not allowed to deny his obligations on the basis that the trust was not stipulated in the will in accordance with the **WA 1837**. This is the application of the maxim, above: *McCormick v Grogan* (1869) L.R. 4 H.L. 82. However, as there are two types of such trusts—the fully and the half secret trust, the application of the maxim is strictly applicable in the former only. This is because in the case of the fully secret trust there is no mention of the trust in the will—it takes the form of an absolute gift on the face of the will. In the case of the half secret trust, the will mentions that there is a trust which is held by the secret trustee, but, the terms are not disclosed. Hence, there is no possibility of the secret trustee taking the property absolutely or using the **WA 1837** to avoid the secret trust.

The modern view for the basis of the secret trust is that the trust *dehors* the will, namely, that it exists outside and is independent of the will. The secret trust is therefore not subject to the provision of the **WA 1837**. Such trusts are enforceable by virtue of the personal obligation accepted by the secret trustee and binding on his conscience: *Re Young* [1951] Ch. 344. This was reaffirmed by the Supreme Court in Canada in *Chinn v Hanrieder* 11 I.T.E.L.R. 1009 where Loo J. (at p.1033) stated that "secret trusts arise from the court's equitable jurisdiction and operate independently of the terms of a will".

FULLY SECRET TRUSTS

Key Principle

The trust must be communicated to the secret trustee before the testator's death.

> ### WALLGRAVE V TEBBS 1855
>
> Property was left to the defendants as joint tenants. The action was brought to declare the transfer void on the basis that the transfer had been made upon trust for the defendants to carry out certain charitable purposes intended by the testator. It was alleged that the defendants knew of this intention and that a letter setting this out had been drafted, albeit never signed. The defendants denied that they had any communication with the testator about his will.

Held

❖ (VCC) There was no evidence of understanding between the testator and the defendants; there was no communication between them, which could be construed as a trust to give effect to the testator's intent. The transfer to the defendants was valid. They held the property absolutely for their own purposes. (1855) 2 K.&J. 313.

Commentary

The Supreme Court in Canada in *Chinn v Hanrieder* 11 I.T.E.L.R. 1009 in summarising the law in this area stated that to find the existence of a secret trust, in addition to the three certainties required for a trust to be created, the court must satisfy itself on the balance of probabilities, where there was no question of fraud, that the testator intended to subject the donee to an obligation in favour of the beneficiary. An example where the claim failed because the parties could not provide the evidence for the existence of a secret trust can be seen in *Fry v Densham-Smith* [2010] EWCA Civ 1410.

The intention must have been communicated to the donee who accepted that obligation. A person cannot be bound by an obligation unless it is communicated to him. This must be before the death of the testator because it is from that point that the trustee will be bound. If a trustee did not wish to be bound he must communicate this to the testator. It does not matter whether the communication is made before or after the will has been made: *Moss v Cooper* (1861) I S.&H. 352. This was applied in *Re Gardner* [1920] 2 Ch. 523 where a wife left her estate to her husband "knowing he will carry out my wishes". On the evidence it was found that she had communicated those wishes to her husband after the will. There was a valid secret trust. In *Gold v Hill* (1999) 1 F.L.R. 54 the deceased had nominated the plaintiff as beneficiary of his life policy and asked him to look after his wife and children. It was held that this was a sufficient communication of a trust. It was also decided that the nomination did not need to be in writing under s.53(1)(c) of the **Law of Property Act 1925** because at the time of nomination there was no subsisting equitable interest. The interest only came into existence upon the death of the policyholder. In *Marguiles v Marguiles*, above, the Court of Appeal found that a father's letters to his solicitors may have shown evidence of a change in attitude to his son but did not communicate any binding secret trust to the benefit of the claimant.

Key Principle

The terms of the trust must be communicated to the secret trustee.

RE BOYES 1884

A testator instructed his solicitor to draft a will leaving all his property to the solicitor absolutely, but to be held by him and distributed according to instructions that were to be subsequently given to him. The will was so drafted but no further instructions were given to the solicitor during the testator's lifetime. After the testator's death, an unattested paper was found indicating the testator's wish that the property should be given to X and Y with a small amount for the solicitor. The solicitor accepting this agreed to hold all but his indicated share on trust for X and Y.

Held

❖ (Ch) The terms of the trust were not communicated during the testator's lifetime. No valid trust was created in favour of X and Y. The solicitor held the property on resulting trust for the estate with the consequence that it would go to the next of kin. (1884) 26 Ch. D. 531.

Commentary

[1] This result is what the testator precisely wanted to avoid. It is possible for the terms to be constructively communicated by way of a sealed letter: *Re Keen* [1937] Ch. 236. This may make sense in preventing the secret trustee committing a fraud by taking the property absolutely but does not afford the trustee the opportunity to decline the obligation.

[2] Where a trust is communicated to one secret trustee but not the other, whether both are bound depends on whether they take the property as joint

tenants or tenants in common. If they take as tenants in common, only the person to whom the communication was made is bound. Where the property is taken as joint tenants, it depends on whether the communication is made before the will is made or after. If the communication is made before the will, both trustees are bound on the basis that there would be a suspicion that the testator would be fraudulently induced into executing the will which would otherwise not bind the other trustee and would take the whole property beneficially. If the communication is made after the execution of the will, then only the trustee to whom communication was made would be bound as there would be no suspicion of inducement: *Re Stead* [1900] I Ch. 237.

[3] Any addition to the property which is subject to the secret trust must also be communicated to the trustees and where this has not been done, the additional property will not be held on the terms of the secret trust but on a resulting trust: *Re Colin Cooper* [1939] Ch. 811.

Key Principle

A legal obligation as opposed to a moral obligation must be imposed on the secret trustee.

> MCCORMICK V GROGAN 1868
> A testator left all his property to the defendant. He fell ill with cholera. On his deathbed he told the defendant that his will and a letter were in his desk. The letter set out his intended beneficiaries and bequests. The testator concluded the letter saying that he did not expect the defendant to carry out the instructions strictly, but to use his judgment as he thought the testator would decide who was deserving of the bequests. The defendant excluded one of the possible beneficiaries, an illegitimate child, who subsequently sued.

Held

❖ (HL) There was no valid secret trust. The letter imposed a moral obligation as opposed to a legal one. (1869) L.R. 4 H.L. 82.

> RE SNOWDEN 1979
> A testatrix left the residue of her estate to her brother with whom she had lived for the last six months of her life. He died six days after the testatrix leaving his son as sole beneficiary of his will. Nineteen relatives challenged the testatrix's will claiming that the brother had received the legacy on secret trust for them. There was a solicitor"s

note indicating that she meant to leave legacies to her relatives, leaving the brother to split up the remainder of the estate.

Held

❖ (Ch) The standard of proof for establishing a secret trust was the same ordinary civil standard of proof. There was insufficient evidence to show that the testatrix intended to bind the brother by a legally enforceable trust. There was a moral obligation on him to distribute, as she would have done. Consequently, the brother and his son thereafter took the residue absolutely. [1979] Ch. 528.

Commentary

The whole point of a trust, secret or otherwise, is that it affixes to the trustee a legal obligation going beyond a moral one. In *Brown v Willoughby* 14 I.T.E.L.R. 758 the Supreme Court of Australia found on the facts of the case that no secret trust was established as there was no evidence of the intention to impose a legal obligation on the donee. Heenan J. stated at p.771 that

> "[w]hile there are obviously occasions when a testator may wish to establish a secret trust in order to maintain the privacy of certain matters or past events the prospects of the trust being effective, and if necessary being enforced, must depend on the availability of evidence to support the absence of intention to confer the whole beneficial interest in the property upon the object of the apparently absolute gift".

Key Principle

The legal obligation must be accepted by the secret trustee.

OTTAWAY V NORMAN 1972
H bequeathed his house and its contents to E. He intended that she would leave his house to his son. Shortly before her death, however, she made a new will leaving the property to the defendant and his wife. She left her residuary estate, half to the plaintiff and half to the defendant. The plaintiffs (who were the son and his wife) claimed that the house, contents and E's residuary estate should have gone to them.

Held

❖ (Ch) The plaintiffs established that there was a secret trust of the house in their favour and such of its contents which passed in the will from H to E. There was insufficient evidence of a secret trust of the remaining contents or the residuary estate. To establish that a secret trust had been created one had to show that the testator intended to impose an obligation upon the first donee and that such intention was communicated to the first donee, who accepted the obligation. It was not necessary to show any wrongdoing by the donee as the trust was established at the outset. [1972] Ch. 698.

Commentary

Acceptance of the obligations of a secret trustee can be express, implied (*Wallgrave v Tebbs*, above) or by acquiescence (*Moss v Cooper*, above).

HALF SECRET TRUSTS

Key Principle

The trust must be communicated to the half-secret trustee before the testator's will is made.

> BLACKWELL V BLACKWELL 1929
>
> A testator by a codicil gave five persons £12,000 upon trust to invest as they thought fit and to apply the income "for the purposes indicated by me to them" with a power to pay a sum of £8,000 "... to such person or persons indicated by me to them" as they thought fit. Detailed parol instructions were given by the testator to C, one of the trustees. The object and outline was known and accepted by all five before the codicil was executed. On the same day, soon after the codicil was executed, C wrote out and signed a memorandum of the detailed instructions. The income was to be applied for the benefit of a lady and her son. The widow and her son brought an action to test the validity of the legacy.

Held

❖ (HL) Parol evidence was admissible to establish a trust. The codicil and memorandum gave rise to a valid trust. [1929] A.C. 318.

> RE BATEMAN'S WILL TRUSTS 1970
>
> A testator directed his trustees to set aside £24,000 from his estate to pay the income thereof "to such persons and in such proportions as shall be stated by me in a sealed letter in my own handwriting addressed to my trustees".

Held

❖ (Ch) The direction relating to the sealed letter could not be read as referring only to a past letter but clearly envisaged that the testator might give the trustees a letter at some point in the future. The direction was therefore invalid as an attempt to dispose of the estate by a non-testamentary instrument. The subsequent directions as to the giftover of the £24,000 were likewise invalid. [1970] 1 W.L.R. 1463.

Commentary

The requirement for the communication of a half-secret trust before the will is executed is stricter than the rule in relation to fully secret trusts where it is sufficient for the communication to be made before the testator's death.

OTHER ISSUES

Key Principle

The beneficiary under a secret trust can claim the interest under the trust even though he or she was a witness to the will.

> RE YOUNG 1951
>
> The testator gave a bequest to his wife with a direction for her to make small legacies in accordance with his wishes. Prior to the execution of the will, the testator told his wife that he wished his chauffeur to receive a sum of £2,000. The chauffeur was one of the witnesses to the will.

Held

❖ (Ch) The chauffeur was entitled to take the legacy as the secret trust operated outside the **Wills Act 1837**. [1951] Ch. 344.

Commentary

[1] Under s.15 of the **WA 1837**, a witness to a will cannot take a benefit under the will. In the present case, the chauffeur was allowed to take the legacy because of the principle that the secret trust operated outside (or *dehors*) the will and therefore did not infringe s.15 of the **WA 1837**.

[2] Where the attestation of the will is by the secret trustee, the difficulty in the case of a fully secret trust is that there is no reference on the face of the will to the existence of the trust. Therefore s.15 of the **WA 1837** may apply preventing the trustee from taking under the will. In the case of a half secret trust as it is apparent on the face of the will that the secret trustee is taking

as a trustee, it is argued that s.15 would not apply. See by analogy *Creswell v Creswell* (1868) L.R. 6 E.Q. 69.

Key Principle

Where the beneficiary under a secret trust predeceases the testator, his estate may nonetheless benefit under the trust.

RE GARDNER (NO. 2) 1923

A testatrix left her estate to her husband stating that he would carry out her wishes. The testatrix wished the estate to be divided on her husband's death between three beneficiaries, one of whom had predeceased the testatrix.

Held

❖ (Ch) The beneficiary's personal representative could claim on behalf of the deceased beneficiary under the secret trust. [1923] 2 Ch. 230.

Commentary

The normal rule of succession is that a beneficiary under a will must survive the testator. However, in this case, the court's view was that as the secret trust existed outside the will, the fact the beneficiary predeceased the testatrix did not matter. The court decided that a secret beneficiary becomes entitled upon the creation of the secret trust not on the death of the testatrix. This is unsatisfactory as it ignores the fact that the will could be changed by the testatrix at any time prior to the death and could terminate the trust.

Key Principle

Unless there is clear evidence, the secret trustee cannot take a beneficial interest under the secret trust.

RE REES 1950

A testator died and appointed a friend and a solicitor as his executors and trustees, stating that they knew his wishes as regards the property. The testator had told them to make certain payments but to keep the remainder for themselves. There was a surplus after these payments were made. The executors argued that they were entitled to keep the surplus.

❖ (CA) The executors could not keep the surplus as a fiduciary obligation had been imposed on them. Evidence of the testator's intention was not admissible, as the will clearly showed an intention to create a trust. Evidence that the executors were to take the remainder of the property absolutely would contradict the will. [1950] Ch. 204.

Commentary

The court suggested that, since one of the executors was a solicitor, he should have ensured that the will was drafted in a clear manner so that the executors could take a benefit under the will rather than by use of a secret trust. See also *Re Pugh's Will Trusts* [1967] 1 W.L.R. 1262.

PROTECTIVE TRUSTS

Introduction

The protective trust is a device by which the testator or settler can give the beneficiary a life interest in the property which would terminate on the happening of a specific event, such as, the beneficiary becoming a bankrupt. Once this happens, a discretionary trust will take its place where the trustees then have the discretion to distribute the property amongst the beneficiaries. This could include the life tenant and his family. The purpose of such a trust is to protect the trust property and to avoid it falling into the hands of others such as the trustee in bankruptcy, in the event of the bankruptcy of the life tenant.

Key Principle

The life interest will determine on the principal beneficiary's bankruptcy or where an attempt is made to alienate his interest.

> RE BALFOUR'S SETTLEMENT 1938
> At the life tenant's request, the trustees advanced capital monies to him in breach of trust. In order to replace the trust funds, the trustees impounded his beneficial interest. The life tenant subsequently became bankrupt.

Held

❖ (Ch) The lifes tenant's interest had determined when the beneficial interest was impounded by the trustees. The life tenant's interest was therefore saved from the bankruptcy. [1938] Ch. 928.

> ### RE DENNIS'S SETTLEMENTS TRUSTS 1942
> The settlor's son had a protective life interest under a settlement. Upon attaining 21 years of age, a rearrangement of the settlement occurred. This made provision for the trustees to pay part of his income and accumulate the rest for the following six years.

Held

❖ (Ch) The effect of the rearrangement was to vest the right to receive part of the income on some other person. Accordingly, it brought the forfeiture clause into operation. [1942] Ch. 283.

Commentary

Other examples of determining events include a sequestration order, *Re Baring's Settlement Trusts* [1940] Ch. 737, and a court order to pay maintenance to the principal beneficiary's wife on the security of his life-interest in the trust and to execute a deed to this effect, *Re Richardson's Will Trusts* [1958] 1 Ch. 504. However, in *General Accident, Fire and Life Assurance Corp. Ltd v IRC* [1963] 1 W.L.R. 1207, a court order which diverted part of the income from a life tenant in favour of his wife on their divorce did not result in forfeiture. The court in that case was of the view that it was not the type of event, which the settlor would have intended to be a determining event.

Key Principle

The effect of legislation can be a determining event.

> ### RE GORJU'S WILL TRUSTS 1943
> The principal beneficiary under a protective trust was resident in France. This was under German occupation during the Second World War. The issue was whether the **Trading With the Enemy Act 1939** and the **Trading with the Enemy (Specified Areas) Order 1940**, which provided that persons living in enemy occupied territory would not be entitled to income from Britain, would result in the forfeiture of the principal beneficiary's interest.

Held

❖ (Ch) Upon the coming into force of the Act and Order, an event occurred which deprived the principal beneficiary of her income under the protective trust. The property was thereafter held on a discretionary trust in accordance with s.33 of the Trustee Act 1925. [1943] 1 Ch. 24.

Commentary
The trustees were also prevented from retaining the income for the principal beneficiary until the end of the war. However, in *Re Halt* [1944] Ch. 46, the beneficiary's interest had not been determined by residence in enemy occupied territory. The reason was that the wording used in the instrument as amounting to a determining event restricted it to where the income was payable elsewhere as a result of what she did or suffer any act to be done. As her residence in enemy occupied territory was not as a result of anything she did there was no forfeiture.

Key Principle
The settlor is not permitted to settle his own property on a protective trust on himself until bankruptcy but could do so on the occurrence of other events.

RE DETMOLD 1889
S, by his marriage settlement, settled property on trust to pay the income to himself for life, or until he should become bankrupt or assign, charge or encumber the life interest, or the occurrence of an event whereby the income would be payable to some other person by his own acts, default or operation of law. The settlement provided that after the determination of the trust in favour of the settlor, the property was to be held on trust with the income to be paid to his wife for life.

Held
❖ (Ch) The trust in favour of the wife was valid in the event of an involuntary alienation by operation of law. (1889) 40 Ch. D. 585.

Commentary
North J. (at 587–588) stated that

> " ... a settlement by a man of his own property upon himself for life, with a clause forfeiting his interest in the event of alienation, or attempted alienation, has never, so far as I know, been defeated in favour of a particular alienee; it has only been defeated in favour of the settlor's creditors generally, on the ground that it would be a fraud on bankrupt law".

Therefore, where the alienation is as a result of some other reason, apart from bankruptcy, the protective trust would be valid.

THINK POINT

If a secret trust exists outside the will, what type of trust is it—an express or a constructive trust?

If the secret trust is an express trust, how was the court able to find the existence of a valid secret trust in *Ottoway v Norman* [1972] Ch. 698, where there was a trust of land but there was no compliance with the requirements of s.53(1)(b) of the **Law of Property Act 1925** which required such trusts to be evidenced in writing?

Charitable and Non-Charitable Trusts

4

Charitable Trusts

INTRODUCTION

The Charities Act 2011 received royal assent on December 14, 2011 and came into force on March 14, 2012. The new Act consolidates the 1993 and 2006 Act and the Recreational Charities Act 1958 but does not change the law in a significant manner. As this change is recent and for ease of reference the original provision has been retained with the new provisions in brackets in respect of where this is discussed in the case law but the commentary will refer to the new provisions.

The Charities Act 2006 made important changes to the categories of charitable purposes and the requirement of public benefit. Until this Act there was no legal definition of a charity. This has been retained by the **Charities Act 2011**. Section 1 of the **Charities Act 2011** states that a "charity" means an institution which is established for charitable purposes only, and is subject to the control of the High Court in the exercise of its jurisdiction with respect to charities. It therefore excludes charities outside England and Wales. Section 2 goes on to provide that a purpose is charitable if it falls within the list of charitable purposes set out in s.3 and satisfies the requirement of public benefit in s.4. Section 3(1) sets out a non-exhaustive list of heads of charitable purposes which are as follows:

(a) the prevention or relief of poverty;
(b) the advancement of education;
(c) the advancement of religion;
(d) the advancement of health or the saving of lives;
(e) the advancement of citizenship or community development;
(f) the advancement of the arts, culture, heritage or science;
(g) the advancement of amateur sport;
(h) the advancement of human rights, conflict resolution or reconciliation or the promotion of religious or racial harmony or equality and diversity;
(i) the advancement of environmental protection or improvement;
(j) the relief of those in need because of youth, age, ill-health, disability, financial hardship or other disadvantage;

(k) the advancement of animal welfare;

(l) the promotion of the efficiency of the armed forces of the Crown or of the efficiency of the police, fire and rescue services or ambulance services; and

(m) any other purposes—

   [i] that are not within paragraphs (a) to (l) but are recognised as charitable purposes by virtue of section 5 (recreational and similar trusts, etc.) or under the old law;

   [ii] that may reasonably be regarded as analogous to, or within the spirit of, any purposes falling within any of paragraphs (a) to (l) or sub-paragraph (i); or

   [iii] that may reasonably be regarded as analogous to, or within the spirit of, any purposes which have been recognised, under the law relating to charities in England and Wales, as falling within sub-paragraph (ii) or this sub-paragraph.

The Act emphasizes in s.4 that public benefit has to be proved and is not merely to be presumed from a description of the purpose of the trust. As provided in s.17, the Charity Commission has issued guidance on public benefit (see below).

The Act also strengthens the regulatory regime for charities and widens the powers of trustees in regard to cy-près schemes.

CHARITABLE PURPOSES

Key Principle

Prior to the **Charities Act 2011**, charity in its legal sense comprised of trusts for the relief of poverty, trusts for the advancement of education, trusts for the advancement of religion and trusts for other purposes beneficial to the community.

> THE COMMISSIONERS FOR SPECIAL PURPOSES OF THE INCOME TAX V PEMSEL 1891
> Land was conveyed upon trusts whereby any surplus rents and profits were to be used, amongst other purposes, for the maintenance, support and advancement of missionary establishments abroad of the Moravian Church.

Held

❖ (HL) "Charitable" purposes were not restricted to the relief of poverty. [1891] A.C. 531.

Until the **Charities Act 2011,** the courts were able to use the relative breadth of the formulation and the analogy to the Charitable Uses Act 1601 to allow for sensible flexibility and responsiveness to modern demands. In *Scottish Burial Reform and Cremation Society Ltd v Glasgow Corporation* [1968] A.C. 138, the House of Lords held that cremation was for the public benefit within the "spirit and intendment" of the preamble to the 1601 Act. Under s.3 of the **Charities Act 2011,** the categories or heads of charitable purposes have now been clarified and now cover a whole range of purposes under each description of the charitable purpose. As the Act has not changed the purposes which have been recognised as charitable under case law, the previous case law will still be relevant—albeit in some instances it has attempted to clarify the law.

PREVENTION OR RELIEF OF POVERTY

Key Principle

Poverty does not mean destitution but is a wide term implying deprivation in a relative sense having regard to the circumstances.

> RE COULTHURST 1951
> A testator directed that income from the trust fund be applied
>
> > "... for the benefit ... of the ... widows and orphaned children of deceased officers and ex-officers of the bank as the bank shall in its absolute discretion consider ... to be most deserving of such assistance ...".

Held

❖ (CA) The trust was charitable. The intent was that the money was to be given to persons having the quality of poverty within the meaning of the 1601 preamble. [1951] Ch. 661.

> RE NIYAZI'S WILL TRUSTS 1978
> The testator left the residue of his estate in trust to be used "towards the construction of some working men's hostel" in Famagusta, Cyprus.

Held

❖ (Ch) The trust was charitable. The terms "working men's" and "hostel" had sufficient connotation of poverty. [1978] 3 All E.R. 785.

Commentary ....

[1] In *Re Coulthurst*, it was said that poverty did not mean destitution:

> "it is a word of wide and somewhat indefinite import; it may not be unfairly paraphrased for present purposes as meaning persons who have to 'go short' in the ordinary acceptance of that term, due regard being had to their status in life".

Poverty is therefore a relative concept. Other examples of gifts which have been held to be charitable for the relief of poverty include *Biscoe v Jackson* (1887) 35 Ch. D. 460 (a gift to establish a soup kitchen in Shoreditch), and *Shaw v Halifax Corp* [1915] K.B. 170 (a home for ladies in reduced means).

[2] Although the **Charities Act 2011** does not provide any explanation of what poverty is, the Charity Commissioners have provided some guidance and has stated that

> "...[t]he prevention or relief of poverty is not just about giving financial assistance to people who lack money; poverty is a more complex issue that is dependent upon the social and economic circumstances in which it arises".

It went on to state that

> ".... '[p]eople in poverty' does not just include people who are destitute, but also those who cannot satisfy a basic need without assistance... [i]n essence, 'people in poverty' generally refers to people who lack something in the nature of a necessity, or quasi-necessity, which the majority of the population would regard as necessary for a modest, but adequate, standard of living".

The Charity Commission went to say that poverty and financial hardship were not the same and that "... not everyone who is in financial hardship is necessarily poor, but it may still be charitable to relieve their financial hardship". In conclusion it stated that it

> "... is likely to be charitable to relieve either the poverty or the financial hardship of anyone who does not have the resources to provide themselves, either on a short or long-term basis, with the normal things of life which most people take for granted".

ADVANCEMENT OF EDUCATION

Key Principle

Education is to be interpreted broadly to include connected activities.

> **RE MARIETTE 1915**
> A testator bequeathed money for the purpose of building squash or Eton Fives courts and for the provision of school sports prizes.

Held

❖ (Ch) The bequests created valid charitable trusts. Daily sports activities were part of the daily routine of a school. [1915] 2 Ch. 284.

Commentary

Gifts to schools and colleges would normally be charitable provided they are used for charitable educational purposes including activities associated with academic education. Similarly, in *Re Dupree's Deed Trusts* [1945] Ch. 16, a gift to promote chess tournaments for schoolboys was held to be charitable. Gifts to educational bodies other than schools may be charitable: *Re Webber* [1954] 1 W.L.R. 1500.

Key Principle

There must be some element of teaching, instruction or dissemination of knowledge to count as education.

> **RE SHAW 1957**
> George Bernard Shaw bequeathed a fund, the income from which he directed to be used for research into replacing the present alphabet with another of at least 40 letters, to transliterate one of his plays into the new alphabet and to persuade the government and public to use the new alphabet.

Held

❖ (Ch) The trusts were not charitable. An increase in knowledge is not a charitable purpose unless accompanied by teaching or education. Whilst research and propaganda may increase knowledge, any time saved in using the new alphabet was not for the advancement of education. [1957] 1 W.L.R. 729.

RE HOPKINS 1965

A testator left part of her estate to the Francis Bacon Society, whose aims included the encouragement of the reading of Bacon's work and research to establish whether Shakespeare's works were in fact written by Bacon.

Held

❖ (Ch) Research into Shakespeare's scripts was a charitable purpose, as any definitive identification of the author would contribute to knowledge. In order for research to count as educational for the purposes of being charitable, it must be of educational value to the researcher or be directed to the dissemination of material so as to improve the sum of communicable knowledge in an area which may be covered by education. [1965] Ch. 669.

Commentary

[1] *Re Hopkins* broadened the courts' approach to education to allow for research provided it involved teaching or instruction or the dissemination of educationally valid material. It would be strange if, for instance medical research organisations were barred from charitable status on the grounds that they were not teaching bodies. Education can be extended to education of artistic taste: *Royal Choral Society v Commissioners of Inland Revenue* [1943] 2 All E.R. 101. For the purpose of determining whether VAT is payable "education" has been defined more narrowly in the sense of some formal instruction rather than a more general broadening or improving of the mind: *North of England Zoological Society v Customs and Excise Commissioners*, *The Times*, November 2, 1999.

[2] The Charity Commission in its decision on the *Agnostic Centre* decided that the Centre's goals which were to encourage others to adopt its viewpoint based on the principles of Gnosticism could not be said to be in advancement of education. The Commission stated that in order for it to be for the advancement of education, the education

> "does not have to be value free and completely neutral. It can be based on broad values that are uncontroversial which would be generally supported by objective and informed opinion".

It would also allow those being educated to make their own minds up. However, as in this case, if the purpose is for providing information or education in order to persuade others to form specific conclusions or accept certain beliefs then this is not in the advancement of education.

Key Principle

There is a threshold of merit in assessing the charitable status of an educational gift.

> **RE PINION 1965**
> A testator left his studio and its contents including paintings and other objets d'art to be endowed as a museum to display his collection. Experts gave evidence that the collection had no educational merit whatsoever.

Held

❖ (CA) Where the utility of a gift is in question, the court had to hear expert evidence on the quality and merit of the proposed exhibits in order to judge whether they would be conducive to the education of the public. Although the merit of the collection was a matter of taste, there was an accepted canon of taste. The overwhelming evidence was that the collection was worthless as a means of education and no purpose would be served by foisting on the public a "mass of junk". [1965] Ch. 85.

Commentary

The test of merit is fairly minimal but in cases of doubt the court should hear expert evidence. In *Re Delius* [1957] Ch. 299 the merit of Delius's work was clear. Increasing the public's knowledge of Delius's works was held to be charitable within the principles of *Royal Choral Society v Commissioners of Inland Revenue*, above.

ADVANCEMENT OF RELIGION

Key Principle

Religion for the purpose of charitable status means a theistic belief.

> **BOWMAN V SECULAR SOCIETY LTD 1917**
> The Secular Society was a limited company whose main object was
>
> > "to promote ... the principle that human conduct should be based upon natural knowledge and not upon supernatural belief, and that human welfare in this world is the proper end of all thought and action".

Held

❖ (HL) There was a valid trust in favour of the Society although not a charitable one. [1917] A.C. 406.

Commentary

[1] Lord Parker stated that a trust for the purpose of any kind of monotheistic theism would be a valid charitable trust. Before the **Charities Act 2011** there was uncertainty as to the extent of religion in that although it included the Christian religion the extent of non Christian religions which were recognized was not clear. The courts recognized as charitable a trust in respect of the Jewish faith: *Neville Estates v Madden* [1962] Ch. 832. The courts have accepted as charitable peculiar sects, provided that they are not adverse to the foundations of all religion or subversive of morality: *Thornton v Howe* (1862) 31 Beav. 14 and *Re Watson* (Deed) [1973] 1 W.L.R. 1472. Faith healing has been found to be a charitable purpose in *Re Le Cren Clarke* [1996] 1 W.L.R. 288. In contrast, ancestor worship has been denied charitable status in *Yeap Cheah Neo v Ong Cheng Neo* (1875) L.R. 6 P.C. 381.

[2] In *Re South Place Ethical Society* [1980] 1 W.L.R. 1565 the society was held not to have charitable status because, although its objects included the study and dissemination of ethical principles, its beliefs were non-theistic. In *United Grand Lodge of Ancient Free & Accepted Masons of England & Wales v Holborn Borough Council* [1957] 1 W.L.R. 1080, the freemasons were denied charitable status.

[3] Under s.3(2)(a) of the **Charities Act 2006**, religion is now defined to include a religion which involves the belief in more than one God and that which does not involve the belief in a God.

The Charity Commission in its guidance, "The Advancement of Religion for the Public Benefit" (issued 2008 and updated 2011), stated that for the purposes of the law of charity, in deciding whether a system belief is regarded as a religion, the courts have identified a number of characteristics which include:

- "belief in a god (or gods) or goddess (or goddesses), or supreme being, or divine or transcendental being or entity or spiritual principle, which is the object or focus of the religion (referred to throughout this guidance as 'supreme being or entity');
- a relationship between the believer and the supreme being or entity by showing worship of, reverence for or veneration of the supreme being or entity;
- a degree of cogency, cohesion, seriousness and importance;
- an identifiable positive, beneficial, moral or ethical framework".

The Commission is also required to have regard to Art.1 of the First Protocol (peaceful enjoyment of possessions), Art.9 (freedom of thought, conscience and religion and freedom to manifest one's religion or belief) and Art.14 (freedom from discrimination on the grounds of religion or belief) of the European Convention for Human Rights.

[4] In two recent cases, the Charity Commission has applied its guidelines. The first is *The Druid Network* [2010] where the Commission was asked to consider if the Druid Network could be registered as a charity. The Druid Network was an unincorporated association and its objects were

> "to provide information on the principles and practices of Druidry
> for the benefit of all and to inspire and facilitate that practice for
> those who have committed themselves to this spiritual path".

The Charity Commission were satisfied that within Druidry there was a sufficient belief in a supreme being to constitute a religion for the purposes of the charities law; there was evidence of worship of or reverence for and veneration of the supreme being or entity; there was a sufficient element of core practices and beliefs to conclude that the characteristics of cogency, cohesion, seriousness and important of religion were met; and there was evidence of an identifiable positive beneficial ethical framework that is capable of having a beneficial impact on the community at large. The Commission also concluded that the practices and beliefs were being advanced through the provision of information about Druidry and inspiring and facilitating that practice. Hence the Druid Network could be registered as a charity.

The second is the *Gnostic Centre* [2009], where the Charity Commission refused its application for registration as a charity as it was not established exclusively for charitable purposes for public benefit. The Commission found that whilst the Centre satisfies a number of the requirements of a religion it was not shown that all of the required characteristics were established. In particular it had not identified that a positive, beneficial, moral or ethical framework was being promoted and therefore it could regard the Centre as having been established for the advancement of religion.

THE ADVANCEMENT OF ANIMAL WELFARE

Key Principle
Trusts for the advancement of animal welfare must be for their benefit and enhance human behaviours.

RE GROVE-GRADY 1929
Money was left in a will to

> "provide a refuge or refuges for the preservation of all animals, birds or other creatures not human ... so that they shall be safe from molestation and destruction by man".

Held

❖ (CA) The trust would not have charitable status as the animals were free to harass each other at will and therefore did not promote their welfare. There was no advantage to the animals nor protection from cruelty. Further there was no public benefit as the public was excluded from the sanctuary. [1929] 1 Ch. 557.

Commentary

[1] Lord Hanworth MR stated that

> "one characteristic of the refuge is that it is free from the molestation of man, while all the fauna within are free to molest and harry one another ... It does not denote any elevating lesson to mankind".

Animal charities have been accepted as being charitable as it enhances humane behaviour as in *Re Wedgwood* [1915] 1 Ch. 1 13 and *Re Moss* [1949] 1 All E.R. 495. Animal homes and hospitals are normally accepted as being charitable as in *Re Douglas* (1887) 35 Ch. D. 472.

[2] In *Re Foveaux* [1895] W.N. 29, the anti-vivisection society was held to be charitable but this was successfully challenged in *National Anti-Vivisection Society v Inland Revenue Commissioners* [1948] A.C. 31. In the latter case, it was found that the alleviation of animal suffering was outweighed by the public benefit of vivisection in advancing medical research.

OTHER PURPOSES

Key Principle

The purposes of a trust could satisfy two or more of the charitable purposes.

The primary purpose of the Incorporated Society was

> "[t]he preparation and publication ... at a modest price and under gratuitous professional control, of reports of judicial decisions of the superior and appellate courts in England".

Held

❖ (CA) The Society was an educational charity. It was also said that it could be regarded as being for purposes beneficial to the community. [1972] Ch. 73.

Commentary

[1] This case which was pre-**Charities Act 2011** fell within two of the four heads of charities under the *Pemsel v IRC* categories. The decision would likely be the same under the Act.

[2] Gifts for the preservation of places of historical importance or beauty (*Re Cranstones Will Trusts* [1949] 1 Ch. 523) have also been held to be charitable. This is now covered by s.3(1)(f) of the **Charities Act 2011** —the advancement of the arts, culture, heritage or sciences.

[3] Gifts for a voluntary fire brigade (*Re Wokingam Fire Brigade Trusts* [1951] Ch. 373) and a gift to an officer's mess (*Re Good* [1905] 2 Ch. 60) have been held charitable. These two cases now fall within the ambit of s.3(1)(l) of the 2006 Act.

[4] In *Re Harding (Deceased)* [2007] EWHC 3, the court decided that a non specific gift to the black community of four London Boroughs could be construed as being implicitly limited to charitable purposes. Lewison J. accepted that this principle was probably to save an otherwise invalid gift. However, the reference to the race or colour would be removed under s.34 of the Race Relations Act 1976 otherwise it would invalidate the gift. This is explicitly stated in the guidance issued by the Charity Commission's guidance on public benefit where is states that

> "...although beneficiaries can be defined by reference to race, nationality, ethnic or national origin, the **Race Relations Act 1976** prevents charities from defining their beneficiaries by skin colour. Where a charity defines its beneficiaries by reference to their skin colour in its objects, the effect of the Race Relations Act is that the objects are treated as if that reference were omitted".

It gives the example of a charity for the benefit of black women in financial need would be construed as having objects "for the benefit of women in financial need".

[5] An organisation to promote a profession and benefit its members is not charitable (*General Nursing Council for England and Wales v St Marylebone Borough Council* [1959] A.C. 540).

[6] In *Helena Partnerships Ltd (formerly Helena Housing Ltd) v Revenue and Customs Commissioners* [2012] EWCA Civ 569, Helena Partnerships was incorporated in 2001 and its new memorandum and articles of association provided that its objects included the provision of housing, accommodation, assistance to house people; associated facilities and amenities; and any other object that could be carried out by a company registered as a social landlord with the Housing Corporation, for the benefit of the community. The Court of Appeal held that its purpose was not exclusively charitable as the provision of housing was not restricted to those with a particular need of the class eligible to occupy it. As the issue was with reference to circumstances before the **Charities Act 2006** came into force, the court decided that the purpose was not charitable as it was not beneficial to the community within *Pemsel v IRC* categories.

TRUSTS FOR RECREATIONAL PURPOSES

Key Principle

Trusts for recreational purposes may be charitable provided they are exclusively charitable or come within the terms of the **Recreational Charities Act 1958** (now s.5 of the **Charities Act 2011**).

INLAND REVENUE COMMISSIONERS V CITY OF GLASGOW POLICE ATHLETIC ASSOCIATION 1953
The association claimed exemption from tax on the profits of their sports event.

Held

❖ (HL) The association was not exempt, as it was not established "for charitable purposes only". Though improving police efficiency through athletic activity could be regarded as charitable, the purpose of providing recreation for members was not exclusively charitable and was not merely incidental to the charitable purposes. [1953] A.C. 380.

Land was conveyed on trusts to be used for the purpose of the

> "promotion of the religious, social and physical well-being of persons resident ... in West Ham and Leyton ... by the provision of facilities for religious services and instruction and for the social and physical training and recreation of such ... persons who ... are in the opinion of such leaders, members or likely to become members of the Methodist Church and of insufficient means otherwise to enjoy the advantages provided by these presents ...".

Held

❖ (HL) The trusts were not charitable. They did not fall within the fourth head of charity of other purposes beneficial to the community (under the *Pemsel v IRC* catergories). The language of the conveyances was too vague and allowed the property to be used for purposes which were not charitable or if prima facie charitable, was not of sufficient public benefit. The restriction to members or future members of the Methodist Church within a given area constituted a class within a class, which did not satisfy the test of public benefit. [1955] A.C. 572.

Commentary

[1] In both cases, the purposes in themselves could be charitable, but could only be enjoyed by a limited class of persons. In both cases there was no genuine benefit to a section of the community. As a response to cases such as these, the **Recreational Charities Act 1958** was introduced which is now superseded by the **Charities Act 2011**.

Section 5 of the **Charities Act 2011** provides that it would be charitable (and is to be treated as always having been charitable) where there is provision or assistance in the provision of facilities for recreation or other leisure time occupation. Section 5(3) stipulates the basic condition that needs to be made in order for it to be recognised as being charitable. They are (a) that the facilities are provided with the object of improving the conditions of life for the persons for whom the facilities are primarily intended; and (b) that those persons have need of the facilities because of their youth, age, infirmity or disability, poverty, or social and economic circumstances, or the facilities are to be available to members of the public at large or to male, or to female, members of the public at large.

It further goes on to explain in s.5(4) that s.5(1) applies in particular to (a) the provision of facilities at village halls, community centres and women's institutes; and (b) the provision and maintenance of grounds and buildings to be used for purposes of recreation or leisure-time occupation, and extends to the provision of facilities for those purposes by the organising of any activity. The section makes it clear that this is subject to the requirement that the facilities are provided in the interests of social welfare.

[2] The cases also illustrate the point that some of the requirements for charitable status overlap. The causes here did not satisfy the public benefit test, in that, it was incidental in *Inland Revenue Commissioners v City of Glasgow Police Athletic Association* and was limited to an insufficient class in *IRC v Baddeley*. Moreover, to the extent that the purposes were charitable, they did not satisfy the test of being exclusively charitable as the funds could be used for purposes other than charitable ones.

Key Principle

Under the **Recreational Charities Act 1958** (now superseded by **Charities Act 2011**), facilities for recreation provided with the object of benefiting a given group could be charitable even where the persons benefiting are not in a position of relative deprivation.

GUILD (EXECUTOR NOMINATE OF THE LATE JAMES YOUNG RUSSELL) V INLAND REVENUE COMMISSIONERS 1992

A testator left the residue of his estate

> "to the town council of North Berwick for the use in connection with the Sports Centre in North Berwick or some similar purpose in connection with sport".

The IRC argued that this bequest was not charitable and thus not tax exempt.

Held

❖ (HL) On the true construction of s.1(2)(a) of the **Recreational Charities Act 1958,** facilities for recreation or other leisure time occupation could be provided for improving the conditions of the persons for whom they were primarily intended, notwithstanding, that those persons were not in a position of relative social disadvantage or suffering a degree of deprivation. The facilities concerned were provided in the interests of social welfare, within the meaning of s.1 of the Act. [1992] 2 W.L.R. 397.

Commentary

The Act provides that facilities for recreation are deemed to be charitable if they are in the social interest and for the public benefit. This would be the case if they were provided to a group in need such as the young or infirm or if the facilities were available to the public at large. The Act has been amended by the **Charities Act 2011** to the extent that the facilities will be regarded as charitable provided it is available either to the public as a whole or to men or women only – s.5(3). In addition, trusts for the advancement of amateur sport are specifically listed as a separate charitable purpose under s.3(1)(g) of the **Charities Act 2011**.

TRUSTS FOR POLITICAL PURPOSES

Key Principle
Political trusts aiming to change the law are not charitable.

> **MCGOVERN V ATTORNEY-GENERAL 1982**
> Amnesty International was founded with the object of securing the observance of the human rights of prisoners of conscience throughout the world. It sought charitable status for part of its activity including the relief of prisoners of conscience and their families, securing the release of prisoners, campaigning for the abolition of torture and other inhuman treatment, and promoting research into the observance of human rights. It set up a trust deed to cover these objects for which it claimed charitable status.

Held
❖ (Ch) Though the relief of human suffering was charitable in its nature, it would not be charitable if any of its main objects were political. Trusts seeking to change the law of the UK or another country or seeking to alter government policy or administrative decisions were of a political nature. The object of securing the release of political prisoners through lawful persuasion to change the law, policy or administration of a country was political. That object affected all the other objects in the deed thus making it non-charitable. In particular, the object of procuring abolition of torture and inhuman treatment was a political purpose as it sought to change legislation. Further, the objects of researching into human rights would add to the sum of knowledge and be of public benefit but in the context they were merely adjunct to the other political purposes. [1982] Ch. 321.

Commentary

[1] Historically, the courts have been wary of trusts that use the accepted heads of charity as a guise for advancing political aims that are not charitable. In *Re Hopkinson* [1949] W.N. 29, a trust to advance education in accordance with the Labour Party manifesto was held not to be charitable. In *Re Strakosch* [1949] Ch. 529, it was held that a trust to strengthen unity in South Africa through improving relations between the English and Dutch communities was not charitable as it had a political character. In *Southwood v HM Attorney-General*, Lawtel, June 28, 2000, it was held that an organisation whose purpose was "the advancement of education of the public in the subject of militarism and disarmament and related fields" should not have charitable status. The court could not determine between differing views as to how peace should be secured. The promotion of pacifism was not necessarily charitable.

[2] The **Charities Act 2011** did not change the principle that a trust would not be recognized as charitable if its purpose was to advocate for a change in the law: *Hanchett-Stamford v HM Attorney General* [2008] 4 All E.R. 323 (see below).

[3] In *Re Koeppler's Will Trusts* [1984] 2 W.L.R. 973, a gift was made to the Wilton Park Centre which was a prestigious body which organised conferences on international political affairs with representatives from institutions such as NATO, OECD and the EEC. The Court of Appeal found that the trust was valid as advancing education and that any political content was incidental as the centre had no political affiliation. A similar approach can be seen in the Australian decision of where the court was able to separate the educational purpose from the political purpose.

[4] The Charity Commissioners in their guidance on Charities and Public Benefit stated that

> "... a political purpose cannot meet the public benefit requirement and so cannot be a charitable purpose. However, charities do have a great deal of freedom and flexibility to undertake political activities and campaigning as a way of carrying out their charitable aims".

Public Benefit in the Relief of Poverty

Key Principle

A gift which is primarily for the relief of poverty, albeit for a particular class of poor people, is for the public benefit and thus charitable.

> **DINGLE V TURNER 1972**
> A testator directed that the income of a trust be applied in paying pensions to poor employees of E Ltd, a company jointly owned by the testator.

Held

❖ (HL) A trust for "poor employees" was capable of being a valid charitable trust. The distinction between charitable trusts and private trusts depended, as a matter of construction, on whether the gift was for the relief of poverty amongst a particular description of poor people or was merely a gift to particular poor persons. [1972] A.C. 601.

Commentary

[1] In *Re Scarisbrick* [1951] Ch. 622, the Court of Appeal made clear that a different test was to be applied to trusts for the relief of poverty. The House of Lords in the present case followed this view. This has been reiterated in *Re Cohen* [1973] 1 W.L.R. 415 (a gift for relatives "in special" need) and *Re Segelman* [1995] 3 All E.R. 676 (a gift for "poor and needy" members of the family "in order to relieve hardship").

[2] This is now subject to the Charity Commission's guidance under s.17 of the **Charities Act 2011** and to s.4(2) of the Act which states that public benefit has to be proved and is not merely to be presumed from a description of the purpose of the trust. Hence a trust for the relief of poverty will now need to prove the public benefit requirement and cannot be presumed from the fact that it is for the relief of poverty in itself. However, the Attorney General lodged a reference to the First Tier Tribunal which asks whether a benevolent fund for the relief of poverty can have charity status if it benefits only

- those people related to a certain individual, or
- employees of a particular employer or employers, or
- the members of a particular society or organisation.

The reference also asks whether the public benefit requirement applies to charities set up to prevent poverty in the same way that it applies to those set up to relieve poverty. In its decision the Upper Tribunal FTC/84/2011 (it was referred from the First Tier to the Upper Tier Tribunal) stated that there were two aspects to public benefit. The first is that the nature of the purpose itself must be such as to be a benefit to the community – the Tribunal referred to this as public benefit in the first sense. It went on to state that public benefit in the second sense is that

> "those who may benefit from the carrying out of the purpose must be sufficiently numerous, and identified in such manner, as to constitute what is described in the authorities as 'a section of the public'".

The Tribunal decided that

> "*a trust for the relief of poverty which had a narrow class of direct beneficiary, the trust was nonetheless charitable under the law prior to the 2006 Act even though the class was not wide enough to establish public benefit in the second sense as applied to poverty trusts. In order that a trust for the relief of poverty with a narrow class of beneficiary should be charitable, the public benefit requirement as applied to such a trust required only that public benefit in the first sense be established. The 2006 Act has not, in our judgment, changed that. The 'public benefit' as that term was understood for the purposes of the law of charity required, in the context of a trust for the relief of poverty, only that public benefit in the first sense should be shown. Of course, a trust for the relief of poverty might be one which is also for the public benefit in the second sense because the class of potential beneficiary is, on any view, a sufficient section of the community. But it does not follow from that consideration that every trust for the relief of poverty must be for the public benefit in the second sense*".

In answering the questions that were referred by the Attorney General the Upper Tribunal provided the following answers:

"Question 2.1: Whether a trust for the relief of poverty amongst a class of potential objects of the trust's bounty defined by reference to the relationship of the potential objects to one or more individuals is capable of being a charitable trust. — YES

Question 2.2: Whether a trust for the relief of poverty amongst a class of potential objects of the trust's bounty defined by reference to their or a member of their family's employment or former employment by one or specified commercial companies is capable of being a charitable trust. — YES

Question 2.3: Whether a trust for the relief of poverty amongst the members of an unincorporated association or their families is capable of being a charitable trust — YES

Question 2.4: Whether Part I of the **Charities Act 2006** operates so as statutorily to reverse the decisions in any, and if which, of the following cases:
  (a) *Att Gen v Price* (1810) 17 Ves. 371.
  (b) *Re Scarisbrick* [1951] Ch. 622.
  (c) *Gibson v South American Stores (Gath & Chaves) Ltd* [1949] Ch. 572 (Harman J.), [1950] Ch. 177 (C.A.).
  (d) *Dingle v Turner* [1972] A.C. 601.
  (e) *Spiller v Maude* (1886) L.R. 32 Ch. D 158.

Answer: No in all cases. Our analysis of the cases and the principles demonstrated that none of the decisions referred to in this Question is affected by the 2006 Act because it is not necessary to show public benefit in the second sense, the absence of which is the only ground on which it could be argued that the 2006 Act has changed the position."
    The position under the **Charities Act 2011** will be the same as under the 2006 Act as the provisions are the same.

[3] In its guidance on Public Benefit and Charities (issued in 2008 and amended in December 2011) the Charity Commission has identified two key principles and a number of factors which must be considered. The first key principle is that there must be an identifiable benefit and in applying this it must be clear what the benefits are, that they are related to the charity's aims and must be balanced against any possible detriment or harm. The second principle is that the benefit has to be for the public or a section of the public. The factors to be considered under this are that it is important that the beneficiaries are appropriate to the aims and that the benefit must not be restricted by geographical or other restrictions and that those in poverty must not be excluded. It further states that any private benefit can only be incidental.
    The Commission has also recognised that "... what constitutes public benefit can change over time, as modern needs and circumstances change ... influenced ... by social and economic conditions". It also made clear that it will take necessary action against charities which do not meet the public benefit requirement in terms of helping them amend their stated purposes,

and if the charity refuses to cooperate then the Commission will use its regulatory powers to enforce change.

The Charity Commission in explaining the concept of the public or a section of the public stated that it

> "... is not a simple matter of numbers, but the number of people who can potentially benefit (now or in the future) must not be negligible. What is important is who could benefit, as well as who is benefiting. The class of people who can benefit must be a public class. In general, the public class must be sufficiently large or open in nature given the charitable aim that is to be carried out. The actual number of people who can benefit at one time can be quite small provided that anyone who qualifies as a beneficiary is eligible to be considered. A charity is for the public benefit if the benefits it offers are made widely available, even though in practice only a few people from time to time are able to benefit".

Part of the Charity Commission's guidance on public benefit has had to be withdrawn following the decision of the Upper Tribunal about the Commission's guidance on public benefit and fee-charging in relation to educational charities – *The Independent Schools Council v The Charity Commission for England v Wales* [2011] UKUT 421. The Commission is in the process of revising the guidance about what trustees must now have regard to in relation to fee charging charities and this was expected to be issued in the summer of 2012 but at the date of writing this has not yet been released. It is now expected to be issued in early 2013.

Key Principle

A scheme can still be of public benefit where beneficiaries might make incidental profits.

JOSEPH ROWNTREE MEMORIAL TRUST HOUSING ASSOCIATION LTD V ATTORNEY GENERAL 1983

The plaintiff charitable housing trust wished to build dwellings for elderly people. The terms of the scheme were that applicants would have to be of a certain age. They would have to pay a capital sum, be able to pay service charges, live independently and be in need of the type of accommodation provided. The Charity Commissioners argued that the scheme was not charitable in that benefits were conferred by contract not bounty.

❖ (Ch) In applying the spirit of the 1601 preamble, the beneficiaries could be aged or poor and not necessarily both, though there had to be "relief" of one or other of those conditions. A charitable gift did not have to be made solely by bounty. That the beneficiaries contributed towards the cost of the benefit on a contractual basis and the absence of a termination provision for when a beneficiary ceased to qualify did not prevent the scheme being charitable. The security of tenure was part of the need for accommodation for the elderly, which the scheme was relieving. Any profit the beneficiary might make was incidental and not at the expense of the charity; it did not make the scheme as a whole non-charitable. [1983] 2 W.L.R. 284.

Commentary

The court took a broad view of the way in which a need can be relieved within the bounds of public benefit. The court's concern was to give effect to the underlying intent of the scheme notwithstanding that to give proper effect to the aim of providing secure housing would stretch the benefit to the indivi-dual beyond that which is normally acceptable. This is subject to the guidance issued by the Charity Commission which states that any private benefit must be incidental.

Public Benefit in the Advancement of Education

Key Principle

The test of public benefit is not satisfied where the beneficiaries are iden-tified on the basis of a personal nexus with the settlor.

OPPENHEIM V TOBACCO SECURITIES TRUST CO LTD 1951
Trustees were directed to apply certain income "in providing for the ... education of children of employees or former employees" of a British company and its subsidiaries or allied companies. There were 110,000 such employees.

Held

❖ (HL) Although the group was large, the nexus between them was employment by particular employers. Therefore, the trust did not satisfy the public benefit test to be charitable. [1951] A.C. 297.

Commentary

Where there is a personal nexus between the beneficiary and settlor then the test of public benefit is not satisfied. As a matter of public policy, it is difficult to justify tax exemption for trusts where they are limited by the nature of a person's employment. In *Re Compton* [1945] 1 All E.R. 198, a gift for the education of the descendants of three named people was not charitable as they could not be regarded as a sufficient section of the community. In *Re Koettgen's Will Trusts* [1954] Ch. 252, a trust for the education of members of the public who could not do so at their own expense with a preference to the employees of a particular organization was held to be charitable. This decision has however been criticised and Pennycuick J. in *IRC v Education Grants Association Ltd* [1967] Ch. 123 affirmed in [1967] Ch. 993, expressed difficulty with *Re Koettgen*.

Public Benefit in the Advancement of Religion

Key Principle

The public benefit of a gift for the purpose of advancement of religion must be capable of proof.

> **GILMOUR V COATS 1949**
> Money was to be held on trust for the purposes, if charitable, of a Roman Catholic priory consisting of cloistered nuns who "devoted their lives to prayer, contemplation, penance and self-sanctification". Evidence was given as to Roman Catholic doctrine of the benefit to the public through intercessory prayers and the example of their self-denial.

Held

❖ (HL) The purposes of the priory were not charitable. The benefits of intercessory prayer were not susceptible to proof and the value of the example of self-denial was too vague. The court needed proof of tangible public benefit. [1949] A.C. 426.

Commentary

[1] The House of Lords made the important point that the requirement of public benefit applied equally to the advancement of religion as to other heads of charity. In *Neville Estates v Madden* [1962] Ch. 832 it was said that the court was entitled to assume that some benefit arose from attendance at a place of worship. In *Re Hetherington* [1989] 2 W.L.R. 1094, it was held that gifts for the saying of masses, a religious purpose, were prima facie charitable. There was sufficient public benefit so long as the masses were said in public and stipends thereby payable to priests relieved the Church's other funds.

[2] The Charity Commission in its guidance in the Advancement of Religion for Public Benefit has stated that in order to advance religion for public benefit, charities could do this in a number of ways. This could include firstly,

" ... seeking new followers: it is not necessary for all charities whose aims include advancing religion to seek new followers or adherents. In the case of some religions (such as Sikhism), followers or adherents are born into the religion and people who are not born into the religion are not able to convert to it. In those cases, the 'advancement' of the religion will not be concerned with encouraging people to join the religion, since that is determined by birth, but may be concerned with the personal and social effects of the religion being practised by such followers or adherents".

Secondly, it would also encompass

" ... promoting particular tenets of religion: some charities whose aims include advancing religion might choose to concentrate on promoting particular tenets of the religion in order to further what they believe to be an inherently important aspect of that religion. Provided the purpose is not so narrow as to produce either insufficient public benefit or have little consideration for the broader teachings of the religion, this should not affect the organisation"s charitable status".

EXCLUSIVELY CHARITABLE

Key Principle
A gift must be devoted to solely charitable purposes to acquire charitable status.

> CHICHESTER DIOCESAN FUND AND BOARD OF FINANCE V SIMPSON 1944
> A testator left the residue of his estate to be applied "for such charitable institution or institutions or other charitable or benevolent object or objects in England".

Held
❖ (HL) The bequest was void for uncertainty. The word "benevolent" had a wider meaning than charitable. The word "or" permitted a choice between "charitable" and "benevolent". Thus, non-charitable benevolent purposes

could be selected, meaning that the bequest was not exclusively charitable. In the absence of exclusive charitable intent, the gift also failed as a trust because there was no certainty of beneficiaries. [1944] A.C. 341.

Commentary

[1] Similarly, in *Blair v Duncan* [1902] A.C. 37, a bequest "for such charitable or public purposes as my trustee thinks proper" failed because some or all of the funds could have been used for "public purposes which were not charitable". The Privy Council in *Att-Gen of the Bahamas v Royal Trust Co* [1986] 3 All E.R. 423 also read the bequest disjunctively. One might think that the courts might take a more "charitable" reading of such bequests, but, in the absence of certain words and evidence, the court cannot second-guess a testator's intent.

[2] Where non-charitable purposes are wholly subsidiary to the charity, the gift may be valid. In *London Hospital Medical College v Inland Revenue Commissioners* [1976] 1 W.L.R. 613, it was held that a Students' Union was charitable although it provided specific benefits to its members because these were incidental to its overall charitable educational purpose.

[3] In *Gaudiya Mission v Kamalaksha Das Brahmachary* [1998] 2 W.L.R. 175 it was confirmed that an English court did not have jurisdiction over a charity unless it was registered in the UK under the **Charities Act 1993**. This is now reflected in the **Charities Act 2011**.

[4] Words in a gift cannot be construed as being limited to charitable purposes only where there was no evidence that such a limitation was intended. *Attorney-General of the Cayman Islands v Even Wahr-Hansen* [2000] 3 W.L.R. 869. The gift provided for any one or more religious, charitable or educational institution or any organisations or institutions operating for the public good. The second clause was held not to be exclusively charitable. Its extent was not limited by the first clause. Public good was not synonymous with charitable at law. A somewhat different conclusion was reached in *Archbishop Torkom Manoogian v Sonsino*, Lawtel, May 7, 2002. It was held that a gift to the Armenian Patriarch for the purpose of education and advancement in life of Armenian children or for such other charitable purpose or purposes as he may consider allied thereto was a valid charitable gift.

THE CY-PRÈS DOCTRINE

A charitable fund may be applied cy-près to give effect to the spirit of the gift.

> **PEGGS V LAMB 1994**
> Ancient rights of grazing on certain areas of land existed in favour of the freemen of Huntingdon. By 1829, these included the right to income from other uses of the land. Later, the land became vested in Huntingdon Corporation upon trust for the freeman. Parts of the land were sold; the capital was placed in a separate fund the income of which also being held on trust for the freemen. By 1960, the trusts were recognised as charities for the provision of income for the freeman and their widows. By 1991, there were only 34 possible beneficiaries yet the annual income was £550,000 and the assets were £4 million in cash and 700 acres of agricultural land. The trustees believed that annual distribution amongst the class was no longer consistent with a charitable application. They proposed an application to only freemen and their widows in need with the surplus applied to the sick and needy of the borough.

Held

❖ (Ch) The provision of funds to a class was not of itself charitable and had to be interpreted within the preamble to the **Charitable Uses Act 1601**. The size of the fund and decline in number of freemen had led to an equal distribution falling outside that spirit. Having regard to the spirit of the gift the freemen had now ceased to be a suitable class by reference to which the charitable purpose could be carried out. Consequently, a cy-près scheme under s.13 of the **Charities Act 1993** would be settled so as to extend the class to all the inhabitants of the borough. [1994] Ch. 172.

> **VARSANI V JESANI 1998**
> A charity was established to promote the faith of a sect of the Hindu religion. In 1990, a minority group in the sect sought a declaration that the majority group's leader was no longer the sect's spiritual leader, that the members who followed him could no longer worship in the London temple and the members should no longer have the benefit of the assets of the charity. These proceedings were stayed. In 1997, the majority group applied for a cy-près scheme under s.13(1)(e)(iii) of the **Charities Act 1993**. The judge at first instance determined that it was not possible to determine which group of the sect were the true followers of the original faith. He also decided that it was not necessary to

do so because he had wide jurisdiction under s.13 to make a regulatory scheme. He ordered the assets of the charity to be held on two separate trusts for the furtherance of the sect's faith as practised by the two groups. The minority group appealed arguing that the judge should have directed enquiries to determine if either group had ceased to profess the faith which the charity had been established to promote. The Attorney General also contended that the judge lacked jurisdiction under s.13 until the exact original purposes of the charity had been determined. The scheme approved by the judge in his opinion was not justified because the purpose of the charity can only be fulfilled by those professing to the original faith.

Held

❖ (CA) The judge did have jurisdiction under s.13(1)(e)(iii). Section 13 did not depend on the original purposes being impossible or impractical but whether the case fell within one of the sub-heads of s.13. The true test to be found in s.13(1)(e)(iii) was whether the original purposes had ceased to provide a suitable and effective method of using the property, regard being had to the spirit of the gift. The impasse between the groups meant that the original purpose of the charity had ceased to be a suitable and effective method of using the property. Thus, the court did have jurisdiction to apply a cy-près scheme. [1999] 2 W.L.R. 255.

Commentary

Section 13 of the **Charities Act 1960** (now the **Charities Act 1993**) extended the jurisdiction to apply a cy-près scheme beyond instances of impossibility or impracticality to allow for the spirit of bequests to be given effect. In *Versani v Jesani*, Lawtel, September 13, 2001 it was not necessarily relevant to the question of jurisdiction whether one group or the other had ceased to profess the original faith. It was because of the schism and impasse that the spirit of the gift could not be properly implemented and that the court had the jurisdiction to make a new scheme. See also *White v Williams* [2010] EWHC 940.

The case of *In the Matter of Clara Broadbent*, Lawtel, May 17, 2001, illustrates the importance of avoiding uncertainty in the terminology of bequests. A bequest provided for various gifts including to the Vicar and Church Wardens of St Matthews Church for the general purposes of the church with the request that the money be used primarily for the upkeep of the fabric of the church. Notwithstanding that the church never had a Vicar or wardens and that the particular church had been demolished, the Court of Appeal found that there could still be a gift for the general purposes of the church.

Under the **Charities Act 2011**, it is made clear in s.62 that a trust for charitable purposes places a trustee under a duty, provided the circumstances so permit, and requires the property or some part of it to be applied cy-près, to secure its effective use for charity by taking steps to enable it to be so applied. In s.63, the Act provides that the circumstances under which the original purposes of a charitable gift can be altered to allow the property given or part of it to be applied cy-près are:

(a) where the original purposes, in whole or in part (i) have been as far as may be fulfilled, or (ii) cannot be carried out, or not according to the directions given and to the spirit of the gift;

(b) where the original purposes provide a use for part only of the property available by virtue of the gift;

(c) where (i) the property available by virtue of the gift, and (ii) other property applicable for similar purposes, can be more effectively used in conjunction, and to that end can suitably, regard being had to the appropriate considerations, be made applicable to common purposes;

(d) where the original purposes were laid down by reference to (i) an area which then was but has since ceased to be a unit for some other purpose, or (ii) a class of persons or an area which has for any reason since ceased to be suitable, regard being had to the appropriate considerations, or to be practical in administering the gift; or

(e) where the original purposes, in whole or in part, have, since they were laid down (i) been adequately provided for by other means, (ii) ceased, as being useless or harmful to the community or for other reasons, to be in law charitable, or (iii) ceased in any other way to provide a suitable and effective method of using the property available by virtue of the gift, regard being had to the appropriate considerations.

These provisions now supersede the provisions on cy-près in the **Charities Act 1993** as amended by the **Charities Act 2006**.

Key Principle

Where a gift fails from the outset, the court will not direct a cy-près application unless they are satisfied that the testator had a general charitable intention.

Re Rymer 1895

A testator bequeathed £5,000 to the rector for the time being of St Thomas' Seminary for the education of priests in the diocese of

Westminister for the purposes of such seminary. The seminary closed just before the testator's death.

Held

❖ (CA) The bequest was for the particular institution. The institution having ceased to exist during the testator's lifetime, the legacy could not be applied cy-près and fell into the residue. [1895] 1 Ch. 19.

KINGS V BULTITUDE 2010

The settlor S, was an active member of a church and by clause 8 of her will left a gift of residue of around £449,000

> "to the person who ... shall act as the Trustee of the Ancient Catholic Church known as the Church of the Good Shepherd ... for the general purposes of the said Church ...".

She was the designated keeper of the church archives, and from 1995 until just before she died, she conducted services in the church as a minister of the church. Just before she died, the church closed down and the building was used by another church with the congregation going its separate ways. Following S's death, probate of her last will was granted. The claimant who was a solicitor and executor of the will sought a declaration from the courts as to a number of questions in respect of the residuary estate.

Held

❖ (Ch D) The rule that was applicable was that if the purposes of the particular church carried on in another premises and only the building ceased to be available for its use then the church could be regarded as carrying on its purpose and the gift would not be allowed to fail. However, in this case S was a crucial part of the church and when she was not able to continue to take part in its activities, the church itself and its purposes then became defunct. It was clear from the evidence that S had intended to make the gift to this particular church as a distinct institution and as there was nothing in the will that indicated that she had a general charitable intention. The residuary estate was not subject to a valid charitable gift which had failed subsequently or one in which the initial purpose had failed but that could be applied cy-près as there was a lack of the general charitable intent. [2010] EWHC 1795.

Commentary

[1] In *Re Rymer*, it was clear from the evidence that the testator's gift was specific and did not evince a general charitable intention. This was the same conclusion in *Kings v Bultitude*. In *Biscoe v Jackson* [1887] 35 Ch. D. 460, money was left to establish a soup kitchen in Shoreditch. The intended land was not available upon the testator's death but it was held that the money could be re-applied as the general charitable intention existed to benefit the poor and sick of the area.

[2] Where a gift is to a corporate charity, there is a tendency to assume that the gift is for that specific body. Where the gift is to an unincorporated charity the assumption is usually that the gift is to the purpose of that charity and is more easily re-applied to another charity with the same purpose. See *Re Vernon's Will Trusts* [1972] Ch. 300 and *Re Fingers Will Trusts* [1972] Ch. 286. In *Re Spence* [1979] Ch. 483, this line was followed where a gift to a specific old folks' home was held to be for that institution and not for the general purpose of providing for the elderly. In the absence of a general charitable intention, no cy-près scheme could be applied. A gift to a specific institution can be applied to successor bodies or amalgamated bodies even if the purposes are slightly wider though not if they are significantly different: *Re Faraker* [1912] 2 Ch. 488.

[3] Where the gift can take effect but later fails because the object ceases to exist, then that is known as subsequent failure. Where there is subsequent failure, there is no need to establish general charitable intention in order to make a cy-près application.

Non-Charitable Trusts

INTRODUCTION

Key Principle

A private trust must have a beneficiary capable of enforcing the trust.

> RE ASTOR 1952
> A settlement contained trusts which included the
>
> > "maintenance of ... good understanding ... between nations, ... the preservation of the independence and integrity of newspapers ... and the protection of newspapers ... from being absorbed or controlled by combines".

It was agreed that the purposes were not charitable but were within the rule against perpetuities.

Held

❖ (Ch) The trusts were invalid because they were not for the benefit of individuals but for non-charitable purposes, which no one could enforce. The purposes were also void for uncertainty. [1952] Ch. 534.

Commentary

In *Morice v Bishop of Durham* (1805) 10 Ves. 522, the court was clear that there must be a human beneficiary capable of enforcing the trust in the case of a non charitable private trust. Where there is no beneficiary then the trust is void. This has been followed by the Canadian court in *Ernst & Young v Central Guaranty Trust Co (No.2)* [2004–2005] 7 I.T.E.L.R. 69. Where a gift is intended to be for a charitable purpose but which is held not to be charitable then the gift to the non-charitable purpose will not take effect as a trust, as in *Re Shaw*, above. Where the trust is invalid then the property will go to the giftover, if any, or on resulting trust or ultimately become bona vacantia if there is no other potential recipient.

Key Principle

There are exceptions to the rule that a private trust requires a human beneficiary.

RE HOOPER 1932

A testator bequeathed money out of which income was to be applied "so far as they legally can do so and in any manner that they may in their discretion arrange" for the care and upkeep of certain graves, a vault, certain monuments, a tablet and a window.

Held

❖ (Ch) The trust would be valid for a period of 21 years from the testator's death. [1932] 1 Ch. 38.

RE DEAN 1889

The testator left an annual sum of £750 for the upkeep of stables and kennels for his horses and hounds.

Held

❖ (Ch) The money was not given to the trustees beneficially but was held on trust for the horses and hounds so long as they shall live. (1889) 41 Ch. D. 552.

Commentary

[1] The rule against perpetual trusts did not apply to the church tablet and window. The court kept the other parts of the bequest within the rule by restricting the validity of the gift to 21 years. The result in allowing for a non-charitable purpose trust still leaves the question as to who could enforce the trust. It may have been better to attribute by analogy charitable status to the purposes. In *Re Dean*, the time limit was thought to satisfy the rule against perpetual trusts.

[2] Section 15(4) of the Perpetuities and Accumulations Act 1964 provides for the period in respect of the rule against perpetual trust to be lives in being plus 21 years. The section states as follows:

> *"Nothing in this Act shall affect the operation of the rule of law rendering void for remoteness certain dispositions under which property is limited to be applied for purposes other than the benefit of any person or class of persons in cases where the property may be so applied after the end of the perpetuity period".*

The Perpetuities and Accumulations Act 2009 replaced the common law perpetuity period with a fixed period of 125 years. However this does not apply to purpose trusts as this was excluded from the review of the perpetuity rule by the Law Commission. Section 18 of the Perpetuities and Accumulations Act 2009 states that the Act does not affect the rule of law which limits the duration of non-charitable purpose trusts.

[3] In addition to trusts for the erection and maintenance of monuments and graves, and maintenance of animals, other types of purpose trusts which have been recognised include:

(a) trusts for saying of mass (*Bourne v Keane* [1919] A.C. 815) though these can now be regarded as charitable anyway as in *Re Hetherington*, above;

(b) possibly, trusts for unincorporated associations, see *Re Lipinski's Will Trust* below; and

(c) other miscellaneous trusts (*Re Thompson* [1934] Ch. 342, a bequest to be applied for the promotion and furtherance of fox-hunting).

Key Principle

The court will not extend the class of anomalous purpose trusts unless they have a sufficiently certain purpose.

> RE ENDACOTT 1960
> (See Ch.3.)

Held

❖ (CA) The bequest did not fall within the class of non-charitable purpose trusts, as it was too wide and uncertain in nature to be enforceable. [1960] Ch. 232.

Commentary

For a non-charitable purpose trust to be accepted it must fall clearly within the recognised classes of purpose trusts otherwise it will not be valid. The court in *Re Endacott* made it clear that the exceptions were not to be extended as they were regarded as "troublesome, anomalous and aberrant".

Key Principle

A gift for an unincorporated association may be valid if, though, described for a purpose, there is a benefit for ascertained or ascertainable beneficiaries.

> RE DENLEY'S TRUST DEED 1969
> Trusts were declared of land to be used for recreation, primarily as a sports ground for employees of the company and such other persons as the trustees may allow. If less than 75 per cent of employees sub-scribed to use the sport ground, the land was to be conveyed to a hospital. The trustees sought a determination as to whether there was a valid trust or whether the giftover to the hospital should take effect.

Held

❖ (Ch) The trust was valid because, though the trust was not charitable and expressed for purposes rather than beneficiaries, the purpose was directly or indirectly for the benefit of individuals. The class of employees was suffi-ciently ascertainable and the class of other persons was a valid power from which every member need not be identified. The court could enforce the trust by restraining improper use of the land or by ordering the trustee to allow employees and others to use the land for recreation. [1969] 1 Ch. 373.

Re Lipinski's Will Trusts 1976

A testator left part of his estate to the Hull Judeans (Maccabi) Association to be used solely in constructing and improving the new buildings for the association. At the time of his death, the association was not charitable. It did not have premises of its own at that time but did acquire its own premises subsequently. Another part was left to the Hull Hebrew Board of Deputies, which was charitable, for the sole purpose of constructing and improving the new buildings for the "association". The executors sought a determination as to whether the bequests were valid or void for impracticality.

Held

❖ (Ch) The gift (though to a non-charitable unincorporated association) was valid as there were ascertainable beneficiaries, i.e. the members of the association and the purpose of the bequest was within the powers of the association. Notwithstanding the word "solely", they could vary the trust. The term "new buildings" meant whatever buildings the association had or chose to build or buy; the reference to improvements did not mean such continuity so as break the rule against perpetuities. The rules of the association were sufficient to regulate the purpose in the bequest. [1976] Ch. 235.

Commentary

[1] The modern approach to purpose trusts of non-charitable unincorporated associations is that they are valid if there are individuals who benefit, a clear purpose and some way of regulating the bequest within the intended purpose. The regulation may in fact be self-regulation.

[2] Earlier cases had considered a variety of possible interpretations of gifts to non-charitable unincorporated associations. *Re Recher's Will Trusts* [1972] Ch. 526 and *Neville Estates v Madden* [1962] Ch. 832, indicate four possibilities:

(a) a gift to the current members to be distributed amongst themselves;

(b) a gift to present and future members (though such a gift would have to be phrased to come within the rule against perpetuities);

(c) a gift to the officers of the association to be held on trust to carry out the purposes of the trust; and

(d) a gift to the existing members to be managed according to the rules of the association but not divisible amongst existing members; each member's "share" accruing to future members.

In *Re Recher's Will Trusts* an absolute gift to an anti-vivisection society was held to be a gift to the members of that society (not those of the larger society into which it later amalgamated). The gift was not to the individual members to distribute amongst themselves but was to be treated as an accretion to the funds, which constituted the subject matter of the contract between the members. However, since the society had dissolved before the will was made, the gift failed. The fourth interpretation, which was applied in the case, is reconcilable with the approach in *Denley* and *Lipinski*, though, in the latter case, the court seems to have allowed more leeway to the members in applying the purpose than was intended in the bequest.

In *Re St Andrew's (Cheam) Lawn Tennis Club Trust* 15 I.T.E.L.R. 105, the court held that land which was purchased with the assistance of various donations and gifts, for the Club for use as tennis courts, was to be for the benefit of present and future members of the association. However this failed as it was not a charitable trust. It infringed the rule against perpetuities. As a result the land was held on a resulting trust in favour of the estate of T who was the largest single donor for the club in the acquisition of the land as the other smaller donations were predicated on that one donation.

Note also *Re Horley Football Club* [2006] W.T.L.R. 1817 where the court applied the fourth interpretation in dealing with a gift of land on trust to be used as a football ground.

[3] In deciding how to construe the gift or trust in favour of an unincorporated association, the court may take into account various factors. This includes the character of the recipients as in *Leahy v Attorney-General of New South Wales* [1959] A.C. 457 where the trust was in favour of an order of contemplative nuns such that the possibility that they would take the property beneficially was an unlikely outcome. In addition, the court will consider the association's rules as seen in *Re Grant's Will Trust* [1980] 1 W.L.R. 360. Here, the association rules made it clear that the members of the association—the Chertsey Labour Party—did not control the property of the association nor could they change the rules in order to gain control of the property. Its rules were subject to the approval of the National Executive Committee of the Labour Party. Hence the trust was for a non charitable purpose which failed.

[4] Gifts to associations that are incorporated, (there being no possibility of a trust or a Recher type solution) have been treated on an agency or mandate basis, i.e. the gift is deemed to be given for a given purpose, which if not satisfied is returnable on the ground that the agency or mandate has not been performed. See *Conservative and Unionist Central Office v Burrell* [1982] 1 W.L.R. 522.

Key Principle

Where the assets are owned by the members of the unincorporated association on a contractual basis, the last surviving member is entitled to the assets absolutely.

> **HANCHETT-STAMFORD V HM ATTORNEY GENERAL 2008**
> The claimant was the sole surviving member of an unincorporated association and sought a declaration that its objects were charitable with an order appointing herself and her solicitor as trustees of the funds to transfer it to another charity. The claimant and her husband were the only two members of the association and the latter died in 2006. The association has as its purpose
>
> > "to make illegal performances by animals by cruelty in the 'training'" and to "make unprofitable the infliction of cruelty in the production of animal films shown on the British screen".
>
> The court had to decide whether the association was a charity, and, if it was not, to whom its assets should be transferred.

Held

❖ (Ch) The association could not be and was never a charitable in nature as it had as one of its objects to change the law. The **Charities Act 2006 (Charities Act 2011)** did not alter the rule that a trust could not be charitable if one of its purposes was to change the law. The claimant as the last surviving member of the association was therefore entitled to its assets since the association ceased to exist upon the death of the husband. [2008] 4 All E.R. 323.

Commentary

Lewison J. suggested that ownership of the assets of the association by the members was not a traditional joint tenancy but as the collective ownership of property had to be either a joint tenancy or tenancy in common, the ownership by the members of an unincorporated association was therefore a sub-species of a joint tenancy. This type of co-ownership was however subject to the contractual limitations imposed by association. The rights of the members were contractual in nature which therefore ceased upon death and their interest accrued to the remainder of the co-owners based on the survivorship principle.

THINK POINT

In the context of a charitable trust, in which the guidance on the requirement of public benefit suggests that there should be no restriction for the public to benefit by the payment of fees, what would the status be of a racing club which charges a high fee to join because of the equipment costs? Would it not be possible for it to be charitable?

Why did Parliament leave the guidance as to what is public benefit to the Charity Commission? Do you think that this is the correct approach?

In *Re Lipinski's Will Trusts*, do you think the court's decision was correct in concluding that the gift was for human beneficiaries even though ostensibly for a purpose?

Resulting Trust

5

INTRODUCTION

A resulting trust is one type of implied trust, the constructive trust being the other. A conventional classification of resulting trusts includes the automatic and presumed resulting trusts. The main feature of a resulting trust is that the transferor or settlor becomes the beneficial owner because of the inability to determine what the transferor intended. This arises by operation of various presumptions (the presumed resulting trust) and by operation of law as a result of a gap of ownership (the automatic resulting trust).

In *Westdeutsche Landesbank Girozentrale v Islington Borough Council* [1996] A.C. 669, Lord Browne-Wilkinson stated, obiter, that

> "a resulting trust arises in two sets of circumstances: (A) where A makes a voluntary payment to B or pays (wholly or in part) for the purchase of property which is vested either in B alone or in the joint names of A and B, there is a presumption that A did not intend to make a gift to B: the money or property is held on trust for A ….or in the case of a joint purchase by A and B in shares proportionate to their contributions. (B) Where A transfers property to B *on express trusts*, but the trusts declared do not exhaust the whole beneficial interest."

His Lordship went on to say that

> "[b]oth types of resulting trust are traditionally regarded as examples of trusts giving effect to the common intention of the parties … [and] gives effect to his presumed intention".

His Lordship did not agree that resulting trusts could arise automatically. However, this view is not consistent with existing case law such as *Re Vandervell's Trusts (No. 2)* [1974] 1 All E.R. 47 where an automatic resulting trust was found to exist on the facts.

AUTOMATIC RESULTING TRUSTS

Key Principle

An automatic resulting trust arises where the purpose of a trust fails.

> BARCLAYS BANK LTD V QUISTCLOSE INVESTMENTS LTD 1970
> R Ltd decided to declare dividends on its share but was unable to pay for it. The defendant provided R Ltd with a loan for the purpose of paying for this dividend. The money was deposited in a separate account with the plaintiff. The plaintiff agreed that the money was to be used for the payment of the dividend. R Ltd went into liquidation with substantial debts before the dividend was paid. The defendant claimed to be entitled to the money in the separate account.

Held

❖ (HL) The arrangement for payment of creditors (the shareholders) by the defendant constituted a trust for the shareholders, which if it failed, would lead to a resulting trust for the defendant. That the transaction was a loan did not prevent it from simultaneously being a trust. As the money was not used for its intended purpose, there was a resulting trust. There was evidence that if the primary use of the money was not fulfilled, the money should return to the lender. The plaintiff could not withhold the money from the defendant but held it as constructive trustee. [1970] A.C. 567.

> CARRERAS ROTHMANS LTD V FREEMAN MATTHEWS TREASURE LTD 1984
> The plaintiff paid a monthly sum to its advertising agent to pay invoices incurred in placing the plaintiff's adverts. The money was put into a separate account specifically for the purpose of paying the previous month's invoices. The defendant went into liquidation.

Held

❖ (Ch) The money in the separate account was transferred for a purpose which was not fulfilled. Therefore, the money should revert back to the plaintiff. [1984] 3 W.L.R. 1016.

> TWINSECTRA LTD V YARDLEY 2002
> The appellant solicitor acted for Y and negotiated a loan of £1 million from the lender. Another firm of solicitors acted on behalf of Y with the lender who received the money with an undertaking that the money was to be retained until it was used for the acquisition of property and was to be released solely for that purpose. The second firm of solicitors in breach of the undertaking released the money to the appellant on

receipt of an assurance from Y that it would used for the stated purpose. The appellant did not ensure that the money was used for the stated purpose and merely paid it out on Y's instructions. Y used £358,000 for other purposes and defaulted on his loan. The lender brought an action against the appellant alleging the payment was in breach of trust and that he had dishonestly assisted in the breach of trust. The Court of Appeal found in favour of the lender and the appellant appealed.

Held

❖ (HL) There was a Quistclose type resulting trust of the loan in favour of the lender. As it was clear that the lender had explicitly made the loan subject to the requirement that it be used for the stated purpose by virtue of the undertaking, there was a trust of the money in favour of the lender. Payment of the money in breach of the undertaking amounted to a breach of trust. [2002] 2 W.L.R. 802.

Commentary

[1] In *Westdeutsche Landesbank Girozentrale v Islington Borough Council* [1996] A.C. 669, it was held that the Council must return with compound interest, money received under an ultra vires interest swap agreement. One of the reasons was that there was a resulting trust of the money for the bank in the light of the incomplete transfer for the Council given its ultra vires nature.

[2] *Barclays Bank Ltd v Quistclose Investments Ltd* [1970] A.C. 567 also illustrates the need to distinguish the basis for implied trusts. There was an automatic resulting trust because the purpose having not been completed, there was an incomplete transfer. The bank also held the property on trust for them, but as a constructive trustee based upon them having had notice of the agreement. See *R v The Common Professional Examination Board Exp Sally Mealing-McCleod, The Times,* May 2, 2000.

[3] In *Twinsectra v Yardley* [2002] 2 W.L.R. 802, the House of Lords made it clear that not every payment made by a lender to a borrower would be subject to a Quistclose type trust. Most lenders would ask the borrower as to the use of the monies loaned but this did not give rise to a trust. The payment must have been made on the basis that it is to be used only for the stated purpose and there was no freedom on the borrower to use it for any other purpose before a Quistclose type trust could arise.

[4] In *Hurst Bannister v New Cap Reinsurance Corp Ltd*, Lawtel, December 14, 1999, the court held that the Quistclose principle could be applied widely. In

that case, the principle applied to money given to pay insurance premiums. However, in *Dubey v HM Revenue & Customs* [2007] B.C.L.C. 1 the court held that money paid to a savings scheme with Farepak Food and Gifts Ltd for hampers and other festive gifts did not give rise to a Quistclose trust. The money paid into the scheme created the situation of creditor and debtor not that of trustee and beneficiary. Similarly, in *Azam v Iqbal* [2007] EWHC 2025, the court did not find the existence of Quistclose trust in respect money paid to a money transfer facility. The relationship was one of creditor and debtor.

[5] The Quistclose principle was applied in *Cooper v PRG Powerhouse* [2008] EWHC 498 where it was extended to cover a contractual situation. A Managing Director of a company who was leaving the company paid money to the company to be paid to the leasing company in order for him to purchase his company car. The court found a Quistclose trust in favour of the managing director when the company became insolvent. The question has arisen as to whether it was right to give the managing director priority over the company creditors.

[6] Other instances of where a resulting trust automatically arises include:
   (a) Where an express trust fails: *Re Ames' Settlement* [1946] Ch. 217.
   (b) Where an attempted charitable trust fails: *Chichester Diocesan Fund and Board of Finance v Simpson* [1944] A.C.341.
   (c) Where the settlor has failed to dispose of the entire beneficial interest in a property. This can arise where a trust is created for a beneficiary for life but there is no giftover on the beneficiary's death; at that point there is a resulting trust to the settlor. See *Vandervell v IRC* (see Ch.3).
   (d) Where the Law Society held money in a solicitor's client account it did not hold it on behalf of the client but on trust for the persons from whom the client had obtained the money by fraud. *Halley v Law Society*, Lawtel, February 13, 2002. See also *Re Ahmed & Co* [2006] EWHC 480.
   (e) Where the beneficial interest is not wholly exhausted, for example, where money is advanced to an unincorporated association which subsequently ceases to exist, the money could revert to the settlor on resulting trust (see below). A similar situation can arise where money is donated for a purpose, which is no longer necessary. In *Re Gillingham Bus Disaster Fund* [1958] Ch. 300, funds were raised following a disaster in which 24 marine cadets were killed. Later, the funds were proved unnecessary. The court held that the funds should revert to the donors on a resulting trust and that money from unidentified donors should be paid into court rather than to the Crown. In *Davies v Hardwick* [1999] 6 C.L.Y. 554, surplus donations for A, who was born with biliary artesia, were not held on a resulting trust. The donations were for a

liver transplant. Although this had taken place, there was a need for continued medical treatment and the evidence was that the donors had intended to make out and out gifts of the donations.

Key Principle

Upon the dissolution of an incorporated association any surplus funds should be distributed to its surviving members according to their contractual rights.

RE BUCKS CONSTABULARY WIDOWS' AND ORPHANS' FUND FRIENDLY SOCIETY (NO. 2) 1979

The Society was open to serving members of the Bucks constabulary. In 1968 the constabulary was amalgamated with others. The members resolved to wind up the society, continue to pay benefits to its existing beneficiaries until dissolution and realise its assets for the purchase of annuities for all current members and the transfer of some of its assets to the Thames Valley Constabulary Benevolent Fund. The instrument of dissolution provided for the purchase of the annuities and the transfer of £40,000 to the Thames Valley Fund with the surplus going to another benevolent fund. The trustee sought a determination as to whether the society's funds could be distributed according to the terms of the instrument of dissolution.

Held

❖ (Ch) There was a general principle applicable to all unincorporated societies that any surplus funds remaining upon a society's dissolution should belong to the existing members. Subject to contrary expression, such a term should be implied in the contract between the members. The entitlement of the members was governed by the contract between them. The instrument of dissolution signed by some members did not constitute directions by all members as to how their interest in the surplus funds should be distributed. [1979] 1 W.L.R. 936.

Commentary

[1] Where an unincorporated association ends, the remaining funds should be distributed to existing beneficiaries according to the contract between the association and the members. When there are no beneficiaries left, any surplus may go to the Crown as bona vacantia. However, before that happens, it is not open to the association to give funds, which should be held on trust for the members, to third parties. In *Re GKN Bolts and Nuts (Automotive*

Division) Birmingham Works, Sports and Social Club [1982] 1 W.L.R. 774, it was held that where surplus funds were to be distributed to surviving members, this was to be done equally, regardless of the duration of membership or value of contributions.

[2] There are three main approaches as to how funds from a dissolved unincorporated association should be distributed:

(a) The property should be distributed upon resulting trust to those who contributed the property: *Re Printers and Transferors Amalgamated Trades Protection Society* [1899] 2 A.C. 386. This approach is often not used in the situation of unincorporated associations, though it prevails in situations of imperfect dispositions. A recent example is *Re St Andrew's (Cheam) Lawn Tennis Club Trust* 15 I.T.E.L.R. 105 (see Chapter 4).

(b) The property should be distributed on a contractual basis. Prior to *Re Bucks Constabulary Widows' and Orphans' Fund Friendly Society*, it was held in *Re St Andrews Allotment Association* [1969] 1 W.L.R. 229 that the contributions of donors including members ceased to be their property once the contribution was made and were not held on trust for those contributors. The contributions were complete and became the property of the association and should be distributed upon dissolution in accordance with the association's rules to the members. In *Re Sick and Funeral Society of St John's Sunday School* [1973] Ch. 51, the same approach was taken.

(c) The property goes as bona vacantia to the crown. In *Re West Sussex Constabulary Widows, Children and Benevolent (1930) Fund Trusts* [1970] Ch. 1, the association was wound up. The court held that identified legacies should revert to the donors on resulting trust and unidentified donations should go to the Crown as bona vacantia. Here the members were not beneficiaries so distribution amongst surviving members was not appropriate. In *Re St Andrew's (Cheam) Lawn Tennis Club Trust* 15 I.T.E.L.R. 105, the court held that land which was purchased with the assistance of various donations and gifts for the Club for use as tennis courts failed as it was not a charitable trust. As a result the land was held on a resulting trust in favour of the estate of T who was the largest single donor for the club in the acquisition of the land as the other smaller donations were predicated on that one donation. The court held that it would not pass to the Crown as bona vacantia.

In *Davis v Richards & Wallington Industries Ltd* [1990] 1 W.L.R. 1511 the winding up of a pension scheme was considered. It was said obiter that employer's contributions could go on resulting trust where the contributions were for a limited purpose and that the surplus of employees' contributions could go as bona vacantia as the employees were limited by statute as to the benefit they could receive. However, in *Air Jamaica Ltd v Charlton* [1999] 1 W.L.R. 1399, the Privy Council was of the view that upon the dissolution of Air Jamaica's pension fund, the surplus was held on a resulting trust for the members of the fund and Air Jamaica in equal shares. This was different from *Davis v Richards & Wallington Industries Ltd* because there was no statutory basis for the pension fund and also because the members had not received all that they had bargained for.

PRESUMED RESULTING TRUSTS

Key Principle

A resulting trust may arise from a voluntary conveyance where there is no intention to make a gift.

> HODGSON V MARKS 1971
> In 1960, the plaintiff executed a voluntary conveyance in favour of E, her lodger. E was registered as the new proprietor though there was an oral agreement that the plaintiff retained beneficial ownership. The plaintiff and lodger continued to live in the house. In 1964, E sold the property to the first defendant who mortgaged it to the second defendant. The first defendant was registered as the new owner subject to the second defendant's charge. When the plaintiff discovered the situation, she applied for a declaration that the first defendant should transfer the property to her free of the charge against it.

Held

❖ (CA) On the evidence, the transfer to E was not intended to be a gift. A resulting trust of the beneficial interest arose. In addition, the plaintiff was in actual occupation for the purposes of s.70(1)(g) of the Land Registration Act 1925 and so had an overriding interest against the defendants. [1971] Ch. 892.

Commentary

[1] This is notwithstanding s.60(3) of the **Law of Property Act 1925** which provides that in a voluntary conveyance, a resulting trust shall not be implied merely by reason that the property is not expressed to be conveyed for the use or benefit of the grantee. In *Lohia v Lohia* [2001] W.T.L.R. 101 the court at first instance suggested that s.60(3) of the **Law of Property Act 1925** had abolished the presumption of resulting trust and hence there has to be some evidence in order to give rise to a presumption of resulting trust in case of

transfers of realty. However this point was not considered on appeal as the court did not hear a full argument on the matter and decided the case on the evidence alone.

[2] Other instances where presumed resulting trusts arise include:

(a) Where a purchaser buys a property and puts it in the name of another person who provides no consideration a resulting trust is presumed in favour of the purchaser: *Dyer v Dyer* (1788) 2 Cox. E.Q. 92, *Abrahams v The Trustee of the Property of Anthony Abrahams (A Bankrupt)*, *The Times*, July 26, 1999, and *Poojary v Kotecha* (2002) 21 F.G 144(CS).

(b) Where a purchaser buys a property and puts it in the names of himself and another person, who provides no consideration, a resulting trust is presumed whereby the purchaser and other person hold the property on trust for the purchaser. The same applies where the owner of property transfers property into joint names: *Re Vinogradoff* [1935] W.N. 68. See also *Goodman v Carlton* (2002) F.L.R. 259.

(c) Where two purchasers buy a property together but transfer the title to one of their names only, a resulting trust will be presumed whereby the title owner holds the property on trust for both purchasers: *Bull v Bull* [1955] 1 Q.B. 234.

(d) The issue of the purchase money resulting trusts has given rise to disputes in respect of the ownership of an ex-council house which was purchased with the assistance of one of the party's right to buy discount. The issue is with regards to the size of the beneficial share. In *Laskar v Laskar* [2008] EWCA Civ 347, a mother and daughter purchased the ex-council home together using the mother's right to buy discount. However the daughter jointly purchased the house with her because the mother would not have been able to obtain a mortgage. The issue here was whether the right to buy discount was considered a contribution by the mother. The court decided that the discount was to be attributed solely to the mother and hence the mother was entitled to a two thirds share in the property. The daughter was entitled to a one third share by virtue of the fact that she was co-mortgagor of the property and should be treated as having made a contribution via the mortgage which would not have been otherwise available to the mother.

[3] After the decisions of *Stack v Dowden* [2007] UKHL 17 and *Jones v Kernott* [2012] 1 All E.R. 1265 (see Ch.6), it could be argued that the presumed resulting trust would apply to land held in one person's name or in the joint names except in the case of the family home.

Key Principle

A presumption of a resulting trust may be rebutted by evidence of intention.

> ### FOWKES V PASCOE 1875
> A testator bought shares in the name of herself and the defendant, the son of her daughter-in-law. By her will, she left the residue of her estate to her daughter-in-law for life and thereafter to the defendant and his sister. The question arose as to whether the shares bought in the name of the defendant and the testator were gifted to the defendant or held by him on resulting trust for the testator.

Held

❖ (CA) On the evidence, the shares had been gifted to the defendant. At the same time as the purchase of the shares, she purchased other shares in the name of herself and her companion. If she had intended all the shares to be held beneficially for herself, there would have been no point in the separate but contemporaneous transactions. (1875) L.R. 10 Ch. App. 343.

Commentary

There are frequently evidential problems in providing proof of intention that would rebut the presumption of a resulting trust. See *Sekhon v Alissa* [1989] 2 F.L.R. 94. In *Vajpeyi v Yusaf*, Lawtel, September 24, 2003, the presumption of resulting trust was rebutted by evidence that the defendant to whom the property was transferred to had kept the rental income for 20 years without accounting to the claimant who had contributed 25 per cent of the original purchase price.

Key Principle

A presumption of a resulting trust may be rebutted by the presumption of advancement.

> ### RE ROBERTS 1964
> A father took out an insurance policy on his son. The father paid the premiums. On the father's death, the estate claimed repayment of the premiums.

Held

❖ (Ch) The presumption of advancement was applicable. Each payment of the premium was to be regarded as a separate advancement during the father's lifetime. However, premiums paid after the father's death would be recoverable as the relationship had ended by his death. [1946] Ch. 1.

Commentary

[1] The presumption of advancement means that in certain situations where one party transfers property to another there is a legal presumption that the transfer was intended as a gift. The presumption can be rebutted by evidence to the contrary. In *Cox v Jones*, Lawtel, June 25, 2004, the claim for the return of an engagement ring failed as the claimant could not establish that he had wanted the ring back if the engagement ended. The claimant could not rebut the presumption of advancement.

[2] Instances where the presumption of advancement arises include:
  (a) A transfer from father to his legitimate children (*Re Roberts*, above and *Lavelle v Lavelle* [2004] EWCA Civ 223), or a transfer from a person standing in loco parentis to the children (*Shephard v Cartwright* [1955] A.C. 431).
  (b) A transfer from a husband to his wife: *Re Eykyn's Trusts* (1877) 6 Ch. D. 115.

[3] Instances where the presumption of advancement does not arise include:
  (a) A transfer from a wife to her husband: *Mercier v Mercier* (1903) 2 Ch. D. 98.
  (b) A transfer from mother to her children: *Bennet v Bennet* (1879) 10 Ch. D. 474.

[4] However in *Kyriakides v Pippas* [2004] EWHC 646, the court stated that the position of the courts now was that it would strive to discover the parties' real intention and will only rely on the presumptions of advancement or of resulting trusts in cases where the intention cannot be established or as a default position. The court followed the dicta of Lord Phillips M.R. in *Lavelle v Lavelle*, above.

[5] By s.199 of the Equality Act 2010, the presumption of advancement (by which, for example, a husband is presumed to be making a gift to his wife if he transfers property to her, or purchases property in her name) is abolished. However, this is applicable only to anything done before the commencement of this section, or anything done pursuant to any obligation incurred before the commencement of this section: s.199(2) of the **Equality Act 2010**. However, this has yet to come into force and even if it does the old law still applies to acts done before its commencement.

Key Principle

The presumption of advancement can itself be rebutted by evidence.

> **RE GOOCH 1890**
>
> A father bought shares in his son's name in order to allow him to be a director of a company. The son passed all the dividends back to his father who kept the share certificate.

Held

❖ Ch D On the evidence, the presumption of advancement was rebutted. (1890) 62 L.T. 384.

> **CLOSE INVOICE FINANCE LTD V ABAOWA 2010**
>
> A mother purchased a property in the name of her daughter. The mother had paid the deposit and all the expenses on the property. However the mortgage was put in the daughter's name. The claimant sought a declaration against the daughter that the daughter held the legal title of the property on trust for her mother absolutely. The issue arose as to the beneficial interest in the property. The mother argued that she was the sole beneficial owner in respect of the property inter alia because there was a resulting trust in her favour as she had provided the deposit together with the mortgage instalments, the mortgage in the daughter's name and the expenses.

Held

❖ (QBD) The mother was the beneficial owner under a resulting trust. This was as a result of the deposit which she had paid which equated to 32.20 per cent of the property. As regards the remaining 67.80 per cent this was beneficially owned by the daughter. [2010] EWHC 1920.

Commentary

This presumption of advancement is historically based in a time when it was assumed that a man would provide for his wife and children. In today's more equal and complex family situations, it has been argued that the presumption may be weaker. In *McGrath v Wallis* [1995] 2 F.L.R. 114, the Court of Appeal suggested that the presumption was a judicial instrument of last resort. In *Lavelle v Lavelle*, above, the presumption of advancement was rebutted by evidence that the transfer was for avoidance of inheritance tax rather than intended as a gift from a father to his son.

The issue was considered recently by the Privy Council and the

Supreme Court of Canada. In *Pecore v Pecore* [2007] 9 I.T.E.L.R. 873, the Supreme Court of Canada was of the view that both the presumptions of resulting trusts and advancement were still relevant and applicable. Rothstein J. stated that

> "[t]he presumptions provide a guide for courts in resolving disputes over transfers where evidence as to the transferor's intent in making the transfer is unavailable or unpersuasive".

The other point that was stressed by the court was that the presumption of advancement applied equally to mothers making a gift to her children as it does to fathers and his children. Rothstein J. felt that

> "[a]s women now have both the means as well as obligations to support their children, they are no less likely to intend to make gifts to their children than fathers. The presumption of advancement should thus apply equally to fathers and mothers".

In *Antoni v Antoni* [2007] All E.R. [D] 335, the Privy Council decided that the Appellate Court in Bahamas had erred in not considering the application of the presumption of advancement where there was a transfer from the father to his daughter. It is therefore clear that the presumption of advancement is still relevant to the modern family situation and has been extended to take into account the changing role of the mother.

In *Close Invoice Finance Ltd v Abaowa*, above, the court suggested that there was a presumption of advancement between the mother and the daughter but that it was a weak presumption. However, on the facts of the case the presumption of advancement was rebutted in respect of the deposit and a presumption of resulting trust arose in favour of the mother. As regards the remaining 67.80 per cent this was held by the daughter as she was responsible for the mortgage and hence the contribution was by the daughter not the mother and therefore in respect of this part of the property there was no resulting trust in favour of the mother.

Key Principle

A transferor may not rely on an illegal transaction to support a claim to a property by a presumption of a resulting trust or rebuttal of a presumption of advancement.

The parties bought a house in the plaintiff's name on the under-standing that they were joint beneficial owners. This was for the pur-pose of perpetrating various frauds, which continued over a period of time. The defendant later admitted the frauds. The plaintiff moved out of the house and claimed possession. She sought a declaration that she was the sole owner. The defendant counter-claimed for an order of sale of the house and a declaration that the house was held on trust by the plaintiff for both of them in equal shares.

Held

❖ (HL) A claimant to an interest in a property was entitled to succeed if the claim did not rely on pleading an illegality notwithstanding that the title was acquired in the course of an illegal transaction. The defendant's contribution to the purchase price, along with the understanding of joint beneficial interest, was sufficient to establish a resulting trust in her favour. The public conscience test was not appropriate in determining to what extent illegal transactions should be recognised. [1994] 1 A.C. 340.

TRIBE V TRIBE 1995

The plaintiff owned 459 out of 500 shares in the family company. The landlords of two premises served schedules of dilapidations requiring substantial repairs. As he was the tenant of the premises, he was given legal advice that if the claims were valid he might have to sell the company or dispose of his shares. The plaintiff transferred his shares to the defendant, expressed to be for consideration of £78,030, which was not intended to be paid. In the end, the repairs were not needed. The plaintiff sought the retransfer of the shares but the defendant refused.

Held

❖ (CA) A transferor who transferred property for illegal purposes was entitled to withdraw from the transaction before the illegal purpose was carried out and cite the illegal purpose as evidence to rebut the presumption of advancement. This would be an exception to the principle that a court will not aid a person who relies on an illegal act. The plaintiff had in fact not defrauded the creditors. The evidence clearly rebutted the presumption of advancement. [1995] 4 All E.R. 236.

Commentary

[1] The underlying rule is that a claimant cannot rely on the evidence of an illegal act in order to sustain a claim to a beneficial interest in property either

in support of the presumption of a resulting trust or in rebuttal of the presumption of advancement. In *Tinsley v Milligan*, the defendant was able to sustain the presumption of a resulting trust because she was not relying on an illegal act to support her claim. She had already acquired a beneficial interest in the property, notwithstanding that this was to be used for an illegal purpose. In *Tribe v Tribe*, the plaintiff was able to rebut the presumption of advancement because the evidence used to support it, though illegal in intent was never carried out. The decision in *Tribe v Tribe* was followed in *Painter v Hutchison* [2007] All E.R. [D] 45. See also *Woodman v Tracey*, Lawtel, May 22, 2001.

[2] In *Lowson v Coombes* [1999] 2 W.L.R. 720, the Court of Appeal decided that property transferred into the defendant's name in order to prevent the plaintiff's wife from having a claim on it was on all fours with *Tinsley v Milligan*. As in *Tinsley*, although the purpose was illegal, the plaintiff could rely on the presumption of resulting trust to claim back the property. As the parties were not married, the presumption of advancement did not apply. It should be noted that in *Barrett v Barrett* [2008] EWHC 1061 the court was of the view that this approach only applied to cases of resulting trusts and not constructive trusts. See also *Collier v Collier*, Lawtel, July 30, 2002.

[3] Other cases include *Tinker v Tinker* [1970] P. 136, where a husband transferred property to his wife in order to defeat his creditors, and it was held that the presumption of advancement applied. The unlawful purpose could not be used to rebut the presumption. A similar conclusion was reached in *Collier v Collier* [2003] W.T.L.R. 617. In *Heseltine v Heseltine* [1971] 1 W.L.R. 342, a wife transferred property to her husband to enable him to qualify as a "name" at Lloyds. Notwithstanding that this purpose was a deception, the court held that the husband should hold the property on resulting trust for the wife.

THINK POINT

Do you think the court was correct in holding that the surplus funds should have gone to the Crown as bona vacantia in *Re West Sussex Constabulary Widows, Children and Benevolent* (1930) *Fund Trusts* [1970] Ch. 1?

Do you consider that the presumption of advancement is still relevant as a way to rebut the presumption of advancement?

Constructive Trusts

6

INTRODUCTION

A constructive trust arises generally by operation of law rather than by the intention of the parties. In *Paragon Finance Plc v Thakerar & Co* [1999] 1 All E.R. 400, Millett L.J. explained that a constructive trust arises

> "by operation of law whenever the circumstances are such that it would be unconscionable for the owner of property (usually but not necessarily the legal estate) to assert his own beneficial interest in the property and deny the beneficial interest of another".

Megarry V.C. in *Re Montagu's Settlement Trusts* [1987] Ch. 264, has also suggested that

> "the fundamental question is whether the conscience of the recipient is bound in such a way as to justify equity imposing a trust on him".

A constructive trust is different from an express trust in that the trustee is not usually subject to the duties and obligations normally imposed on a trustee such as the duty to invest. However, the extent of the duties and obligations owed by a constructive trustee are still unclear but in *Tackaberry v Hollis* [2007] EWHC 2633 the court held that in the context of a constructive trust of a family home there must also be certainty of objects given that it is usually the case that the beneficial interest is to be shared.

There are different aspects of constructive trusts and the key areas considered here are in respect of profits from a trust, liability as a stranger and the beneficial ownership of the family home.

PROFITS FROM A TRUST

Key Principle

Where a trustee or fiduciary makes a profit from the trust, a constructive trust will be imposed.

> KEECH V SANDFORD 1726
> (See Ch.8.)

Held

❖ (Ch) The trustee held the renewed lease on trust for the infant beneficiary. (1726) Sel. Cas. Ch. 61.

Commentary

[1] The trust in that case was a constructive trust for the infant beneficiary. In *Boardman v Phipps* [1967] 2 A.C. 46 (see Ch.8), the majority of their Lordships held that a constructive trust was imposed. However, the House of Lords did not appear to distinguish between the duty to account and the imposition of a constructive trust. The distinction is important in cases where the profit has been invested successfully resulting in further profits or where the trustee or fiduciary is adjudicated a bankrupt. In these situations, the constructive trustee can claim the profit or priority over the unsecured creditors.

[2] There has been a suggestion in *Sinclair Investment Holdings SA v Versailles Trade Finance Ltd*, Lawtel, May 12, 2005 that a fiduciary obligation could arise as a result of a person giving an undertaking of loyalty with regard to property even though he was not in a fiduciary position.

[3] It has been stressed by the Court of Appeal in *Re Polly Peck International Plc (No.5)* [1998] 3 All E.R. 812, that it did not have jurisdiction to grant a remedial constructive trust. It was noted that this was a concept recognised by the American and Canadian courts and despite dicta in some English cases this was not a concept that is recognised by the English courts. The jurisdiction to grant a constructive trust is based on proprietary rights between the parties and not merely as a means of preventing unjust enrichment.

RECEIPT OF BRIBES

Key Principle

Where a bribe has been received by a fiduciary to betray his fiduciary obligations, the fiduciary is accountable under an equitable account rather than as a constructive trustee.

SINCLAIR INVESTMENTS (UK) LTD V VERSAILLES TRADE FINANCE LTD (IN ADMINISTRATIVE RECEIVERSHIP) 2011

A director of a company sold his shares in a company prior to its collapse and made a substantial profit. Evidence showed that the company had implemented a fraudulent investment scheme. The monies needed from the scheme were from a group of investors through an investment company (TPL) and via loans from banks. As a result of the fraud TPL and the banks suffered substantial losses. The issue arose as to whether the director held the proceeds of sale of the shares and the property he subsequently acquired with a mixture of his own monies and the share profits he made on the sale on a constructive trust for TPL. The dispute was between TPL and the banks.

Held

❖ (CA) It was clear from previous case law that a beneficiary could not claim a proprietary interest against a bribe received by a fiduciary in order to induce him to treat the bribe payer more favourably. The beneficiary was entitled to claim an equitable account in respect of the monies or assets acquired by the fiduciary as a result of his breach of fiduciary obligation. The beneficiary could claim the monies or assets where they were the property belonging to the trust or the beneficiary or the fiduciary acquired the asset or money by taking advantage of an opportunity which properly belonged to the trust. Accordingly, TPL had no proprietary claim to the proceeds of sale of the shares. [2011] EWCA Civ 347.

Commentary

In *Lister & Co v Stubbs* (1890) 45 Ch. D. 1, it was decided that where bribes were received, the liability of the fiduciary was personal, giving rise to a relationship of creditor and debtor only rather than that of trustee and beneficiary. In *Attorney-General for Hong Kong v Reid* [1994] A.C. 324, *Lister & Co v Stubbs* was disapproved of. In that case the defendant breached his fiduciary duty to the Crown and was convicted of corruption. An application was made by the Attorney-General to renew the caveats on property in New Zealand on the basis that the titles to these properties were held on a constructive trust for the Crown. The Privy Council was of the opinion that where a fiduciary accepted a bribe to betray his fiduciary obligations, the bribe and the property representing the bribe including any profit resulting from the use of the money, is held on a constructive trust for the person to whom the duty is owed.

It has been suggested in *Attorney-General v Blake* [1996] 3 W.L.R. 741 that *Lister & Co v Stubbs* is still binding on the High Court. However, in *Daraydan Holdings Ltd v Solland International Ltd* [2005] Chan. 119 it was held that the courts were free to follow the decision in *Att Gen for Hong Kong v Reid* instead of *Lister v Stubbs*.

The position has now been clarified by the Court of Appeal in *Sinclair Investments (UK) Ltd v Versailles Trade Finance Ltd (in administrative receivership)* [2011] EWCA Civ 347 which did not follow *Att Gen for Hong Kong v Reid*. Lord Neuberger stated:

> "...We should not follow the Privy Council decision in *Reid* ....in preference to decisions of this court, unless there are domestic authorities which show that the decisions of this court were *per incuriam*, or at least of doubtful reliability. Save where there are powerful reasons to the contrary, the Court of Appeal should follow its own previous decisions, and in this instance there are five such previous decisions. It is true that there is a powerful subsequent decision of the Privy Council which goes the other way, but that of itself is not enough to justify departing from the earlier decisions of this court: see *Re Spectrum Plus Ltd (in liquidation)* [2004] EWCA Civ 670".

The consequence of this is that it will be difficult to trace the bribes into the hands of third parties and recover it from them as the bribes are not regarded as trust property.

LIABILITY OF STRANGERS TO THE TRUST

Key Principle
Strangers to the trust can be liable as constructive trustees.

BARNES V ADDY 1874
A, the surviving trustee of a trust fund, where one part was settled upon A's wife and his children and the other part upon B's wife and children, appointed B as sole trustee of half of the fund. B misappropriated that half of the fund and was adjudicated a bankrupt. A's solicitor had advised A against the appointment of B as sole trustee of half the fund

but nonetheless prepared the deeds of appointment and an indemnity for B's execution. B appointed another solicitor who warned B's wife of the risk of the transaction but B's wife confirmed that she had no objections to it. The issue was whether the solicitors were liable to make good the loss to the trust.

Held

❖ (HL) As neither of the solicitors had any knowledge of, or reason to suspect, any dishonest design in the transaction and as the funds had not passed into their hands, the action against them would be dismissed. (1874) L.R. 9 Ch. 244.

SATNAM INVESTMENTS LTD V DUNLOP HEYWOOD & CO LTD 1999

The plaintiff acquired an option to purchase a site for development subject to the site owner's right to terminate the option if the plaintiff went into receivership. The plaintiff was placed in receivership. The defendants, who had acted for the plaintiff, told M Ltd, a rival, about the plaintiff's receivership and the option. The owners of the site terminated the option and sold the land to M Ltd. The plaintiff sued the defendants and M Ltd contending that the defendants had breached their fiduciary duty by the disclosure to M Ltd, and M Ltd who had received the information was a constructive trustee.

Held

❖ (CA) Mere knowledge of a breach of fiduciary duty was not sufficient to make a person, who was not a trustee nor in a fiduciary position, a constructive trustee of property acquired through taking advantage of an opportunity arising from a breach of fiduciary duty. M Ltd could not be liable as constructive trustee on the basis of knowing receipt of the information because there was a lack of nexus between the information and the site. Although the information disclosed was confidential, it was readily available to M Ltd from other sources. The claim against M Ltd would be dismissed. [1999] 3 All E.R. 652.

Commentary

The dictum of Lord Selborne L.C. in *Barnes v Addy* is important. His Lordship stated (at 251–252) that

> "... strangers are not to be made constructive trustees merely because they act as the agents of trustees in transactions within their legal powers ... unless those agents receive and become chargeable with some part of the trust property, or unless they

assist with knowledge in a dishonest and fraudulent design on the part of the trustees".

The liabilities of strangers were categorised until recently as "knowing assistance" and "knowing receipt". However, as a result of the Privy Council decision in *Royal Brunei Airlines Sdn Bhd v Tan* [1995] 2 A.C. 378, the first category is now called dishonest assistance. It has been suggested that it would also be inappropriate to call the second category knowing receipt but rather as "liability for receipt".

Key Principle

A stranger is liable as a constructive trustee where there has been dishonest assistance in the trustee's breach of trust.

> ### ROYAL BRUNEI AIRLINES SDN BHD V TAN 1995
> The plaintiff appointed Borneo Leisure Travel ("BLT") as its agent for the sale of passenger and cargo transportation. The defendant was the principal shareholder and managing director of the company. It was agreed that BLT was to hold in trust for the plaintiff money received from its sales of tickets until it was accounted to the plaintiff. However, BLT, with the knowledge and assistance of the defendant, paid the money into its current account instead of a separate account. BLT subsequently became insolvent and the plaintiff commenced an action against the defendant to recover monies due to it.

Held

❖ (PC) A stranger who dishonestly assisted a trustee to commit a breach of trust or procured him to do so would be liable as a constructive trustee for the loss to the beneficiary. The stranger must, however, have acted dishonestly and not merely negligently. It did not matter that the trustee may not have been dishonest or fraudulent nor had received trust property. The defendant was liable to the plaintiff for the whole amount owed by BLT. This was because he had allowed BLT to commit a breach of trust by using the money, which it was to hold on trust for the plaintiff when he knew that BLT did not have the authority or power to do so. [1995] 2 A.C. 378.

Commentary

[1] The Privy Council was of the view that the term "dishonest assistance" was to be used rather than "knowing assistance", as the word "knowingly" was open to different interpretations. Lord Nicholls (p.392) stated that

"dishonesty is a necessary ingredient of accessory liability. It is also a sufficient ingredient. A liability in equity ... attaches to a person who dishonestly procures or assists in a breach of trust ... It is not necessary that ... the trustee ... was acting dishonestly, although this will usually be so... Knowingly is better avoided as a defining ingredient of the principle and in the context of this principle the [*Baden v Societe Generate Pour Favoriser le Developpement du Commerce et de L'industrie en France SA* [1993] 1 W.L.R. 509] ... scale of knowledge is best forgotten."

His Lordship went on to state that an objective test for dishonesty should be adopted but in determining this it would be useful to consider the stranger's personal "experience and intelligence, and the reason he acted as he did". Hence, a stranger would not be able to avoid liability merely because he thought he was acting honestly—the issue would be whether the stranger had been dishonest and this is adjudged by looking at whether he was acting in a way that an "honest person would in the circumstances".

In *Twinsectra Ltd v Yardley* [2002] 2 W.L.R. 802 (see Ch.5 for the facts of the case), the House of Lords held the Court of Appeal was wrong to interfere in the trial judge's ruling in respect of accessory liability. The judge had seen and heard the witness and ruled that the defendant had not acted dishonestly when he had deliberately shut his eyes in paying out money without concern to its application. The Court of Appeal was wrong in equating shutting ones eyes with dishonesty. The House of Lords endorsed the principle in *Royal Brunei Airlines Sdn Bhd v Tan* that dishonesty was a necessary ingredient of liability. However, the court set a dual test that the defendant's conduct must be dishonest by the ordinary standards of reasonable and honest people and that the defendant himself realised that by those standards his conduct was dishonest.

There has been some ambiguity as to the effect of the decision in *Twinsectra Ltd v Yardley*. One interpretation is that it reinterpreted the decision in *Royal Brunei Airlines Sdn Bhd v Tan* and that there was both a subjective and objective element in proving dishonesty i.e. the stranger must have been aware that his actions were below what was normally accepted. In *Barlow Clowes International Ltd v Eurotrust International Ltd* [2006] 1 All E.R. 333 the Privy Council suggested that this approach was wrong as there was no requirement to prove that the stranger was aware that what he was doing was dishonest.

In *Abou-Rahmah v Abacha* [2007] 1 Lloyd's Rep. 115, the Court of Appeal was faced with a dilemma as to whether to follow Privy Council's interpretation of *Twinsectra*. In this case, the appellants were a victim of a

Nigerian money transfer scam and had transferred US$600,000 to a Nigerian bank. The money was then transferred out and the transferees disappeared. The appellants commenced an action against the bank on the basis that it had knowingly assisted in the breach of trust as its employee was suspicious that the transferee was involved in money laundering but was not suspicious about the specific transactions in question. The issue was whether the bank's state of knowledge made them liable as a constructive trustee for knowingly assisting in the breach of trust. On the facts, the Court refused the appeal as the first instance judge did not find any dishonesty on the part of the respondent and the decision should not be overturned. Arden L.J. was of the view that *Barlow Clowes International Ltd v Eurotrust International Ltd* merely indicated how *Twinsectra* should be interpreted and therefore it was not wrong to follow the decision. Arden L.J. went on to state that the test of dishonesty was predominantly objective but with subjective elements namely, what the defendant actually knew at that time. Hence, the present position appears to be that there is merely an objective standard and the stranger's own view as to whether his actions were dishonest or not is not relevant although what he knew is relevant in deciding whether he was dishonest.

[2] The Court of Appeal in *Heinl v Jyske Bank (Gibraltar)* (1999) Lloyd's Rep. 511, re-emphasised the need to prove dishonesty in order to make a stranger liable as a constructive trustee. The case goes on to suggest that the standard of proof of dishonesty in this type of situation requires proof to a high level of probability. In *Starglade Properties Ltd v Glade* [2010] EWCA Civ 1314, Sir Andrew Morritt stated (at para.25) that

> "…there is a single standard of honesty objectively determined by the court. That standard is applied to specific conduct of a specific individual possessing the knowledge and qualities he actually enjoyed".

See also *Houghton v Fayers*, *The Times*, February 9, 2000 and *Satnam Investments Ltd v Dunlop Heywood & Co Ltd*, above.

Key Principle
Dishonesty is taken to mean conscious impropriety and would include closing one's eyes to the obvious.

LIPKIN GORMAN V KARPNALE LTD 1989

A partner in a firm of solicitors had used money in its client account for gambling. The firm inter alia, attempted to recover this money from the bank where the money had been deposited.

Held

❖ (CA) The bank was not liable as a constructive trustee unless it was also in breach of its contractual duty of care. As the bank had no reason to believe that there was a possibility that the money was being withdrawn in breach of trust, it was not liable. [1989] 1 W.L.R. 1340.

AGIP (AFRICA) LTD V JACKSON 1991

The plaintiff signed a payment order in favour of a shipping company but the plaintiff's chief accountant fraudulently altered it by substituting Baker Oil Services Ltd ("Baker Oil"). Baker Oil was a company in which the first and third defendants were the sole directors and shareholders. The first and second defendants were partners in a firm of chartered accountants trading under the name of Jackson & Co in the Isle of Man. The third defendant was an employee of the firm. The money was paid by the plaintiffs through its account with their bankers in Tunisia ("Tunis Bank"). The Tunis Bank instructed Citibank, their correspondents in New York, to credit Baker Oil's Bank, through the New York Clearing system. Jackson & Co then ordered the bank to transfer the money to its account with the same branch of the bank. The money was subsequently transferred to a client account of the firm in the Isle of Man. Most of this money was subsequently transferred out on the instructions of clients. After the discovery of the fraud, the plaintiff sought to recover the money on the basis that money had been received at common law or on the basis that the defendants were constructive trustees.

Held

❖ (CA) In equity, the defendants were liable as constructive trustees because they assisted the chief accountant in his fraud. [1991] Ch. 547.

Commentary

[1] *Lipkin Gorman v Karpnale Ltd* went on appeal to the House of Lords but this concerned the liability of the casino.

[2] In *Agip (Africa) Ltd v Jackson*, at first instance (reported at [1990] Ch. 265), Millet J. decided that the defendants were liable for knowing assistance (see now *Royal Brunei Airlines Sdn Bhd v Tan*) in a dishonest and fraudulent

design. On the facts of the case, Millet J. held that this was dishonest because of their indifference to the state of affairs that existed. The Court of Appeal affirmed the decision of Millet J. on appeal.

Key Principle

Liability of a stranger as a constructive trustee can arise by virtue of receipt of trust property.

RE MONTAGUE'S SETTLEMENT TRUSTS 1987
Chattels, which were subject to a resettlement, were transferred to the 10th Duke of Manchester by trustees in breach of trust. Before they transferred the chattels, the trustees failed to ensure that the chattels were not subject to the resettlement. The 10th Duke sold some of the chattels. After the death of the 10th Duke, the plaintiff, who was the 11th Duke, commenced an action alleging, inter alia, that the 10th Duke held the chattels as a constructive trustee.

Held

❖ (Ch) Although the trustees were in breach of their fiduciary duty in transferring the chattels to the 10th Duke, the 10th Duke was not liable as a constructive trustee. This was because at the relevant time when the chattels were transferred to him he did not know that the chattels were subject to a trust. [1987] 1 Ch. 264.

Commentary

A stranger could be liable as a constructive trustee where he or she has received trust property. Here, the 10th Duke was not liable, as he did not know the items were transferred in breach of trust. Megarry V.C. suggested (at 285) that

> "... knowledge ... includes at least ... actual knowledge that would have been acquired but for shutting one's eyes to the obvious, or wilfully and recklessly failing to make such inquiries as a reasonable and honest man would make; for in such cases there is a want of probity which justifies imposing a constructive trust".

Other cases (see below) have, however, suggested that constructive notice is sufficient.

Key Principle

In order for a stranger to be liable as a constructive trustee on the basis of knowing receipt, some authorities have suggested that constructive notice will suffice.

> ### BELMONT FINANCE CORPORATION V WILLIAMS FURNITURE LTD (NO. 2) 1980
> A company received money from the illegal sale of a subsidiary company. The receiver of the subsidiary company subsequently claimed that the parent company was a constructive trustee of the proceeds of sale. This was on the basis that the illegal transaction occurred as a result of the director's breach of their fiduciary duties.

Held

❖ (CA) The parent company was a constructive trustee of the proceeds of sale on the basis of knowing receipt. [1980] 1 All E.R. 393.

> ### EAGLE TRUST PLC V SBC SECURITIES LTD 1992
> The defendant agreed to underwrite a takeover bid initiated by the plaintiff. The chief executive of the defendant agreed to sub-underwrite part of it. The plaintiff commenced an action to recover monies taken by the chief executive from the plaintiff for his own use. The plaintiff argued that the defendant was liable as a constructive trustee because the circumstances were such that it ought to have known or was put on enquiry that the chief executive would use the plaintiff's monies for his own purposes.

Held

❖ (Ch) For the defendant to be liable as a constructive trustee of money received, it must be shown that it had actual knowledge of the breach of trust, wilfully shut its eyes to the obvious or wilfully and recklessly failed to make inquiries that an honest and reasonable person would make. There was no evidence here that the defendant had the requisite knowledge and accordingly would not be liable as a constructive trustee. [1992] 4 All E.R. 488.

Commentary

[1] Earlier cases such as *Belmont Finance Corporation v Williams Furniture Ltd (No. 2)*, above, and *International Sales and Agencies Ltd v Marcus* [1982] 3 All E.R. 551, suggested that something similar to constructive notice on the part of the stranger, who received trust property, would suffice, i.e. that the stranger knew or ought to have known that the property was subject to a

trust. In *Re Montague's Settlement Trusts*, Megarry V.C. appeared to have restricted this to actual knowledge. Other cases such as *Eagle Trust Plc v SBC Securities* have required inferred knowledge as opposed to constructive notice. See also *Cowan De Groot Properties Ltd v Eagle Trust Plc* [1992] 4 All E.R. 700.

Key Principle

There should be a single test of knowledge for knowing receipt.

BCCI (OVERSEAS) LTD V AKINDELE 2000
The defendant had entered into a contract with a company to purchase shares in BCCI Holdings. The contract, inter alia, guaranteed a high rate of return for the investment. However the contract was a sham in order to mask dummy loans in order to enable BCCI Holdings to purchase its own shares. Under this contract the defendant received around US$6.6m and when the company went into liquidation, the liquidators claimed against the defendant on the basis of knowing assistance in the fraud and knowing receipt of money fraudulently obtained.

Held

❖ (CA) The defendant was not liable for knowing assistance as the court was able to find that he had not been dishonest. In respect of knowing receipt, it was clear from the authorities that dishonesty was not required and on the facts of the case, the defendant did not have the requisite knowledge to make him liable. [2000] 4 All E.R. 221.

Commentary

The Court of Appeal stated that there ought to be a single test of knowledge for knowing receipt. The court suggested that the test is that the recipient's state of knowledge must be such as to make it unconscionable for him to retain the benefit arising from the receipt. The court recognised that the test in this form could cause difficulties in application but would enable the court to make common sense decisions in commercial contexts where such claims usually arise. This approach was followed in *Charter Plc v City Index* [2008] 3 All E.R. 126 where the court stated that *BCCI (Overseas) Ltd v Akindele* represented the law. Carnwarth L.J. stated that

> "liability for 'knowing receipt' depends on the defendant having
> sufficient knowledge of the circumstances of the payment to

make it 'unconscionable' for him to retain the benefit or pay it away for his own purposes".

See also *Pulvers v Chan* [2007] EWHC 2406.

Key Principle
Knowledge on the part of an employee of the stranger, who was its directing mind and will, would suffice for liability as constructive trustee.

EL AJOU V DOLLAR LAND HOLDINGS PLC 1994
The plaintiff placed substantial funds and securities under the control of his investment manager based in Geneva. The investment manager was bribed to invest the plaintiff's money in fraudulent share selling schemes operated by three Canadians through two Dutch companies. The proceeds of these schemes were invested in the first defendant. S was the Managing Director of a subsidiary of the first defendant. F was a Swiss fiduciary agent who acted for the Canadians but who was also the Chairman of the first defendant. The plaintiff subsequently discovered the fraud and commenced proceedings against the first defendant to recover the money received by it, on the basis, inter alia, that the money was received with the knowledge that it represented the proceeds of fraud.

Held
❖ (CA) The first defendant would be liable as a constructive trustee. F had the de facto management and control of the relevant transactions and as such was its "directing mind and will". F's knowledge could be imputed to the first defendant and therefore a constructive trust on the basis of knowing receipt could be enforced. [1994] 2 All E.R. 685.

Key Principle
A partnership may be vicariously liable for the acts of one of the partners including liability for dishonest assistance.

DUBAI ALUMINIUM V SALAAM 2003
"Amhursts", a partnership settled a claim with the claimant on the basis of the assumed dishonest assistance of one of the partners in a complex fraud. The partner's involvement had been in respect of drawing up agreements in respect of the fraud. The issue was whether

the other partners were vicariously liable under s.10 of the Partnership Act 1890, for the "wrongful act or omission of any partner ... in the ordinary course of the business".

Held

❖ (HL) The definition of wrongful in the Act included liability in equity for dishonest assistance and was not restricted to tortious claims. The action of the partner was in the ordinary course of business of the partnership even though the motives may have been dishonest. Accordingly the partners of the firm were vicariously liable for the actions of the dishonest partner but the quantum of the contributions by the partners would reflect the fact that neither the dishonest partner nor the partnership received any proceeds from the fraud. [2003] 1 All E.R. 97.

Commentary

The House of Lords overruled the comments of Vinelott J. in *Re Bell's Indenture* [1980] 1 W.L.R. 1217 in respect of the limitation of the liability of partnerships.

LIABILITY OF TRUSTEE'S AGENT

Key Principle

A trustee's agent who innocently deals with trust funds is not liable as a constructive trustee.

WILLIAMS-ASHMAN V PRICE AND WILLIAMS 1942
Trust funds paid into a firm of solicitors' bank account were subsequently invested in unauthorized investments on the instructions of the trustee.

Held

❖ (Ch) The solicitor was not liable as a constructive trustee as he had acted honestly on the instructions of the trustee. [1942] Ch. 219.

Commentary

Mara v Browne [1896] 1 Ch. 199 was regarded as authority for the proposition that where the agent of the trustees acted honestly, he or she is not accountable to the beneficiaries unless he has intermeddled with the duties of a trustee. Where the agent has not acted honestly or acts in a manner that he knows is contrary to the trust, he may be liable for having intermeddled in the trust.

TRUSTS OF THE FAMILY HOME

Interest arising from a resulting trust

Key Principle

A beneficial interest under a resulting trust can only arise where the payments towards the purchase price are made at the time the property was acquired.

> CURLEY V PARKES 2004
>
> The claimant claimed a beneficial interest in a property which was in the defendant's sole name. The initial payment for the deposit was paid by the defendant with the mortgage also in her name. The claimant contributed to mortgage payments out of a joint bank account. After the property was acquired the claimant made a payment of £9,213 to the defendant which he alleged was to cover some of the acquisition costs of the property. The solicitors' fees and removal fees were paid by the claimant's employer as part of his relocation package. The relationship subsequently broke down.

Held

❖ (CA) For a resulting trust to arise, the payments towards to the purchase price had to be made at the time of the acquisition of the property. The payment of the mortgage instalments after the purchase of the property was insufficient as these were made after the acquisition of the property. None of the lump sum payments could be linked to the purchase of the property.

Commentary

The traditional view was that a beneficial interest under a resulting trust arose only where the payments towards the purchase price were made at the time the property was acquired. However, it was thought that this was extended to mortgage payments as this could be regarded as a delayed payment. This case now rules out that possibility. However such payments could give rise to a constructive trust either by detrimental reliance on a common intention or an inferred common intention by virtue of contributions to the purchase in accordance with the view of Bridge L.J. in *Lloyds Bank v Rossett*.

After *Stack v Dowden* [2007] 2 All E.R. 929 and *Jones v Kernott* [2011] UKSC 53 (see below) it would appear that resulting trusts do not apply in cases where the property is in the parties' joint names or where land is held

CONSTRUCTIVE TRUSTS

121

in one party's name in a family home context. However, it still applies in the commercial context— *Laskar v Laskar* [2008] EWCA Civ 347.

Interest arising from a constructive trust

Key Principle

In the absence of an expressed common intention as to the beneficial ownership in a property, the common intention can only be inferred by direct financial contribution to the acquisition of the property.

> LLOYDS BANK V ROSSETT 1991
> A husband and wife purchased a semi-derelict property with the husband's family trust providing the purchase price. The title to the property was put in the husband's name on the insistence of the trustees of the family trust. The purchasers were given access to the property before completion of the purchase. Renovation work was commenced with the wife doing some decorating and supervising the builders. Shortly after the work commenced, the husband obtained an overdraft facility for the renovation work. Upon default, possession proceedings were instituted. The wife claimed an interest in the property.

Held

❖ (HL) The wife's activities in respect of the property were not sufficient evidence on which an inference of common intention that the wife was to have a beneficial interest in the property could be drawn. In the absence of an expressed intention, the husband held the property for his own use and benefit. [1991] 1 A.C. 107.

Commentary

[1] Lord Bridge (at 132–133) suggested that in the absence of an expressed common intention as to the beneficial interest in the property, it was doubtful that any conduct short of direct financial contribution to the purchase price would suffice. The position is that where there are direct financial contributions to the purchase price after the date of the acquisition of the property, for example, by payment of mortgage instalments, a beneficial interest in the property will arise. This beneficial interest will be held by way of a constructive trust (*Drake v Whipp*, below). Where there is an expressed common intention and the representee acted in reliance of it to his or her detriment (which can take the form of direct or indirect financial contribution), a beneficial interest could arise which would be held by way of a constructive trust

(see below). See also *Halifax Building Society v Brown* [1996] 1 F.L.R. 103 and *Goodman v Carlton* (2002) 2 F.L.R. 259.

The principles in *Lloyds Bank v Rossett* were used to resolve a business dispute in *Lloyd v Pickering* [2004] EWHC 1513.

[2] The dicta by Lord Bridge as regards the situation about the inference of the common intention by way of direct financial contributions only, has been criticised as being unfair to the party who made indirect financial contributions which enabled the other party to pay the mortgage. The former will have no interest if there has been no expressed common intention. In *Le Foe v Le Foe* [2001] 2 F.L.R. 970, the court, albeit at first instance, decided that a party's indirect financial contribution by way of payment of the day to day household expenses amounted to an indirect financial contribution to the mortgage payments which gave her an interest in the property. The court stated that it did not think that Lord Bridge intended to exclude all indirect financial contributions where there has been no expressed common intention but was to be allowed in exceptional circumstances. In *Stack v Dowden* [2007] 2 All E.R. 929, Lord Walker was of the view that Lord Bridge's dicta has been criticized as giving rise to potential injustice and regardless of whether it was right to conclude as he did in that decision, the law has since moved on. Baroness Hale in *Abbot v Abbot* [2008] 1 F.L.R. 1451 went on to say that the House of Lords in *Stack v Dowden* had agreed that a "common intention trust could be inferred even where there was not evidence of an actual agreement" and referred to her own judgment in that case where she stated that

> "the law has …. moved on in response to changing social and economic conditions … [t]he search is to ascertain the parties' shared intentions, actual, inferred or imputed with respect to the property in light of their whole course of conduct …".

See also *James v Thomas* [2007] 3 F.C.R. 696.

[3] In *Aspden v Elvy* [2012] EWHC 1387, the court decided that the claimant was entitled to a 25 per cent share in a property which he had originally transferred to the defendant. The defendant had converted the property which was a barn into a dwelling house with some help from the claimant who provided some monies as well as work on the conversion. The court found that the

> "proper inference from the whole course of dealing is that there was a common intention that the claimant should have some

interest in [the property] as a result of the very substantial contributions made to the conversion works".

See also *Geary v Rankine* [2012] EWCA Civ 555 where the court refused to
recognise the defendant's claim to a beneficial share in the property as she
failed to prove that there was a common intention either express or inferred
that she would have a share in the property.

Key Principle

An uncommunicated intention as to the beneficial ownership was not relevant, as evidence of intention can be established either as communicated or
manifested by the parties.

MOLLO V MOLLO 1999

The second and third claimants were the children of the first claimant
and the defendant who were divorced. A property, which required
substantial refurbishment, was acquired in the defendant's name to
provide a home for the children. The defendant wished the first claimant to contribute equally towards the cost of the work but he was
unable to do so. The first claimant contributed £9,000 towards the
purchase price and spent time refurbishing the house. The claimants
argued that the contribution in cash and kind was pursuant to a
common intention that the defendant held the property beneficially for
either, the two children, or herself and the first claimant. The defendant
denied such common intention existed.

Held

❖ (Ch) There was insufficient evidence to establish a common intention that
the property was to be held on trust for the children. The defendant had
wanted the first claimant to contribute equally to the purchase price. It was
difficult to believe the defendant's contention that the contribution was made
gratuitously. Also, the defendant's claim that the money had been repaid was
not credible. Therefore there was a clear agreement that the first claimant and
the defendant should share the property beneficially. (1999) E.G.C.S. 117.

Commentary

The court assessed the first claimant's share at 25 per cent representing the
value of his contribution. There was no clear evidence that the defendant and
the first claimant were to share the property equally.

Where the owner of the property represents to the non-owning party that the latter was to have an interest in the property and the latter acted in reliance of it to his or her detriment, a constructive trust in favour of the latter may arise.

> **GRANT V EDWARDS 1986**
> The plaintiff and first defendant moved into a house bought by the first defendant. At the time of the purchase, the first defendant told the plaintiff that her name would not be on the title because it would complicate her divorce proceedings. The house was put into the first defendant's and his brother's name. The first defendant paid the mortgage instalments with the plaintiff paying substantial household expenses. The parties separated in 1980 and the question arose as to the plaintiff's beneficial interest in the property.

Held

❖ (CA) A trust would be inferred where there was a common intention that both parties were to have a beneficial interest in the property and the non-owner had acted in reliance of this to his or her detriment. The excuse made by the first defendant gave rise to an inference of common intention, that, the plaintiff should have an interest in the property. Since she had acted in reliance of it to her detriment by her substantial contribution to the household expenses, the plaintiff was entitled to a half share in the property. [1986] 1 Ch. 638.

Commentary

Similarly, in *Hammond v Mitchell* [1991] 1 W.L.R. 1127, the court decided that the defendant had a beneficial interest in the family home. This was because of the express understanding that she was to have an interest in the property together with her contribution as an unpaid business assistant and the other circumstances of the case.

Quantification of beneficial interest in the property— purchase in the name of one owner

Key Principle

Where a constructive trust arises in favour of the person who acted in reliance of the representation of the owner of the property, the court can adopt a "broad brush" approach in deciding the extent of the beneficial interest in the property.

> **DRAKE V WHIPP 1996**
> The plaintiff and defendant bought a barn, which was in the defendant's sole name. The plaintiff provided 40.1 per cent of the purchase price. The parties spent £129,536 on the property out of which the plaintiff contributed £13,000. The parties subsequently split up and the question arose as to the extent of the parties' interest in the property.

Held

❖ (CA) This was a case of constructive trust rather than resulting trust. In order for such a trust to arise, all that was needed was a common intention that the non-owning party should have a beneficial interest in the property and the latter had acted to his or her detriment in reliance of it. In constructive trust cases, the court can adopt a broad-brush approach in determining the parties' share in the property. The plaintiff was entitled to one-third share in the property. [1996] 1 F.L.R. 826.

Commentary

[1] In *Drake v Whipp*, Gibson L.J. (at 827) suggested that the

> "... potent source of confusion, ... has been suggestions that it matters not whether the terminology used is that of the constructive trust, to which the intention, actual or imputed, of the parties is crucial, or that of the resulting trust which operates as a presumed intention of the contributing party in the absence of rebutting evidence of actual intention".

This decision is a welcome source of clarification as to when a constructive or resulting trust will arise although this is now to be read subject to *Jones v Kernott* and *Stack v Dowden* as regards the suitability of relying on resulting trusts in family home cases.

[2] In the case of a resulting trust, the contributing party will be entitled to a beneficial interest to the extent of his or her contribution. In *Springette v Defoe* [1992] 2 F.L.R. 388, a resulting trust arose and the plaintiff was held to be entitled to a 75 per cent share in the property as this represented the extent of her contribution. However, in *Midland Bank Plc v Cooke* [1995] 4 All E.R. 562, the Court of Appeal decided that where a resulting trust arose, it was permissible to look at the whole course of dealings and conduct between the parties with regard to the ownership and occupation of the property.

Although the contribution of the non-owning spouse amounted to 6.47 per cent only, the court found that she was entitled to a beneficial half interest in the property.

[3] Under the Civil Partnership Act 2004, civil partners as defined in that Act will have many of the same property rights as married couples.

Key Principle

In deciding the beneficial interest between two parties where there is no agreement as to the size of the beneficial share the court could adopt an approach based on fairness to the parties.

> ### OXLEY V HISCOCK 2004
> O and H were cohabitees who purchased a property together but registered in H's sole name. H had provided more of the purchase price and the balance was by way of a mortgage. The relationship broke down and O alleged that the registration in H's sole name as at his insistence and that their expressed intention was that they should have an equal share in the beneficial ownership of the property. H alleged that there had been no discussion as to how they should share their beneficial interest.

Held

❖ (CA) It would not be fair to declare that the parties had equal beneficial shares in the property. The court would take into account the fact that H's contribution was greater than O's and accordingly awarded O a 40 per cent share and the remainder to H. [2004] EWCA Civ 546.

Commentary

In this case, the court was of the view that the correct approach was to ask what a fair share between the parties would be, taking into account all the circumstances of the case, including, the course of dealing between the parties. Chadwick L.J. stated that the approach to resolve the issue where a family home is in the sole name of one of the parties and each makes some financial contribution to the purchase but fail to make an express declaration of trust is to ask two questions:

[1] Whether there is a common intention that each shall have a beneficial interest in the property. If there was such a common intention then there is no problem. This can be inferred from the financial contribution made by the

parties. If the answer to this question is yes then as a constructive trust arises, there should be detrimental reliance but this is usually satisfied by a party's financial contribution.

[2] What is the extent of the parties' beneficial interest? Evidence of the discussions between the parties may provide the necessary solution. However, in the absence of such evidence the court will have to look at the course of dealings between the parties including the arrangements in respect of the outgoings for the house, e.g. council tax and utilities payments, mortgage payments etc.

The approach has been followed in *Cox v Jones* [2004] EWHC 1486 where the court found that in respect of a house which was bought in the defendant's name, there was an express agreement between the parties that the property would be jointly owned but not as to proportion of that beneficial ownership. There was evidence that the claimant had acted to her detriment. The court applied the principle of fairness from *Oxley v Hiscock* and having regard to the course of conduct between the parties. Accordingly, it was appropriate to give the claimant a 25 per cent share in the property in light of her contributions. See also *Jones v Kernott* [2011] UKSC 53 which similarly followed this approach (see below) and *Re Piper* [2011] EWHC 3570 where the court found in favour of equal shares between the parties.

Quantification of beneficial interest in the property— purchase in the name of joint owners

Key Principle

Where property is purchased in the parties' joint names, the normal principle is that the beneficial ownership should follow the legal position, namely equal shares, unless there is a contrary intention.

STACK V DOWDEN 2007

The parties, an unmarried couple, bought their family home in joint names. D paid the deposit from the proceeds of sale of a house owned by her and her savings account. S had made alterations and improvements to D's previous property. The rest of the purchase price was from a mortgage in their joint names. S paid the premiums on the mortgage insurance policy and paid some of the interest payments. The utility bills were in D's name and S claimed to have contributed to these. The transfer was on the land registry form which at that time did not contain any declaration of trust. However, it contained a declaration that the survivor could give a good receipt for capital monies arising from a disposition of all or part of the property. Some improvements were made to the property. The parties had throughout their time together kept separate bank accounts out of which they made their own investments and savings. The Court of Appeal applied the decision in *Oxley v Hiscock* and adopted the "fairness" approach enunciated in that decision and ordered that D was to be given a 65 per cent share in the property whilst S got 35 per cent.

Held

❖ (HL) In the domestic context, where there is a conveyance in the parties' joint names, the normal principle was equal beneficial ownership following the legal ownership. Where a party is seeking a different quantification then he or she has to prove that there was a contrary intention. This would require the court to look at all the circumstances of the case so as to be able to ascertain their common intention—actual, inferred or imputed—in light of the parties' conduct in relation to the property. In this case, as the factors which indicated that the parties had a contrary intention, included that the parties were clear that D had contributed more than S and that S would pay the interest payments and the premiums on the insurance policies. Further, the parties had kept their financial affairs separate which was unusual given the duration that the parties were together and even though there were four children from the relationship. This showed that the parties had intended they did not want their shares in the property to be equal and also pointed to their intention not to have a beneficial joint tenancy. The appeal would be dismissed and D would be entitled to her 65 per cent share. [2007] 2 All E.R. 929.

Commentary

[1] Baroness Hale stated that in considering the factors in order to decide what the parties' intentions were, in the domestic context, many more factors than merely financial considerations may be relevant. These included:

- any advice or discussions at the time of the transfer which cast light upon their intentions then;
- the reasons why the home was acquired in their joint names;
- the reasons why … the survivor was authorised to give a receipt for the capital monies;
- the purpose for which the home was acquired;
- the nature of the parties' relationship;
- whether they had children for whom they both had responsibility to provide a home;

- how the purchase was financed, both initially and subsequently;
- how the parties arranged their finances, whether separately or together or a bit of both;
- how they discharged the outgoings on the property and their other household expenses. When a couple are joint owners of the home and jointly liable for the mortgage, the inferences to be drawn from who pays for what may be very different from the inferences to be drawn when only one is owner of the home. The arithmetical calculation of how much was paid by each is also likely to be less important; and
- the parties' individual characters and personalities.

Baroness Hale went on to say that

> "[i]n the cohabitation context, mercenary considerations may be more to the fore than they would be in marriage, but it should not be assumed that they always take pride of place over natural love and affection. At the end of the day, having taken all this into account, cases in which the joint legal owners are to be taken to have intended that their beneficial interests should be different from their legal interests will be very unusual".

This was followed in *Fowler v Barron* [2008] 2 F.L.R. 381 where the property was conveyed in the parties' joint names without any express declaration as to the beneficial ownership. The court decided that it would look at the parties' course of dealing in respect of the property. As the parties were joint legal owners, this gave rise to a presumption of joint beneficial ownership which the appellant failed to rebut. Accordingly, each had a half share in the property.

In *Abbot v Abbot* [2008] 1 F.L.R. 1451, a Privy Council decision, Baroness Hale reiterated that the common intention could be express, inferred or imputed. In this case, the property was in the husband's sole name and the court had to consider whether the wife had a share in the property as there is no property adjustment legislation in Antigua and Barbuda. The court recognized that she had undertaken a joint liability in respect to the mortgage but her contributions were less than 50 per cent. This enabled the wife to have an interest in the property. Baroness Hale criticized the Court of Appeal in not recognizing that the law had moved on since *Lloyds Bank v Rossett* and that in deciding the parties' share in the property the court should take into account their course of conduct. Taking the circumstances of the case into account, the Privy Council decided that they were each to have a half share in the property.

[2] Recent cases which followed the *Stack v Dowden* approach include *Jones v Kernott* [2011] UKSC 53 (see below) and *Williamson v Sheikh* [2008] EWCA Civ 990 where the court took into account an unsigned declaration of trust deed as establishing the parties' common intention as to the beneficial share in the home. In *Akhtar v Hussain* [2012] EWCA Civ 1170 the Court of Appeal rejected an attempt to rely on *Jones v Kernott* to rebut the presumption as there was insufficient evidence to support its rebuttal. See also *Morris v Morris* [2008] EWCA Civ 257.

[3] This approach does not apply in a commercial context. In *Laskar v Laskar* [2008] EWCA Civ 347 where a mother and daughter jointly bought an ex-council property as an investment, the presumption that they held the beneficial interest jointly was not applicable. The eventual dispute was resolved through a purchase money resulting trust.

[4] Where there is an express declaration of trust which provided for the parties to hold the property as tenants in common in equal shares the court will not insert a constructive trust in substitution of that express trust. In the absence of any evidence of fraud or mistake as a ground for setting aside the express trust or as a basis for rectification, the court is compelled to give effect to the express declaration: *Pankhania v Chandegra* [2012] EWCA Civ 1438. Lord Justice Mummery in that case also confirmed that *Jones v Kernott* and *Stack v Dowden* did not apply in such cases.

Key Principle
The presumption of joint tenants in law and equity applicable at the time of the acquisition of the family home can be displaced where there is evidence to show that they later formed the common intention that their shares in the home would change.

JONES V KERNOTT 2011
The parties were cohabitees and shared the family home which was in their joint names. In 1993 the relationship broke down with Mr Kernott leaving the home and Ms Jones remaining in occupation. She met the future expenses in respect of the maintenance of the home as well as payment of the mortgage. Subsequently they cashed in a joint life insurance policy and as a result Mr Kernott purchased a property in his own name with the shared proceeds. In 2006 he claimed a half share of the former family home and Ms Jones sought a declaration under the **Trusts of Land and Appointment of Trustees Act 1996** that she was fully

entitled to the entire beneficial interest in the home. Ms Jones accepted that when they separated there was insufficient evidence to displace the presumption of equal shares but argued that events since then provided evidence that their intentions in respect of the beneficial interest in the home had now changed.

Held

❖ (SC) The starting point in cases such as this was that equity followed the law and as such the parties would be joint tenants both in law and in equity. However the presumption could be displaced where there was evidence of a different common intention at the time of the acquisition of the property or by evidence to show that they had changed their common intention subsequent to the acquisition of the home. This common intention had to deduced objectively from their conduct — the intention in question should be that which was reasonably understood by the other as shown by his or her words or conduct. It does not matter that the party did not consciously formulate that intention or even act differently. In this case although the intention at the time of the acquisition was to provide a home for the family, this intention changed when they cashed in their joint life insurance policy and the acquisition of a separate property by Mr Kernott with the proceeds of the policy. The inference was that they had intended that Mr Kernott's interest crystallised at that stage. A rough calculation showed that the County Court judge decision was on the same basis and hence it would be wrong for the appellate court to interfere with it. Accordingly Ms Jones was entitled to 90 per cent of the beneficial interest in the home and Mr Kernott to the remaining 10 per cent. [2011] UKSC 53.

Commentary

In *Jones v Kernott*, their Lordships went to state that where the parties did not intend a joint tenancy at the time of the acquisition of the home or had changed their intention but it was difficult to ascertain their actual intention either from the evidence available or as an inference from their conduct, the court would assess their entitlement on the basis which was fair having regard to the whole course of dealing between the parties (following *Oxley v Hiscock* [2004] EWCA Civ 546). Lord Walker and Lady Hale stated that

> "...in our judgment, 'the whole course of dealing ... in relation to the property' should be given a broad meaning, enabling a similar range of factors to be taken into account as may be relevant to ascertaining the parties' actual intentions".

Their Lordships also went on to state that each case would be dependent on its own facts and that financial contributions would be relevant but that there were other factors which would assist the court in deciding what the parties were intending or fair in the circumstances.

This decision of the Supreme Court confirms the approach in *Stack v Dowden* and although on the face of it might enable justice to be done in some cases, the risk remains of potential injustice. This is because the finding of the parties' intention is that which is found by the court on a balance of probabilities and as such the outcome of such cases will be hard to predict going forward leading to an increase of litigation.

Key Principle
An interest-free loan made by the non-owning party to the owner of the property may be taken into account in assessing the non-owning party's beneficial interest.

> ### RISCH V MCFEE 1990
> The plaintiff who lived with the defendant made an interest-free loan to the latter but had not sought repayment of it.

Held
❖ (CA) The unpaid interest-free loan could be taken into account in assessing the plaintiff's beneficial interest in the property. *The Times*, July 6, 1990.

CONVEYANCE INDUCED BY FRAUD

Key Principle
Where a conveyance has been induced by fraud, the transferee may have to hold the property on a constructive trust.

> ### ROCHEFOUCAULD V BOUSTEAD 1897
> The plaintiff agreed to sell some lands to the defendant who would hold it upon trust for the plaintiff. Without the plaintiff's consent, the defendant mortgaged the lands and subsequently became bankrupt. The plaintiff argued that the lands were held on trust for her.

Held
❖ (CA) The plaintiff was entitled to prove her claim by parol evidence, despite the requirements of writing. Accordingly, since there was evidence

that the lands were transferred subject to the trust, the defendant held the lands as trustee for the plaintiff. [1897] 1 Ch. 196.

BANNISTER V BANNISTER 1948

The defendant agreed to sell two cottages to the plaintiff subject to an agreement that she was to be allowed to live in one of them. The conveyance made no reference to the agreement. The plaintiff sought to evict the defendant.

Held

❖ (CA) A constructive trust arises to prevent a party from relying on the absolute nature of a conveyance for the purpose of defeating a beneficial interest in the property. The defendant was entitled to a declaration that the plaintiff held the house on a constructive trust during her life for her occupation for so long as she desired. Accordingly, the plaintiff could not evict her. [1948] 2 All E.R. 133.

Commentary

The Court of Appeal in *Rochefoucauld v Boustead*, above, thought that they were enforcing an express rather than a constructive trust. However, later cases such as *Bannister v Bannister*, above, have suggested that these situations give rise to a constructive trust. However the position will be different if there is no subject to an equitable interest. See also *Binions v Evans* [1972] 2 All E.R. 70 and *Lyus v Prowsa Developments Ltd* [1982] 2 All E.R. 953.

MUTUAL WILLS

Key Principle

Where mutual wills are found to exist, a constructive trust arises to enforce the intentions of the parties.

RE CLEAVER 1981

A husband and wife made mutual wills in the other's favour absolutely with gifts in favour of the husband's three children (from an earlier relationship) in the event of the other's prior death. In 1974 they amended their wills to reduce the share of one daughter to a life interest. The husband died and the wife made a new will which was in line with the previous will. She then subsequently made another will which changed the daughter's life interest to an absolute interest. Thereafter she made a third will which left everything to the daughter and her husband without leaving anything for the remaining two children.

Held

❖ (Ch) The wife's executors held her estate on a constructive trust as set out in the 1974 will. There was sufficient evidence to show the agreement between the husband and wife to make mutual wills. This was on the basis of the equitable principle that it would not permit a person to whom property had been transferred on the faith of an agreement to make mutual wills to deal with it in a manner which was inconsistent with that agreement. [1981] 2 All E.R. 1018.

Commentary

Where two or more persons agree that on the death of the first their property will be enjoyed by the survivor but that after the survivor's death the property would go to nominated beneficiaries and they make mutual wills to that effect, a constructive trust will be imposed to prevent the survivor from disposing of the property in a manner inconsistent with that agreement. Lord Justice Mummery on *Olins v Walters* [2008] EWCA Civ 782 stated that

> "...it is a legally necessary condition of mutual wills that there is clear and satisfactory evidence of a contract between two testators...The obligation on the surviving testator is equitable. It is in the nature of a trust of the property affected, so the constructive trust label is attached to it. The equitable obligation is imposed for the benefit of third parties, who were intended by the parties to benefit from it. It arises by operation of law on the death of the first testator to die so as to bind the conscience of the surviving testator in relation to the property affected".

The court in *Charles v Fraser* [2010] EWHC 2154 helpfully summarised the requirements for the existence of mutual wills and the consequences flowing from it as follows:

(i)   Mutual wills are wills made by two or more persons, usually in substantially the same terms and conferring reciprocal benefits, following an agreement between them to make such wills and not revoke them without the consent of the other.

(ii) For the doctrine to apply there has to be what amounts to a contract between the two testators that both wills will be irrevocable and remain unaltered. A common intention, expectation or desire is not enough.

(iii) The mere execution of mirror or reciprocal wills does not imply any agreement either as to revocation or non-revocation.

(iv) For the doctrine to apply it is not necessary that the second testator should have obtained a personal financial benefit under the will of the first testator. See *Re Dale* [1993] 4 All E.R. 129.

(v) It is perfectly possible for there to have been an agreement preventing revocability as to part of the residuary estate only, in which case the doctrine only applies to that part.

(vi) The agreement may be incorporated in the will or proved by extraneous evidence. It may be oral or in writing.

(vii) The agreement must be established by clear and satisfactory evidence on the balance of probabilities.

(viii) The agreement is enforced in equity by the imposition of a constructive trust on the property which is the subject matter of the agreement. The beneficiaries under the will that was not to be revoked may apply to the court for an order that the estate is held on trust to give effect to the provisions of the old will.

(ix) The action relates only to the dispositive part of the will. The new will is fully effective to deal with non-dispositive matters, such as the appointment of executors. Accordingly where the doctrine applies the executors appointed under the final will hold the assets of the estate on trust to give effect to the earlier will.

THINK POINT

Do you consider that Arden L.J. took the correct approach in *Abou-Rahmah v Abacha* [2007] 1 Lloyd's Rep. 115 in following the earlier Privy Council decision in *Barlow Clowes International Ltd v Eurotrust International Ltd* [2006] 1 All E.R. 333?

Do you consider that the court was right in *Sinclair Investments (UK) Ltd v Versailles Trade Finance Ltd (in administrative receivership)* [2011] EWCA Civ 347 in refusing to follow the Privy Council decision in *Attorney-General for Hong Kong v Reid* [1994] A.C. 324?

Appointment, Retirement and Removal of Trustees

7

INTRODUCTION

Trustees are crucial to the effective and efficient administration of a trust. The trust property is vested in trustees who have a fiduciary obligation and must act in the best interest of the trust and its beneficiaries and ensure that they strike a balance between the beneficiaries, both present and future. Hence, the rules in respect of their appointment, retirement and removal are important to ensure that there are appropriate trustees for the trust.

Generally, any person who has legal capacity can be a trustee and this includes a trust corporation. This can also theoretically include the Crown: *Penn v Lord Baltimore* (1750) 1 Ves. Sen. 444 (see Ch.1) and *Civilian War Claimants Association v R* [1932] A.C. 14. A minor, whilst he cannot be a trustee under an express trust, may be a trustee under a resulting or constructive trust of personalty (although not of land—s.20 of the **Law of Property Act 1925**): *Re Vinogradoff* [1935] W.N. 68.

Trustees would be normally appointed under the instrument creating the trust and it is often the case that it will also make provision for the appointment of additional trustees should that be necessary. In addition, the **Trustee Act 1925** provides for the appointment of additional trustees unless it has been expressly excluded.

Other statutory provisions in respect of the appointment of trustees include powers given to donees of enduring power of attorney (s.36(6A) – (6D) of the **Trustee Act 1925**) and where beneficiaries under a trust of land can direct existing trustees to appoint others as trustees (s.19(2)(b) of the **Trusts of Land and Appointment of Trustees Act 1996**).

APPOINTMENT OF TRUSTEES

Key Principle

A person who is resident abroad will be appointed as a trustee only where there are special circumstances.

RE WHITEHEAD'S WILL TRUSTS 1971

Trustees who were resident in the UK applied to court for permission to appoint new trustees who were resident in Jersey. The beneficiaries resided in Jersey.

Held

❖ (Ch) There was no rule preventing the appointment of trustees who were resident abroad. However, the court would only do so rarely. It was appropriate in this case to allow such an appointment, as the beneficiaries were also resident abroad. [1971] 2 All E.R. 1334.

Commentary

It is possible to frame a deed in such a way as to allow the appointment of a trustee resident abroad. The exercise of a power of appointment may be invalid if it fails to take into account the possible adverse capital gains consequences of the appointment: *Green v Cobham* 4 I.T.E.L.R. 784.

Key Principle

Where new trustees are appointed to replace existing trustees under s.36 of the **Trustee Act 1925**, the trustee being replaced, need not be party to the decision.

RE STONEHAM SETTLEMENT TRUSTS 1952

One of two trustees of a family trust was out of the country for more than 12 months but was willing to continue as trustee. His co-trustee, who wished to retire, appointed new trustees in place of himself and the trustee who had been out of the country.

Held

❖ (Ch) The trustee who had been out of the country did not need to have taken part in the decision. The appointment of the new trustees to replace existing trustees under s.36 of the **Trustee Act 1925** was valid. [1952] 2 All E.R. 694.

Commentary

The statutory power to appoint new trustees under s.36 of the **Trustee Act 1925** is available unless it has been expressly excluded. The power is given to persons who have been specifically nominated as persons having the power to appoint new trustees or where there is none, then to surviving and continuing trustees. Section 36(8) of the **Trustee Act 1925** provides that a continuing trustee includes the trustee who is refusing to act or a trustee who wishes to retire, so long as he is willing to appoint new trustees. Therefore, in this case, it was proper for the retiring trustee to appoint new trustees as replacement for himself and the trustee who was out of the country.

Key Principle

Under s.36(1) of the **Trustee Act 1925**, the power of appointment can only be exercised to replace existing trustees, while, s.36(6) allows the appointment of additional trustees up to a maximum of four.

RE POWER'S SETTLEMENT TRUSTS 1951

A tenant for life under a settlement was given the power to appoint new trustees under s.36 of the **Trustee Act 1925**. The tenant for life purported to appoint himself as an additional trustee.

Held

❖ (CA) The tenant for life cannot appoint himself as a trustee under the settlement. Under s.36(1) of the **Trustee Act 1925**, the power to appoint trustees is limited to the replacement of existing trustees. Under s.36(6) additional trustees can be appointed but this did not permit the person given the power to appoint new trustees to appoint himself. [1951] 2 All E.R. 513.

Commentary

The statutory power to appoint new trustees does not allow the appointment of more than four trustees. It is also not available if one of the existing trustees is a trust corporation. In *Adam & Co International Trustees Ltd v Theodore Goddard*, *The Times*, March 17, 2000, the court held that s.36 could not be used to appoint one new trustee in order to discharge two retiring trustees. The second retiring trustees would have to retire under s.39 of the **Trustees Act 1925**.

Key Principle

The court has the power to appoint new trustees under s.41 of the **Trustee Act 1925**.

RE TEMPEST 1866

One of the trustees of a family settlement predeceased the testator. The persons with the power to appoint new trustees could not agree on a replacement. An application to court was made to appoint P. One of the beneficiaries opposed this because the proposed trustee was from a branch of the family with which the testator had not been on friendly terms.

Held

❖ (CA) In the circumstances of the case, P was not a proper person to be appointed as a trustee. (1866) L.R. 1 Ch. App. 485.

Commentary

In exercising its discretion, the court will take into account the wishes of the testator, where this is clear from the trust instrument or will. It would not normally appoint a person as a trustee where there is a risk that the appointed person may not serve the interests of all the beneficiaries by acting impartially. The court may need to take into account the reluctance of the surviving trustee to co-operate with the new trustee but should not refuse to appoint on that basis. However, the court suggested that in this case, this could be a ground for the removal of the existing trustee where he has acted unreasonably rather than as an argument against appointing the new trustee.

DISCLAIMER

Key Principle

A person who has been appointed a trustee can avoid the office of trusteeship by disclaimer.

> RE CLOUT AND FREWERS CONTRACT 1924
>
> An executor trustee did not prove or act under the will for 30 years. He did not apply to take the legacy that the testator had left to him in the will.

Held

❖ (Ch) The executor trustee's inaction amounted to a disclaimer by conduct. [1924] 2 Ch. 230.

Commentary

If the person appointed as a trustee wishes to avoid the office of a trustee, he should disclaim immediately by deed, otherwise, his actions may be taken as acceptance of the office of trusteeship: *Re Tyron* (1844) 7 Beav. 496. However, where the trustee has not done anything with the trust, his conduct can be taken as disclaimer. It is also possible that the trustee could have said to have accepted by acquiescence if he allows other trustees to carry out the trust obligations in his name: *Mountford v Cadogan* (1810) 17 Ves. Jr. 485. It is however not possible to have partial disclaimer: *Re Lord and Fullerton's Contract* [1896] 1 Ch. 228.

Once he is deemed to have accepted the office of trusteeship, he can no longer disclaim but can always retire from the trust under s.39 of the **Trustee Act 1925.**

RETIREMENT OF TRUSTEES

Key Principle

Where a trustee retired from the trust, he will not be liable for subsequent breaches of trust unless he contemplated the breaches when he retired.

> #### HEAD V GOULD 1898
> H and C were the trustees of a marriage settlement, who were subsequently appointed trustees of a postnuptial settlement favouring the same beneficiaries. The trustees made various advances to the widow up to her full entitlement in some instances in breach of trust. The trustees retired and new trustees were appointed. After the appointment of the new trustees, further breaches of trust occurred.

Held

❖ (Ch) The trustees who retired would not be liable for the breach of trust committed by the present trustees. They would only be liable where it can be established that the breaches of trust were contemplated by them. It was not enough to show that the retirement facilitated the breach of trust. [1898] 2 Ch. 250.

Commentary

Upon the appointment of a new trustee or on the retirement of an existing trustee by deed, any chattel, land or chose in action subject to the tryst will automatically vest in the new or continuing trustees as joint tenants without the need for a formal assignment or conveyance. There are exceptions to this including, land conveyed by mortgage as security for trust monies; land held under a legal or equitable lease which has a covenant against assignment or disposition; company shares; and registered land.

REMOVAL OF TRUSTEES

Key Principle

The court has an inherent jurisdiction to remove a trustee.

> LETTERSTEDT V BROERS 1884
>
> Several allegations of misconduct were made against the trustee. The beneficiary asked for the trustee to be removed.

Held

❖ (PC) The court has a general duty to ensure the proper execution of the trust. As part of this duty, the court can remove a trustee if it is satisfied that the continuation of the trustee in office would impede the efficient administration of the trust. Accordingly, the trustee would be removed. (1884) 9 App. Cas. 371.

Commentary

Although the court has a statutory power to remove and replace a trustee under s.41 of the **Trustee Act 1925**, the court also has an inherent discretion to do so. The Privy Council was reluctant to lay down general rules but merely stated that the interest of the beneficiary is paramount. It would ultimately depend on the circumstances of the case. These may include the expense involved and the faith that beneficiaries have in the trustee: *Re Wrightson* [1908] 1 Ch. 789. However Lewison J. in *Thomas and Agnes Carvel Foundation v Carvel* [2008] Ch. 395, suggested (at para.46 of his judgment) that

> "the overriding consideration is ... whether the trusts are being properly executed" or, as he put it in a later passage, the main guide must be "the welfare of the beneficiaries".

The court was prepared to use its inherent jurisdiction to remove the trustees in the *National Union of Mineworkers in Clarke v Heathfield* [1985] I.C.R. 606, where the trustees moved trust funds out of jurisdiction in order to avoid sequestration. The court also removed three out of four trustees in *Jones v Firkin Flood* [2008] All E.R. (D) 175 where the trustees had totally abdicated their responsibilities. A recent example is *Scott v Scott* [2012] EWHC 2397 where the court removed a hostile trustee where the hostility was such as to have a deleterious effect on the administration of the trust and affect the welfare of the beneficiaries. The decision in *Letterstedt v Broers* was also followed in *Walker v Walker*, Lawtel, March 31, 2008.

In exceptional cases, the court can order the removal of trustees without appointing a replacement provided that there is an alternative mode of administration which protected the interests of the beneficiaries: *Gonder v Gonder Estate* 13 I.T.E.L.R. 44.

Key Principle
The Charity Commissioners have the power to appoint, discharge or remove a trustee of a charity.

SCARGILL V CHARITY COMMISSIONERS 1998
The Charity Commissioners ordered the removal of the two appellants who were trustees of two charities. These were the Yorkshire Miners' Welfare Trust Fund ("YMWTF") and the Yorkshire Miners' Welfare Convalescent Homes ("YMWCH"). The appellants arranged for a grant of £800,000 to be made by the former charity to the latter. Such a grant was within the power of the YMWTF to make but it did require the consent of the Coal Industry Social Welfare Organisation ("CISWO"). The main ground for removing the appellants was their decision to make the grant and the implementation of it.

Held
❖ (Ch) The appellants knew that the consent of CISWO was required yet knowingly went ahead with the grant. In doing so they substantially reduced the endowment fund of YMWTF. Whilst the appellants were not motivated by personal gain they were motivated by principles which they used to justify flouting the requirements of the trust and the law. Consequently the removal of the appellants by the Charity Commissioners was justified. Lawtel, September 9, 1998.

Commentary
The Charities Act 1993 strengthened the Charity Commissioners powers to deal with misconduct and mismanagement of Charities. They have the same jurisdiction as the High Court for the purpose of removing trustees of charities. In *Weth v HM Attorney General*, Lawtel, July 10, 2000, the Court of Appeal found that the decision to remove trustees of a charity was justified. This was on the grounds of mismanagement, which consisted largely of protracted disputes between trustees themselves, which diverted their attention and resources from the proper running of the charity to achieve its purposes. Similarly, in *Seray-Wurie v Charity Commission*, Lawtel, September 1, 2008, the Commission removed a trustee of an incorporated charity under s.18 of the **Charity Act 1993** where he had failed to record relevant financial information and properly account for its funds. There was clear evidence that

there was a conscious breach of the law and a failure to comply with the obligations of a charity trustee.

THINK POINT

Re Tempest (1866) L.R. 1 Ch. App. 485 suggested a number of circumstances where the court may refuse to appoint an individual as a trustee under s.41 of the **Trustee Act 1925**. In what other situations will the court refuse to make an appointment under s.41? See *Re Coode* (1913) 108 L.T. 94 and *Re Earl of Stamford* [1896] 1 Ch. 288 as examples.

What is the difference between the judicial trustee and the public trustee?

Trustees' Duties

8

INTRODUCTION

The trustees' fiduciary obligations impose a number of duties on the trustees which they have to carry out—these are either expressly provided in the trust instrument or implied by law. In the event of a failure to carry out the duties the trustees could be liable for breach of trust. The trustees do not have any discretion in the matter and unlike the case of trustees' powers they have to carry out the obligation.

The fiduciary nature of their obligation means that the liability is neither fault nor intent based. So long as there is a breach of their obligation the trustees are liable for a breach of trust and as seen in Chapter 11, will have to make good any loss or account for any profit to the trust.

As part of their duties, the trustees may be compelled to produce trust documents for trial involving beneficiaries or former beneficiaries: *North Shore Ventures Ltd v Anstead Holdings Inc* [2012] EWCA Civ 11.

FIDUCIARY DUTIES

[a] The rule against self-dealing

Key Principle

Where a trustee purchases trust property in his own name, the beneficiary can set aside the sale.

> **WRIGHT V MORGAN 1926**
> The will stated that the property was to be offered for sale to the trustee-beneficiary at a price fixed by an independent valuer. The trustee-beneficiary assigned this option to purchase to another trustee who purchased the property at a price fixed by an independent valuer.

Held

❖ (PC) As there was a conflict of duty and interest, the sale would be set aside on the application of a beneficiary. [1926] A.C. 788.

Commentary

This rule had already been established in earlier cases such as *Ex p. James* (1803) 8 Ves. 337 and *Ex p. Lacey* (1802) 6 Ves. 265. To allow the trustee to purchase trust property would in fact be to allow the trustee to purchase the property from himself. There would be a conflict of interest and duty and, also, the trustee may have been aware of information relating to the property which others may not have been aware of. However, where there is an adequate lapse of time between the retirement and purchase, the purchase may be upheld: *Re Boles and British Land Co's Contract* [1902] 1 Ch. 244 (12-year gap). See also *Kane v Radley-Kane* [1997] Ch. 274 and the New Zealand case of *McNulty v McNulty* 14 I.T.E.L.R. 361.

In *Brucknell-Bruce, Earl of Cadogan v Moore* [2012] All E.R. 108, the court applied the self-dealing rule in setting aside a lease and made it clear that the self-dealing rule can apply where trustees merely concur in a transaction and not only where they acquired the trust property.

Key Principle

A trustee may purchase trust property where the trust instrument authorises it.

> SARGEANT V NATIONAL WESTMINSTER BANK PLC 1990
> A testator appointed his wife and children as his executors and trustees under his will. The will authorised the purchase of the trust property by the trustees. Part of the estate consisted of several farms which he had let to his children to work on as a partnership before he died. The question arose as to whether the trustees could sell the freeholds of the farms to themselves.

Held

❖ (CA) As the trustees' rights pre-dated the will (by virtue of their tenancy of the farms), they had not put themselves in a position of conflict of interest and duty. Further, the express provision in the will allowing the trustees to purchase the trust property excluded the rule that a trustee could not purchase trust property. They could purchase the freeholds of the farm although they had a duty to obtain the best price. (1991) 61 P.&C.R. 518.

Key Principle

The court may allow a trustee to purchase trust property in exceptional cases.

An executor purported to renounce his executorship under a will after having carried out certain acts that amounted to intermeddling. Later, he purchased two farms owned by the estate, but of which he was the tenant, at an auction. He paid a price, which was probably higher than would have been paid by anyone else.

Held

❖ (CA) The sale would not be set aside. The acts of administration which he had undertaken were minimal, and, the knowledge which he acquired about the property was in his position as tenant, rather than as an executor. As he had not influenced the other executors, it was proper in the special circumstances of this case to allow the sale. [1968] Ch. 353.

Commentary

The executor did not take an active part in the administration of the estate, although he acted in a manner which amounted to intermeddling. It was conceded that these acts of intermeddling rendered the renunciation ineffective. However, Danckwerts L.J. suggested that this was a mistake and doubted whether the renunciation was rendered ineffective by the acts of intermeddling. It was felt that the acts of intermeddling were technical and trivial but since the concession was made, the executor technically remained as executor. However, since the evidence was that he took no part in arranging for the sale of the farms and had not influenced the other executor, it was proper to allow the sale.

The Law Commission has recently in its report *Intestacy and Family Provision Claims on Death (Law Commission Report No. 133)* considered whether the self-dealing rule should be modified in the context of intestacy. After consultation they decided not to recommend any change as the risks of reform may outweigh any possible advantages. It suggested that there may be a case for general reform of the rule against self-dealing as their remit only extended to intestacy cases.

[b] The Fair Dealing rule—the purchase of the beneficial interest

Key Principle

A trustee may purchase the beneficial interest from a beneficiary provided there is a clear and distinct contract, and there is no fraud, concealment, or advantage taken of, by the trustee of information obtained as a trustee.

MORSE V ROYAL 1806
A beneficiary who sold his beneficial interest to a trustee subsequently regretted the sale when the price of the property went up. He applied for the sale to be set aside.

Held
❖ (Ch) The sale would not be set aside. (1806) 12 Ves. 355.

Commentary
In *Tito v Waddell (No. 2)* [1977] Ch. 106, Mcgarry V.C. suggested that such a transaction is not voidable *ex debito justitiae*, but can be set aside by the beneficiary unless the trustee can show that he has taken no advantage of his position and has made full disclosure to the beneficiary, and the transaction is fair and honest. See also *Beale v Trinkler* [2009] 11 I.T.E.L.R. 862 where the Court of Appeal in Australia decided that the "fair-dealing" rules did not apply to a dissolution of a partnership. The court stressed that even though a trust had been used in respect of some of the assets of the partnership, this did not change their relationship which was essentially a partnership.

[c] Competition against the trust

Key Principle
A trustee is not allowed to set up a business in competition with the business carried out by the trust.

RE THOMSON 1930
Under the terms of the trust, the trustees were directed to look after the testator's business of a yacht broker. One of the trustees wished to set up a similar business.

Held
❖ (Ch) The trustee would not be allowed to set up the business which would compete with the business of the trust as this would be a breach of his fiduciary duty. [1930] 1 Ch. 203.

Commentary
In such cases, there is the potential conflict of interest and duty. However, in the Irish case of *Moore v M'glynn* (1894) 1 Ir.R. 74, the court refused to restrain an executor from competing with the estate but was prepared to remove the executor.

[d] The rule in Keech v Sandford

Key Principle

A trustee of a lease is not allowed to obtain a renewal of the lease for himself.

> KEECH V SANDFORD 1726
>
> A trustee of a lease applied to the lessor for a renewal of the lease. The lessor refused to renew the lease in favour of the trust where the beneficiary was an infant. However, the lessor agreed to renew the lease in the trustee's own name.

Held

❖ (Ch) The trustee held the lease upon trust for the infant beneficiary and had to account for the profits. (1726) Sel. Cas. Ch. 61.

Commentary

The court refused to allow the trustee to retain the lease because of the potential conflict of interest and duty. There may be a disincentive for a trustee to secure a renewal of the lease for the trust, where there was the possibility that he could obtain it for himself. This rule appears to extend to preventing the trustee from purchasing the freehold reversion: *Protheroe v Protheroe* [1968] 1 W.L.R. 519. Where the person who obtains the renewal of the lease is not in a fiduciary position, the rule in *Keech v Sandford* does not apply: *Re Biss* [1903] 2 Ch. 40.

[e] Remuneration

One of the consequences of the application of the rule that a trustee is not to profit from his position as a trustee is that a trustee is not entitled to remuneration for his work as a trustee. There are a number of exceptions to this rule. Under s.185 of the **Charities Act 2011**, a charity trustee can be remunerated from charity funds by an agreement with the charity or its trustees. Trustees are, however, entitled to out of pocket expense (s.31 of the Trustee Act 2000).

Key Principle

Where a trustee acts on the behalf of the trust in his professional capacity as a solicitor, the trustee may charge for the costs of litigation.

CRADDOCK V PIPER 1850

One of the trustees who was a solicitor acted on behalf of himself and his co-trustees in two legal actions with regard to the trust property. In taxing the costs of the action, the Master refused to allow the trustee-solicitor's costs incurred for professional work.

Held

❖ (Ch) The trustee-solicitor would be entitled to charge for the costs of litigation. (1850) 1 Mac. & C. 664.

Commentary

This rule has now been codified in s.28 of the **Trustee Act 2000** and by virtue of s.28(2) the trustee can receive payment in respect of the services rendered even though the services are of a nature that could have been provided by a lay trustee. The trustee is regarded as acting in his professional capacity if the trustee acts in course of a profession or business which has a connection with the management or administration of trusts: s.28(5). The important point to stress is that s.28 goes further than the rule in *Craddock v Piper* in that the payment for services is not restricted to the work of a solicitor but to any trustee who acts in his professional capacity. By s.29(2) a trustee who acts in a professional capacity is entitled to receive reasonable remuneration out of the trust funds for any services that he provides to or on behalf of the trust. Section 29(1) provides for the payment of reasonable remuneration for the services provided by a trust corporation.

Section 29(3) defines reasonable income as being

"...in relation to the provision of services by a trustee, such remuneration as is reasonable in the circumstances for the provision of those services".

However, the section has no application where the trust instrument provides for the remuneration of the trustee.

Key Principle

The court has an inherent jurisdiction to authorise remuneration in favour of the trustees.

BOARDMAN V PHIPPS 1966
(See below.)

Held

❖ (HL) The appellants had acted openly but had made a mistake as to their rights. Their actions had been highly beneficial to the trust and therefore it was appropriate to allow remuneration for their work and skill. [1966] 3 All E.R. 721.

> ### RE DUKE OF NORFOLK'S SETTLEMENT TRUSTS 1981
> One of the trustees of a settlement was a trust corporation. The trust corporation subsequently became involved in extensive redevelopment of trust property. This, together with the introduction of Capital Transfer Tax, resulted in additional work for the trustees. The trust corporation asked the court to authorise remuneration for the services provided.

Held

❖ (CA) The court had an inherent jurisdiction to order payment of remuneration to trustees where this would be of benefit to the administration of the trust. In exercising this jurisdiction, the court would have regard to the nature of the trust, the expertise of the trustees, the remuneration requested, the circumstances of the case and whether this would be in the best interests of the trust. [1981] 3 All E.R. 220.

Commentary

[1] In the exercise of the court's inherent jurisdiction to award remuneration, the court would balance, on the one hand, the fact that the office of a trustee is normally gratuitous and on the other hand, to ensure that the trust was properly administered. Ultimately, the question is whether it would be in the best interests of the trust. In *Foster v Spencer* [1996] 2 All E.R. 672, the court was prepared to exercise its inherent jurisdiction to order remuneration for the trustees. In *Badfinger Music v Evans*, Lawtel, May 5, 2000, the court exercised its exceptional jurisdiction to award remuneration to a trustee who owed fiduciary duties to his fellow beneficiaries against the general rule barring remuneration unless pre-approved. The claimant had re-mastered tapes of a live concert. His effort and skill had created profits, which the beneficiaries would not have otherwise gained.

[2] Where the court appoints a trust corporation as a trustee, it has the power to authorise remuneration: s.42 of the **Trustee Act 1925**.

Key Principle

Where the trustee receives Director's fees or salary as a result of being appointed to the Board of Directors by virtue of the trust's shareholding, he may have to account to the trust for the monies received.

RE FRANCIS 1905

The trustees became directors as a result of the trust's shareholding in the company. The issue arose as to whether the trustees had to account for the remuneration received.

Held

❖ (Ch) Applying the rule that trustees cannot profit from their position as trustees, the trustees were under a duty to account to the trust for their remuneration. (1905) 74 L.J. Ch. 198.

RE DOVER COALFIELD EXTENSION LTD 1907

Shares owned by D Company in K Company were transferred to one of its directors in order to qualify to be on the Board of Directors. The director executed a declaration of trust in respect of those shares.

Held

❖ (CA) The remuneration received by the director from his directorship in K Company was not profit received from use of property owned by D Company. Therefore, the director was under no liability to account. [1908] 1 Ch. 65.

Commentary

[1] Notwithstanding the benefits of having the trustee on the Board of Directors of a company, the trustees may have to account to the trust for monies received from that position. In *Re Dover Coalfield Extension Ltd* the court decided that the director could retain the fees because he had been appointed a director before the shares was transferred to him. The cases are not entirely consistent. In *Re Macadam* [1945] 2 All E.R. 664, trustees who held directorships in a company on the trust's behalf were held liable to account to the trust.

[2] Where it is clear that the testator intended the trustee to retain the directors' fees, the trustee may do so: *Re Llewellin's Will Trusts* [1949] Ch. 225.

[f] Trustees or fiduciaries cannot make a profit from that capacity

Key Principle

A trustee or fiduciary cannot make a profit from his position as trustee even though the trust may have declined or was unable to make use of the opportunity.

> **BOARDMAN V PHIPPS 1966**
>
> The trust held some shares in a private company. Boardman, who was the solicitor for the trust and one of the trustees wanted new directors to be appointed at the company. This failed and it was decided that the only way to make the company profitable was to take a controlling interest in the company. The trust was unable to acquire further shares in the company. Therefore, with the trustees' consent, Boardman and one of the beneficiaries acquired a controlling interest in the company and made it profitable. This benefited the trust, Boardman and the beneficiary. One of the other beneficiaries claimed that Boardman and the beneficiary had to account for the profits which they made.

Held

❖ (HL) Boardman and the other beneficiary by their actions were put in a fiduciary position. As such, any information they obtained about the company was acquired in that capacity. Therefore, they were not entitled to keep the profit acquired by them and had to account as constructive trustees to the trust for those profits. [1966] 3 All E.R. 721.

> **REGAL (HASTINGS) LTD V GULLIVER 1942**
>
> A company wanted to acquire the leases of two cinemas. In order to do this it set up a subsidiary company. The lessor refused to grant the leases unless the capital of the subsidiary company was fully paid up. The parent company did not have the funds to do this. The directors of the parent company bought some of the shares in the subsidiary company. The leases were granted and when the subsidiary company was subsequently sold, both the parent company and the directors made a profit.

Held

❖ (HL) The directors had to account for the profits which they made from the sale of the subsidiary company notwithstanding that the directors had acted bona fide. [1942] 1 All E.R. 378.

Commentary

In *Boardman v Phipps*, it was clear that there was no question of bad faith on the part of Boardman and the beneficiary. Linked with the fact that the profit resulted from their hard work, the court decided that they were entitled remuneration for the work. Their Lordships further suggested that they could have protected themselves by obtaining consent. Another important point to note is that Boardman and the beneficiary were not trustees but had by their actions put themselves in a position whereby they owed a fiduciary duty to the trust. See also *Gwembe Valley Development Co v Koshy (No. 3)* [2004] 1 B.C.L.C. 131. In *Murad v Al-Saraj* [2005] EWCA Civ 959 (at para.82) Arden L.J. in considering the application of the *Boardman v Phipps* principle suggested that

> "[i]t may be that the time has come when the court should revisit the operation of the inflexible rule of equity in harsh circum-stances, as where the trustee has acted in perfect good faith and without any deception or concealment, and in the belief that he was acting in the best interests of the beneficiary".

In *Crowder v Hodge* [2009] EWHC 786, the court held that a solicitor was held liable to account for profit made in breach of his fiduciary obligation but in that case, following *Boardman v Phipps*, allowed him a claim for the cost of his acquiring shares in a company (in breach of trust), but would not award him any allowance for the work he had put into the company. This was because he had misled the others as to how he came about to acquire to the shares in the company. A similar approach was taken in *Imageview Management Ltd v Jack* [2009] EWCA Civ 63, where the appellant football agent entered an agreement with the respondent where the latter agreed to pay him a proportion of his salary if the appellant was able to arrange the respondent to sign with a UK football club. The appellant was successful in doing so and the respondent started to pay the agreed amount but was not aware that the appellant was also receiving monies from the club for arranging the respondent's work permit. At first instance the court ordered the appellant to repay the fees received less a deduction for work done in securing the work permit. The appellant appealed. The Court of Appeal rejected the appeal and refused to allow the deduction for the work done. This was because the appellant was in breach of his fiduciary duty arising from a conflict of interest. In addition, the deduction for the work permit was not allowed because the respondent had not expected the appellant to do this for him and it had been done surreptitiously.

Key Principle

The court has the discretion to authorise a scheme where there is a conflict between the trustees' duty and their interests.

> **RE DREXEL BURNHAM LAMBERT UK PENSION PLAN 1995**
> The plaintiffs were the trustees of a pension scheme. The first defendant was the principal employer until it was wound up in 1990. The trustees were also beneficiaries under the scheme. The administrators of the first defendant gave notice that the pension scheme should terminate in July 1990 resulting in a substantial surplus. The rules of the scheme gave the trustees the absolute discretion to apply the surplus to secure further benefits within the limits set out in the rules of the scheme and any further balance was to be apportioned among the first defendant and other participating employers. The trustees sought directions from the court. The question arose as to whether the court could give directions in respect of a proposed scheme by the trustees who were beneficiaries as well.

Held

❖ (Ch) The rule that a trustee must not be in position whereby his duty as trustee conflicts with his own interest did not necessarily involve questions of wrongdoing or morality. However, the rules of equity were adaptable with various exceptions to the rules. The court, therefore, had jurisdiction to give directions as to the exercise of the trustees' discretion even though the trustees were in a position of conflict. As the proposed scheme had commended itself to the court and had been examined by counsel and solicitors, the court allowed the trustees to adopt the scheme. [1995] 1 W.L.R. 32.

Commentary

The court accepted that there may be circumstances where it may be proper to allow a proposal even though the trustees may be in a position of conflict. The court recognised that the general rule that trustees must not put themselves in a position of conflict between their interest and duty is riddled with exceptions and relaxation of the rule.

[g] Where the trust has a controlling interest in a company or business

Key Principle

Where the trust owns a controlling interest in a company, the trustees will be expected to take an active part in the management of the company.

RE LUCKING'S WILL TRUSTS 1967
(See Ch.9.)

Held

❖ (Ch) Trustees who hold a majority shareholding in a company on trust should take more care than a normal shareholder and should ensure that they have adequate information regarding the running of the business. [1967] 3 All E.R. 726.

BARTLETT V BARCLAYS BANK TRUST CO LTD (NO. 1) 1980
(See Ch.11.)

Held

❖ (Ch) It was improper for the professional trustee to confine itself merely to the receipt of the company's accounts and to attendance at general meetings. The trustee should have taken a more active role, which if it had, would have enabled it to prevent speculative investments. [1980] 1 Ch. 515.

[h] Failure to take into account relevant matters

Key Principle

Where trustees fail to take into account relevant matters in making their decisions, this may result in their actions being vitiated.

PITT V HOLT 2011

The first claimant's husband received a structured settlement from damages received as a result of a road accident. A lump sum was payable under the settlement as well as monthly payments. Professional advice had been sought and the lump sum and the annuity was put into a trust (a special needs trust) in favour of the husband. The first claimant entered into a deed of settlement where the lump sum was held on a trust and the annuity assigned to the trustees. This was to be held on the same trusts. The settlement had the effect of creating discretionary trusts of the income and capital for the husband's benefit, as well as the benefit of the first claimant, their children and remoter issue during the husband's lifetime. The husband then died and it was realised that the special needs trusts were subject to inheritance tax like any ordinary discretionary trusts. The trusts could have been set up in a manner which avoided inheritance tax. The claimants sought a declaration that the settlement was void or alternatively voidable and should be set aside.

Held

❖ (CA) Normally the trustees' failure to take into account relevant matters could be a breach of their fiduciary duty and this could lead to their actions being avoided. However the trustees' failure to take into account relevant matters is not always a breach of fiduciary duty. In the present case the trustees had made a settlement and assigned an annuity which exposed the trust to inheritance tax, but this was not a breach of fiduciary duty as they had acted on proper advice. [2011] EWCA Civ 197.

Commentary

The Court of Appeal in this case explained the effect of what has been known as the rule in *Re Hastings-Bass* [1974] 2 All E.R. 193 in that not every instance of the failure to take into account a relevant matter resulted in the actions of the trustees being vitiated. The "rule" was designed to protect the trustees' decisions from external challenge and reflects a pragmatism and promotes efficiency. Lloyd L.J. stated that

> "…[t]he cases which I am now considering concern acts which are within the powers of the trustees but are said to be vitiated by the failure of the trustees to take into account a relevant factor to which they should have had regard – usually tax con-sequences – or by their taking into account some irrelevant matter. It seems to me that the principled and correct approach to these cases is, first, that the trustees' act is not void, but that it may be voidable. It will be voidable if, and only if, it can be shown to have been done in breach of fiduciary duty on the part of the trustees. If it is voidable, then it may be capable of being set aside at the suit of a beneficiary, but this would be subject to equitable defences and to the court's discretion. The trustees' duty to take relevant matters into account is a fiduciary duty, so an act done as a result of a breach of that duty is voidable".

It depends on the circumstances of the case and as here there was evidence that they acted as they did on professional advice, which turned out to be materially wrong, there was no breach of a fiduciary duty by the trustees. The court stressed that until it is set aside the interest of the beneficiaries in the trust property continues. The Court of Appeal also overruled the decisions in *Mettoy Pension Trustees Ltd v Evans* [1991] 2 All E.R. 513 and *Sieff v Fox* [2005] 3 All E.R. 693 on this issue. The decision of Pitt v Holt is on appeal to the Supreme Court.

Pitt v Holt was heard with the case of *Futter v Futter* [2011] EWCA Civ 197 where trustees had exercised the power of advancement and assumed that capital gains tax would not be payable. The issue was whether this could be set aside. The court decided that as the trustees had acted within their powers but on erroneous legal advice, they were not in breach of their fiduciary duty and therefore the disposition was neither void nor voidable.

TRUSTEE INVESTMENTS

Key Principle

Where the trustees have been given an express power of investment, the extent of that power is a matter of construction.

> RE HARARI'S SETTLEMENT TRUSTS 1949
> A settlor recited the transfer of some securities to trustees in his set-tlement. In the settlement, he directed the trustees to hold the investments but had the power to retain it in its present form or may realise the investments and invest in such investments as they may deem fit.

Held

❖ (Ch) On a true construction of the settlement, the trustees had power, under the express power of investment, to invest in any investments they deem fit. [1949] 1 All E.R. 430.

> RE WRAGG 1919
> Trustees of a will were given the power to invest in
>
> "... stocks, shares and securities or other investments of what-soever nature and wheresoever as his trustees should in their absolute and uncontrolled discretion think fit with the like power of varying such investments to the intent that his trustees should have the same full and unrestricted powers of investing and transposing investments as if they were absolutely entitled".

Held

❖ (Ch) The trustees had the power to invest in the purchase of real property. [1919] 2 Ch. 58.

Commentary

Where an express power of investment is concerned, the extent of the power is a matter of interpretation. In *Re Power* [1947] Ch. 572, the trustees were given an express power to invest the trust fund including the purchase of freehold land. The court held that the trustees could only purchase freehold land as an investment and not purchase a home to allow the beneficiaries to live there rent-free. This is now subject to s.12 of the **Trusts of Land and Appointment of Trustees Act 1996**. This provides that the trustees of land have the power to allow the beneficiaries to reside in the property, if, the purposes of the trust include making the land available for the occupation by the beneficiary or beneficiaries OR the land is held by the trustees so as to be available for occupation. Where two or more beneficiaries are entitled to occupy the property under s.12, the trustees have the power under s.13 to exclude or restrict the entitlement of anyone or more (but not all) of them. In the absence of an express power of investment, s.3 of the **Trustee Act 2000** provides that the trustees have the same power of investment that a person could make if he were absolutely entitled to the trust property. In the exercise of this power of investment the trustees must have regard to general investment criteria under s.4 of the **Trustee Act 2000**. This requires the trustee to consider the suitability of the investments to the trust and of that investment as an investment of that kind and the need to diversify the trust fund. Under s.5 of the **Trustee Act 2000,** the trustees have to take proper advice about the investments but under s.5(3) the trustees have the discretion not to obtain advice if the trustees conclude that such advice is not necessary.

In *Jeffrey v Gretton and Russell* [2011] W.T.L.R. 809 the court held that the trustees were in breach of trust for failing in their duty to keep the trust portfolio under regular review. The trustees kept a dilapidated property for six years whilst they sought to refurbish it but did not take legal advice. The court was of the view that it did not regard the trustees had acted reasonably by taking a "punt" on the potential increase of property values.

Key Principle
In making investment decisions, trustees are under a duty to take such care as ordinary prudent persons would take if they were minded to make an investment in favour of persons whom they felt morally bound to provide.

LEAROYD V WHITELEY 1886
Trust funds were invested by the trustees in a five per cent mortgage of a freehold brickfield with buildings, machinery and plant. This was on the advice of competent valuers that the property was good security for the loan. The trustees acted on this advice without any further enquiries. The report failed to state whether the valuation was based on the property being a going concern and failed to distinguish between the

value of the land and the buildings and machinery. The borrower defaulted on the loan and the security proved inadequate.

Held

❖ (HL) The trustees had failed to act with ordinary prudence and therefore were liable to repay the loan with interest at four per cent from the date of the last payment. (1887) 12 App. Cas. 727.

NESTLE V NATIONAL WESTMINSTER BANK PLC 1993

In 1986 the plaintiff became entitled to the residue of her grandfather's estate. The estate was originally worth £54,000 in 1922 when her grandfather died. The defendant was the trustee of the estate. When the plaintiff became entitled, the estate was worth £269,203. The plaintiff alleged that the estate would have been worth more if the defendant had managed the trust with proper care. She alleged that the defendant had failed in their duty to conduct periodic reviews of the investments, failed to balance the interests of the remainderman and the life tenant, and failed to diversify the investments.

Held

❖ (CA) Although the defendant had failed to appreciate the scope of its powers of investment, and had failed to conduct a periodic review of the investments, this was not enough to give the plaintiff a remedy. The plaintiff had to show that the decisions made by the defendant were decisions that a reasonable prudent trustee would not have made. Therefore, the plaintiff failed to establish that the defendant had committed a breach of trust. [1993] 1 W.L.R. 1260.

Commentary

In *Learoyd v Whiteley* (reported at (1886) 33 Ch. D. 347), Lindley L.J. stated (at 355) that

> "... [t]he duty of a trustee is not to take such care only as a prudent man would take if he had only himself to consider; the duty rather is to take such care as an ordinary man would take if he were minded to make an investment for the benefit of other people for whom he felt morally bound to provide".

In *Wight v Olswang*, *The Times*, April 18, 2000, trustees having decided to sell shares of a settlement did not carry through the sale. Subsequently the shares dropped in value. The court held, confirming the principle in *Learoyd v Whiteley*, that a trustee has no higher duty than a man of ordinary prudence would exercise in the management of his own affairs. The action could only have succeeded if it could be shown that no ordinary prudent man with the knowledge of the defendant would have retained the shares. The defendant did have genuine if arguable concerns about his legal position in taking part in the sale.

Section 1 of the **Trustee Act 2000** sets out the duty of care imposed on trustees. Trustees are

> "to exercise such care and skills as may be reasonable in the circumstances, having regard in particular, (a) any special knowledge or experience that he has or holds himself out as having, and (b) if he acts as trustee in the course of a business or profession to any special knowledge or experience that it is reasonable to expect of a person acting in the course of that kind of business or profession".

Schedule 1 of the Act stipulates that this duty of care applies to the trustees in the exercise of their powers of investment. Under the **Trustee Act 2000**, a trustee can make any investment (land included though dealt with separately) subject to taking advice, reviewing investments and satisfying standard investment criteria including the suitability of the investment and the diversification of the fund. The effect of the Act is to liberalise and make more commercially practical the investment powers of trustees.

Key Principle

The trustees have to put aside their personal views when investing trust property.

COWAN V SCARGILL 1984

Five out of the ten trustees of the Mineworkers' Pension Scheme refused to approve an investment plan unless it prohibited an increase in foreign investments, provided for the withdrawal of existing foreign investments and prohibited investments in energies which competed with coal. The other five trustees sought a declaration as to whether the refusal to adopt the investment plan amounted to a breach of trust.

Held

❖ (Ch) The duty of the trustees was to act in the best interests of the beneficiaries and since the purpose of the trust was to provide financial benefits, the fund had to be invested so as to yield the best returns both in terms of income and capital appreciation. The trustees' personal views or moral reservations were irrelevant to the choice of investments except that in exceptional cases, the view of the beneficiaries may be taken into account. Accordingly, the trustees who refused to approve the investment plan would be in breach of trust. [1984] 3 W.L.R. 501.

Commentary

Where the object of the trust is financial provision for the beneficiaries, the trustees have to adopt an investment policy that would provide the best returns to the trust. Even though they may have personal or moral beliefs, these have to be set aside where it would be financially detrimental to the trust. In some circumstances, they may take into account the particular views of the beneficiaries. In *Harries v The Church Commissioners for England* [1992] 1 W.L.R. 1241, it was held that if equal alternative investments were available, trustees may avoid investments that are morally inconsistent with the nature of the trust but could not do so if it was financially detrimental to the trust.

DUTY TO BALANCE THE INTERESTS OF PRESENT AND FUTURE BENEFICIARIES

Key Principle

Trustees are under a duty to balance the interests of present and future beneficiaries.

> HOWE V EARL OF DARTMOUTH 1802
> By his will dated October 25, 1774, the testator left all his realty and personalty to his wife for life and thereafter to other persons in succession. Part of his personalty consisted of bank stock, long and short annuities. The stock and annuities were subsequently sold by the trustees and authorised investments purchased in its place.

Held

❖ (Ch) It was proper for the trustees to sell the bank stock and the annuities and convert them into authorised investments. (1802) 7 Ves. 137.

Commentary

The principle established by this case is that trustees are under a duty to ensure that the interests of the future and present beneficiaries are protected. The rule in *Howe v Earl of Dartmouth* is subject to a contrary intention in the will. Further, if the trustees are directed not to sell any of the investments or are given the discretion whether or not to sell the investments, this rule does not apply: *Re Pitcairn* [1896] 2 Ch. 199.

Key Principle

Where the rule in *Howe v Earl of Dartmouth* applies and there is a delay in the sale of the unauthorised, wasting or hazardous investments, the trustees may have to apportion the income from those investments between present and future beneficiaries.

> RE FAWCETT 1940
> Residuary estate was left by a testatrix on trust for the trustees to invest and to divide the income equally among her nephews and nieces and after their death, to divide it equally among their children upon them attaining the age of 21. Part of the residuary estate consisted of unauthorised investments.

Held

❖ (Ch) The rule in *Howe v Earl of Dartmouth* applied. Where the unauthorised investments remained unsold at the end of one year after the testatrix's death, the life tenants were entitled to interest at the rate of four per cent from the date of death till the sale of the unauthorised investments. The excess income from the unauthorised investments, after the interest had been paid to the life tenants, was to be invested in authorised investments. [1940] 1 Ch. 402.

Commentary

The Law Commission in its report – Capital and Income in Trusts: Classification and Apportionment (No. 315) published in 2009 has recommended that all the equitable rules of apportionment such as the rule in *Howe v Earl of Dartmouth* and the rule in *Re Earl's of Chesterfield's Trusts* should be abolished in respect of trusts created after the coming into force of the new Act. The reform proposals also make provision of company distributions to trustees. At the time of writing the Trusts (Capital and Income) Bill is before Parliament and has completed the House of Lords stage of the bill and is currently with the House of Commons.

THINK POINT

In what circumstances would it be appropriate for trustees not to take advice under s.5(3) of the **Trustee Act 2000** as regards the power of investment?

Do you consider that it is now time to revisit the principle enunciated in *Boardman v Phipps* as suggested by Arden L.J. in *Murad v Al- Saraj* [2005] EWCA Civ 959?

Trustees' Powers

9

INTRODUCTION

Equity provides the trustees with a number of powers in order for them to carry out their obligations in the best interests of the beneficiaries. These powers may be excluded or modified by the settlor in the trust instrument. Most modern trusts which are professionally drafted would normally give the trustees the widest possible powers so as to enable them to carry out their obligations but in some instances it is to allow the trust to save on tax. Although the trust instrument may give the trustees various powers, a number of these powers are statutory in nature under the **Trustee Act 1925** and **Trustee Act 2000**.

The trustees have a discretion as to whether they would exercise their powers with the only obligation being to consider whether to exercise the power rather than an obligation to exercise the power itself. Where the trustees decide not to exercise their power, the beneficiaries would not be able to complain so long as the decision was made in good faith after proper consideration of the relevant facts. This is different from the trustees' duties, as discussed in Chapter 8, where there is an obligation on the trustees to perform their duties; otherwise, they may be in breach of trust.

The trustees have a number of powers including the power to give receipts (s.14 of the **Trustee Act 1925**), the power to compound liabilities (s.15 of the **Trustee Act 1925**), and the power to insure (s.34 of the **Trustee Act 2000**) but the emphasis in this Chapter will be on the powers of advancement, maintenance and delegation.

MAINTENANCE

Section 31 of the **Trustee Act 1925** gives the trustees the power to provide maintenance to the beneficiaries from the income. For the power to be exercisable, the legacy or devise must carry intermediate income. This is subject to s.175 of the **Law of Property Act 1925**, which provides that where there is a specific contingent gift of personalty or realty, the gift will carry the intermediate income except where the income is expressly disposed of.

Key Principle

Section 175 of the **Law of Property Act 1925** has no application to a contingent pecuniary legacy and therefore the intermediate income is generally not available for maintenance.

> RE RAINE 1929
>
> Two pecuniary legacies were bequeathed by the testator, contingently upon the legatees reaching the age of 21. The question arose as to whether s.175 of the **Law of Property Act 1925** applied to contingent pecuniary legacies and whether the legacies carried the intermediate income.

Held

❖ (Ch) Section 175 of the **Law of Property Act 1925** has no application to a contingent pecuniary legacy. The statutory provision refers only to bequests or devises of realty or personalty and makes no reference to legacies. As such, the pre-1925 law will apply to legacies in which contingent pecuniary legacies did not carry the intermediate income. [1929] 1 Ch. 716.

Commentary

The court emphasised that there were exceptions to the general rule where the legacy would carry the intermediate income. These are where the testator:

(a) has shown an intention that the legatee should be maintained (*Re Churchill* [1909] 2 Ch. 431);

(b) was the father or stood in loco parentis to the infant legatee (*Re Boulter* [1918] 2 Ch. 40); and

(c) has directed that the legacy be set aside as a separate fund for the benefit of the legatee (*Re Dickson* [1885] 29 Ch.D. 331).

Key Principle

A deferred gift of realty does not carry the intermediate income, and thus the trustees cannot use the statutory power of maintenance.

> RE MCGEORGE 1963
>
> The testator left property to his daughter under his will but directed that the gift was not to take effect until his wife died. The daughter upon attaining the age of 21, applied for the income to be paid over to her.

Held

❖ (Ch) The daughter was not entitled to the income from the property as the gift was a deferred gift of realty and not a contingent gift. Section 175 of the **Law of Property Act 1925** did not apply. The gift did not therefore carry the intermediate income. [1963] 1 Ch. 544.

Commentary

A deferred gift of realty is different from a contingent gift. Only in the case of the latter does the gift carry the intermediate income. Section 175 of the **Law of Property Act 1925** refers to contingent gifts and not deferred gifts therefore the section had no application in this case. The trustees do not have the power of maintenance in the case of a deferred gift.

Key Principle

A deferred bequest of residuary personalty or realty does not carry the intermediate income.

> RE OLIVER 1947
> The testator left his two daughters a deferred vested bequest of his residuary estate. The issue was whether the bequest carried the intermediate income.

Held

❖ (Ch D) A vested deferred bequest of the residuary estate does not carry the intermediate income. [1947] 2 All E.R. 161.

Commentary

Whilst it is clear that a deferred vested devise of residuary realty and personalty does not carry the intermediate income, the position with respect to deferred contingent devise of residuary realty is unclear. There is no authority on this point but it is argued that the position should be the same in that the devise should not carry the intermediate income. In the case of a deferred contingent bequest of residuary personalty, the bequest does not normally carry the intermediate income: *Re Gearing* [1964] Ch. 136.

Key Principle

The statutory power of maintenance can be excluded either expressly or by a contrary intention.

RE TURNER'S WILL TRUSTS 1937

One-fifth of the testator's residue estate was given to the children of his late son living at his death, who had reached or would thereafter reach the age of 28. The will gave the trustees the power to use the income for the education of the grandchildren and to accumulate the surplus. There were three grandchildren, one of whom died before reaching 28. At the date of his death, his share of the accumulated income amounted to £3,421. If this sum passed to his estate, this would have resulted in a substantial increase of the estate duty payable. Those entitled to his estate argued that the accumulated income should go to the other two grandchildren.

Held

❖ (CA) Although s.31(1)(ii) of the **Trustee Act 1925** required the income to be paid to a beneficiary who had attained the age of 18, but had not yet received a vested interest in the income, s.69(2) of the **Trustee Act 1925** allows s.31 to be expressly or impliedly excluded. Where a contrary intention is present in the trust instrument, this would be taken to have impliedly excluded the operation of the statutory power of maintenance. As the statutory power of maintenance had been impliedly excluded, the accumulated income did not go to the deceased grandchild's estate but to the other two grandchildren. [1937] Ch. 15.

Commentary

The statutory power of maintenance is impliedly excluded where there is an inconsistent provision in the trust instrument or where there is an express power of maintenance inconsistent with the statutory power. See also *Re Ransome's Will Trusts* [1957] 1 All E.R. 690 and *Re Erskine's Settlement Trusts* [1971] 1 W.L.R. 162. Where the trustees' express power of maintenance excludes providing a benefit directly or indirectly to the settlor, the trustees are not disabled in the exercise of their powers, including the maintenance and education of children, merely by the fact that the settlor, as a by-product of the exercise of those powers, may gain a benefit: *Fuller v Evans* [2000] 1 All E.R. 636.

By s.31(1) of the **Trustee Act 1925**, the trustees are directed to have regard

> "to the age of the infant and his requirements and generally to the circumstances of the case, and in particular to what other income, if any, is applicable for the same purposes; and where trustees have notice that the income of more than one fund is applicable for those purposes, then, so far as practicable, unless

the entire income of the funds is paid or applied as aforesaid or the court otherwise directs, a proportionate part only of the income of each fund shall be so paid or applied".

The Law Commission has recently in its report *Intestacy and Family Provision Claims on Death (Law Commission Report No. 133)* recommended that this part of s.31(1) of the **Trustee Act 1925** be deleted in its entirety as the view was that it did not serve any substantive purpose and it duplicated the existing law. In addition it was felt that it would not assist the trustees in making their decisions at a practical level.

ADVANCEMENT

The trustees may have the power to make an advancement to beneficiaries for their advancement or benefit, either under the terms of the trust instrument or s.32 of the **Trustee Act 1925**.

Key Principle

Although s.32(2) of the **Trustee Act 1925** restricts the application of s.32 to trust property which is personalty, where the beneficiary intends to acquire realty which is already subject to the trust, the trustees can convey that realty to him rather than give him capital money.

RE COLLARD'S WILL TRUSTS 1961

The trust instrument provided that the trustees had the statutory power of advancement except for the purpose of acquiring a share or interest in any business. The beneficiary was working on a farm owned by the trust. The trustees wished to convey the farm to the beneficiary for the purpose of avoiding estate duty.

Held

❖ (Ch D) In the circumstances of the case, the trustees could transfer the farm to the beneficiary in the exercise of their statutory power of advancement. As the trustees could have given the beneficiary capital monies in order to purchase the farm, there was no objection to the direct conveyance of the farm to the beneficiary. Further, the purpose of the advancement was to avoid estate duty and not to further the beneficiary's business interest. [1961] 1 All E.R. 821.

Commentary

The court was able to reach the conclusion that the transfer of the farm to the beneficiary was not an acquisition of a business interest because the beneficiary already had security of tenure as tenant of the farm under the Agricultural Holdings Act 1948. Therefore, the acquisition of the freehold reversion did not give the beneficiary any added advantage as a farmer.

The Law Commission in its report *Intestacy and Family Provision Claims on Death (Law Commission Report No. 133)* recommended that Section 32 of the **Trustee Act 1925** be amended so that the trustees have power to transfer or apply other property subject to the trust on the same basis as the power to pay or apply capital money to or for the advancement or benefit of a beneficiary. This is contained in the proposed Inheritance and Trustees Powers Bill and is intended to cover all trusts not only to intestacy cases.

Key Principle

The statutory power of advancement must be made for the advancement or benefit of the beneficiary.

PILKINGTON v IRC 1964

The trustees wished to use their statutory power of advancement to settle part of the trust fund on new trusts primarily to avoid estate duty.

Held

❖ (HL) The term "advancement or benefit" meant any use of the capital money which would improve the material situation of the beneficiary. There was nothing in s.32 preventing the creation of new settlement nor which excluded tax avoidance from being a benefit. It did not matter that the new settlement might provide an incidental benefit to other members of the beneficiary's family. However, the new settlement infringed the rule against remoteness of vesting and would therefore not be allowed. [1964] A.C. 612.

Commentary

Where trustees are given the power of advancement, either expressly or by statute, the trustees must ensure that the exercise of their discretionary power is for "the advancement or benefit" of the beneficiary. The term advancement is normally taken to mean making a permanent provision for the beneficiary by for example setting him up in business or buying him a home (*Re Williams' Will Trusts* [1953] 1 All E.R. 36). The term benefit has a wider meaning. In *Lowther v Bentinck* (1874) L.R. 19 E.Q. 166, it was taken to include the discharge of a beneficiary's debts. The decision in *Pilkington v*

IRC was followed in *Southgate v Sutton* [2011] EWCA Civ 637 where the Court of Appeal confirmed that an advancement can take the form of a resettlement.

Further, *Re Evan's Settlement* [1967] 1 W.L.R. 1294 confirms that the statutory power of advancement may be excluded by the contrary intention of the settlor.

In *Pitt v Holt* [2011] EWCA Civ 197, Lloyd L.J. stated that

> "...[i]t is not possible to lay down any clear rule as to the matters which trustees ought to take into account when considering the exercise of a power of advancement or some other dispositive discretionary power. Circumstances will differ a great deal from one trust to another, and even within one trust they may change from time to time or according to the nature of the particular exercise which is under consideration".

Key Principle

A donation to charity giving rise to a temporal or spiritual benefit is to be regarded as being for the benefit of the beneficiary.

RE CLORE'S SETTLEMENT TRUSTS 1966

A settlement was set up for the benefit of the settlor's son and daughter in equal shares on trust to accumulate the income whilst they were minors. The income was then to be paid to them directly until they attained the age of 30. Thereafter, the capital and income was to be held on trust for the son and daughter absolutely or their children if they should die under the age. The trustees had power to advance up to two-thirds of the presumptive or vested share in the trust fund to the beneficiaries. After the settlor's son attained the age of 21, the trustees sought to pay one-seventh of the son's presumptive share to a charity in the exercise of their power of advancement.

Held

❖ (Ch) It was a proper exercise of the power of advancement to make appropriate donations to charity on behalf of the beneficiary. As this was in discharge of a moral obligation to make donations to charity, this would be regarded as a benefit. [1966] 1 W.L.R. 955.

Commentary

The requirement of the advancement being for the advancement or benefit of the beneficiary is not restricted to financial or material benefit. However, in *X v A* [2006] 1 W.L.R. 741 an attempt to advance the whole of the beneficiary's interest to her so that she could donate it to charity in discharge of her moral obligations in the exercise of the trustees' power of appointment was not to be regarded as being for her benefit. It was clear that the court refused to allow such an advancement as this would not be an improvement of her material position. There is an obvious bias towards improvement of the beneficiary's material wealth for it to be regarded as a proper exercise of the power advancement.

Key Principle

Under s.32 of the **Trustee Act 1925,** the consent of the person with a prior life or other interest, whether vested or contingent, who must be in existence and of full age, has to be obtained in writing before the advancement can be made.

HENLEY V WARDELL 1988

By cl.10 of his will, the testator gave the trustees a power of advancement:

> "to the intent that the powers given to trustees by section 32 of the **Trustee Act 1925** shall be enlarged so as to permit my trustees in their absolute and uncontrolled discretion to advance at any time the whole of any expectant or presumptive share to any of my children ...".

The issue was whether this avoided the need to obtain the consent of the person with a prior life or other interest.

Held

❖ (Ch) The consent of the person with a prior life or other interest had to be obtained in writing in accordance with s.32. Clause 10 had the effect of enlarging the share which the trustees could advance to the beneficiary but did not remove the requirement to obtain the consent of the person with a prior interest. *The Times*, January 29, 1988.

Commentary

The court stated that cl.10 could not be construed so as to exclude the need to obtain the consent in writing of the person with a prior life or other interest. Presumably, if the clause was worded properly, the need to obtain the consent in writing of the prior life interest could be excluded.

Key Principle

In exercising their power of advancement, the trustees must ensure that the purpose for which the advancement was made is actually carried out.

RE PAULING'S SETTLEMENT 1964

A marriage settlement gave the trustee a power to make advances to the children of the marriage for their advancement or benefit. Between 1948 and 1954, the trustee made a number of advances to the children, who on some of the occasions obtained independent legal advice purportedly for the children's benefit or advancement. However, some of the advances were used by their parents for their own benefit including the purchase of a family home in the Isle of Man in the parents' name. The children sued the trustee for breach of trust.

Held

❖ (CA) The power of advancement is a fiduciary power and therefore the trustee must weigh the benefit of the advancement against the rights of those who might become entitled under the settlement. If the circumstances warranted it, the trustee was under a duty to ensure that the advancement was used for the benefit for which it was intended and not allow the person to whom the advancement was made the freedom to spend it in any way he chose. [1964] 1 Ch. 303.

Commentary

The obligation on the trustee to ensure that the advancement is used for the purpose for which it is intended depends on the reliability of the beneficiary and the circumstances of the case. Where the beneficiary is reliable and the trustee is satisfied that the beneficiary will use the advance for the stated purpose, the trustee can leave the money in the hands of the beneficiary. However, if some doubt exists then the trustee has to ensure that the money is used for the purpose for which the advancement was made and not leave the money in the hands of the beneficiary.

Key Principle

Where the beneficiary has received one-half of his vested or presumptive share in the trust fund, the trustees are not allowed to make further advances to him where the remainder of the fund has increased in value.

RE MARQUESS OF ABERGAVENNY'S ESTATE ACT TRUSTS 1981

The trustees of a trust fund advanced one half of the beneficiary's share to him in the exercise of their power of advancement. The remainder of the trust fund subsequently increased in value. The question arose as to whether the trustees could make further advances to the beneficiary.

Held

❖ (Ch) The trustees could not make further advances to the beneficiary as they had already advanced one half of the beneficiary's share to him. [1981] 2 All E.R. 643.

Commentary

The point here is that where the power of advancement has been exhausted, even though the remainder of the trust fund increases in value, the trustees cannot make further advancements to the same beneficiary. In *CD (a child) v O* [2004] 3 All E.R. 780, the court permitted an application under the Variation of Trusts Act 1958 which extended the trustees' power of advancement in excess of the limit of 50 per cent of the beneficiary's presumptive share up to the whole capital in her fund in order to pay for her school fees. In reaching this decision the court was of the view that this was for her benefit especially given that the fund was solely for her benefit.

In *Tamlin v Edgar, The Times*, 23 February 2012, the court stressed that where the court's approval is sought for the exercise of the power of advancement in excess of the statutory power, the court is not there to merely rubber stamp the application. It needs to be satisfied from the evidence that the advancement is for the benefit or advancement of the beneficiaries.

The Law Commission in its report *Intestacy and Family Provision Claims on Death (Law Commission Report No. 133)* recommended that the power contained in Section 32 of the **Trustee Act 1925** to pay or apply capital to or for the benefit of a trust beneficiary should be extended to the whole, rather than one-half, of the beneficiary's share in the trust fund. This is contained in the proposed Inheritance and Trustees Powers Bill and is intended to cover all trusts not only intestacy cases.

DELEGATION AND LIABILITY FOR DELEGATION

Key Principle

At common law, the trustees may appoint a broker or solicitor to do that which, in the ordinary course of business, other people would employ brokers and solicitors to do and would not be liable if the broker or solicitor turns out to be dishonest.

> ### SPEIGHT V GAUNT 1883
> The trustee employed a broker to acquire shares on behalf of the trust. The trustee gave the broker money for this purpose. However, the broker used the money for his own purposes and subsequently became insolvent. The beneficiaries sued the trustee claiming that they had breached their fiduciary obligation by giving the money to the broker, although this was in accordance with established practice.

Held

❖ (HL) The trustee was not liable to the beneficiary for the loss of the trust funds caused by the broker's dishonesty. (1883) 9 A.C. 1.

Commentary

[1] At common law the trustees had a power to appoint agents like solicitors and brokers to carry out some of their duties if this was what ordinary people would have done. If the agent turned out to be dishonest, the trustees would not be liable if they had followed the usual and regular course adopted by ordinary men in the course of business.

[2] Section 11 of the **Trustee Act 2000** gives the trustees power to appoint agents to act on their behalf but not to make decisions as to how the trust assets are distributed, whether fees should be paid out of capital or income, the power to appoint a trustee or the power to appoint custodians or nominees. It is clear from this that the trustees can delegate their investment powers to an agent and by virtue of s.15 can delegate their asset management functions. The trustees cannot appoint a beneficiary as an agent (s.12(3)). In the exercise of the power to delegate to agents, the trustees are subject to the standard of care, discussed above, and this is extended to the selection and the terms upon which the agent is to act on behalf of the trust.

[3] Under s.22 the trustee has a duty to keep under review the arrangements under which the agent, nominee or custodian acts and how the arrangements are implemented. The trustees have to consider whether it is appropriate in the circumstances of the case to exercise their power of intervention and this

is defined in s.22(4) to include the power to give directions to the agent or to revoke the appointment. The Act goes on to provide in s.23 that the trustee will not be liable for the acts or defaults of the agent, nominee or custodian unless he failed to comply with his duty of care in the appointment or in carrying out his duties under s.22. It remains to be seen how the court will construe these provisions in determining the extent of the trustees' liability for the acts or default of the agent.

Key Principle

The trustees' liability for the default or misconduct of an agent is based on the test of the ordinary man of business.

RE LUCKING'S WILL TRUSTS 1968

Lucking was the sole trustee of a trust in which he was also one of the beneficiaries. The trust consisted, inter alia, of a majority shareholding in a private company. Lucking appointed Dewar, a friend, as managing director to manage the company. Lucking signed blank cheques for Dewar's expenses. Lucking became aware that Dewar was using company funds for his own purposes but failed to do anything about it. Lucking continued signing blank cheques for Dewar and although the company's profits increased, its debts increased as well. Dewar was dismissed from the company because of his debts to the company and was subsequently adjudicated a bankrupt. The plaintiff commenced an action against Lucking.

Held

❖ (Ch D) The conduct of the trustee in this case was to be judged on the basis of the ordinary prudent man of business as set out in *Speight v Gaunt*. Lucking was liable as he failed to supervise Dewar, when he had known that the latter was dishonest. [1968] 1 W.L.R. 866.

Commentary

The standard of the duty of care expressed in this case is effectively the same as the statutory duty of care found in s.1 of the **Trustees Act 2000**. Schedule 1 to the Act makes it clear that the statutory duty of care in s.1 covers appointment and supervision of agents, nominees or custodians.

It is clear from *Re Clore's Settlement Trusts* [1966] 1 W.L.R. 955 that an advancement can be made for the purpose of enabling the beneficiary to make a gift to charity. However, in *X v A* [2006] 1 W.L.R. 741 the court refused to allow such an advancement where it amounted to the whole of the fund. The Law Commission has recommended the change to the law to allow for an advancement for the whole of the beneficiary's share. Do you think this is advisable or should it be still limited but at a higher percentage so as to preserve some of the beneficiary's interest under the trust?

In *CD (a child) v O* [2004] 3 All E.R. 780, do you think the court was right in allowing the extension of the trustees' statutory power of advancement to allow an advancement up to the whole of the capital in the fund?

Variation of Trusts

10

INTRODUCTION

The general principle is that trustees are obliged to administer the trust in accordance with the terms of the trust instrument and the duties, powers and obligations imposed or granted by statute or equity. Trustees are not allowed to deviate from these duties, powers and obligations as any deviation may amount to a breach of trust regardless of the absence of intent. There are a number of ways in which the powers or duties of the trustees can be varied. These can be by the court's inherent or statutory jurisdiction.

Statutory variation takes place predominantly under the **Variation of Trusts Act 1958**. There are a number of other statutory provisions under which variation may take place:

- Section 57 of the **Trustee Act 1925**—*Re Downshire Settled Estates* [1953] 1 Ch. 218, *Mason v Farbrother* [1983] 2 All E.R. 1078 and *Anker-Peterson v Anker Peterson* [2001] All E.R. 54. The court does not have power to alter the beneficial interests under the trusts (*Alexander v Alexander* [2011] EWHC 2721) nor does it allow for a variation of the trust (*Southgate v Sutton* [2011] EWCA Civ 637*)*;
- Section 64 of the **Settled Land Act 1925**—*Hambro v The Duke of Marlborough* [1994] Ch. 158;
- Section 53 of the **Trustee Act 1925**—*Re Meux* [1958] Ch. 154; and
- Section 24 of the **Matrimonial Causes Act 1973**—*Brooks v Brooks* [1996] 1 A.C. 375.

Applications to vary investment powers will be less common as the **Trustee Act 2000** has extended the trustees' investment powers.

COURT'S INHERENT JURISDICTION TO VARY A TRUST

Key Principle
Where the beneficiaries of a trust are absolutely entitled, of full age, competent and of one mind, they can terminate the trust.

The testator bequeathed his East India stock to his trustees upon trust to accumulate the interest and dividends until Daniel Vautier reached the age of 25 years. Thereafter, the stock, the accumulated interest and dividends were to be transferred to Daniel Vautier absolutely. Upon reaching the age of 21, Daniel Vautier applied for the transfer of the stock, the accumulated interest and the dividends to him absolutely.

Held

❖ (Ch) The trust fund should be transferred to him. (1841) Beav. 115.

Commentary

[1] The case is authority for the proposition that where all the beneficiaries are of full age, sui juris and absolutely entitled to the trust fund, they can terminate the trust and direct the trustees to transfer the trust fund to them even though this may be against the testator's or settlor's intention. This was followed in *Mourant & Co Retirement Trustees Ltd v JG and HK in the matter of the Turino Consolidated Ltd Trust Fund* [2008] J.R.C. 100 where the Jersey Court upheld a letter signed by both the beneficiaries, who were solely entitled under the trust, directing that the property be held in equal shares for them in the event of their divorce.

[2] This is, however, an all-or-nothing process. The effect of the rule is to terminate the existing trust: *Stephenson (Inspector of Taxes) v Barclays Bank Trust Co Ltd* [1975] 1 All E.R. 625.

[3] In *Drescher v Drescher Estate* 10 I.T.E.L.R. 679, the Canadian court decided that it would not extend the rule in *Saunders v Vautier* to allow the holder of a power of attorney to modify or extinguish a trust on behalf of a beneficiary without the court's approval.

Key Principle

The court has an inherent jurisdiction to vary the terms of a trust.

CHAPMAN V CHAPMAN 1954

The appellants who were trustees of various settlements, applied for leave to execute a scheme of family arrangement affecting the trust property or in the alternative, to release the trust property from certain trusts under the settlements. The arrangement would have had certain tax advantages.

Held

❖ (HL) There was no inherent jurisdiction to sanction on behalf of infant beneficiaries and unborn persons, a rearrangement of the settlements for no other purpose than to secure a financial benefit. [1954] A.C. 429.

Commentary

Lord Simonds (at 445) stated that the court's inherent jurisdiction to vary the terms of a trust was limited to:

[a] where property belonged beneficially to an infant, the court has a jurisdiction to change the nature of the property from real to personal and vice versa;

[b] where no provision was made for infant beneficiaries, the court assumed a jurisdiction to provide maintenance for the infant beneficiaries;

[c] to authorise a transaction which is not permitted by the trust by way of salvage; and

[d] where the rights of infants and unborn beneficiaries are in dispute, the court may approve a compromise.

It should be noted that the category [c] would include cases of emergency which the trust has not made provision for. The **Variation of Trusts Act 1958** was subsequently introduced to complement the court's inherent jurisdiction.

Key Principle

The court's inherent jurisdiction to vary trusts includes allowing variation in cases of emergency for which the testator has made no provision.

RE NEW 1901

The trustees of a trust held shares in a company that was undergoing reconstruction. The company proposed that all shareholders in the existing company exchange their shares in return for shares and debentures in a new or reconstructed company. The trustees did not have the power to purchase or retain these types of shares.

Held

❖ (CA) As the evidence showed that the scheme would be of advantage to the beneficiaries of the trust, the court authorised the variation of the terms of the trust to allow the trustees to concur in the scheme and to hold the type of share to be issued. [1901] 2 Ch. 534.

Commentary

Before the court is prepared to exercise its inherent jurisdiction, there must be a genuine emergency or need. In *Re Tollemache* [1903] 1 Ch. 457, the court was not prepared to sanction a variation of the terms of the trust by allowing trust property to be mortgaged. This was because there was no emergency even though this may have been of benefit to the beneficiary.

Key Principle

Where the testator has directed that income from the trust be accumulated but has made no provision for the maintenance or education of the beneficiaries, the court has an inherent jurisdiction to vary the trust to allow for the maintenance or education of the beneficiaries.

RE COLLINS 1886

A testator directed that the income from his estate be accumulated for 21 years. The accumulated estate was to be given to his sister for life, then to her three sons and their male heirs in successive order.

Held

❖ (Ch) The sister should be paid an annual sum out of the income of the estate for the maintenance and education of her sons. (1886) 32 Ch.D. 229.

Commentary

The inherent jurisdiction would only be used in cases where the statutory power of advancement or maintenance given to trustees under ss.31 and 32 of the **Trustee Act 1925** has been excluded.

Key Principle

The court has an inherent jurisdiction to vary the terms of a trust in order to reach a compromise in cases where a dispute has arisen.

CHAPMAN V CHAPMAN 1954

(See above.)

Held

❖ (HL) The court did not have jurisdiction to approve the variation. In order for the court to avail itself of this jurisdiction, there had to be a genuine dispute for which the court could approve a compromise. [1954] A.C. 429.

MASON V FARBROTHER 1983

The applicants were trustees of the Co-operative Society members' Pension and Death Benefit Scheme. The Scheme was constituted by a trust deed executed in 1929 in which the trustees were given power to invest in the society itself and in authorised trustee investments. The trustees were uncertain whether the investment clause in the trust deed required them to invest all the funds either in the Society or in investments authorised by the Trustee Investments Act 1961. They also wished to have wider powers of investment. They applied to the court under its inherent jurisdiction to compromise disputed rights or alternatively, under s.57 of the **Trustee Act 1925,** to insert a wider investment clause.

Held

❖ (Ch) The court did have the jurisdiction to approve a compromise of disputed rights and on the facts of the case there was a dispute as to the interpretation of the investment clause. However, it was doubtful whether the court had jurisdiction to substitute an entirely new investment clause for the existing investment clause in the trust deed. Therefore, the court would not sanction a variation of the terms of the trust under its inherent jurisdiction. [1983] 2 All E.R. 1078.

Commentary

In order for the court to exercise its inherent jurisdiction to approve a compromise of disputed rights, there must in fact be a dispute. Further, even if there is a dispute, there is a further requirement that the compromise must not be a total substitution of existing rights or powers, it must be a compromise.

STATUTORY VARIATION OF TRUSTS—THE VARIATION OF TRUSTS ACT 1958

The purpose of the **Variation of Trusts Act** is to supply a consent on behalf of those who by virtue of infancy or disability or by virtue of being unascertained or unborn cannot themselves consent to a variation of the trusts – per Etherton J. in *S v T1* [2006] W.T.L.R. 1461. It is also clear that the power of the court under the Act is discretionary in nature: *Ridgwell v Ridgwell* [2007] EWHC 2666. The court stressed that

> "...the discretion under the Act does not arise unless the court is satisfied that: (1) the proposed variation is an arrangement within

the meaning of the Act; and (2) the arrangement is for the benefit of the [beneficiaries]".

Key Principle

The **Variation of Trusts Act 1958** does not allow for a complete resettlement of the trust.

Re Towler's Settled Estates 1963

The trust fund of a settlement was held, subject to the applicant's life interest in half of the fund, on trust. The terms of the trust were that the applicant's daughter would be entitled to one-quarter of the fund in possession on reaching the age of 21 and another quarter in remainder on the death of the applicant. The applicant's daughter was about to reach the age of 21 but had proven herself to be immature and irresponsible with money. The applicant applied under s.1 of the **Variation of Trusts Act 1958** for the court to approve the transfer of the daughter's share to new trustees on protective trusts for the daughter for life, with remainder to her children or issue, or in default of children, to the other infant beneficiary interested under the settlement.

Held

❖ (Ch) The court would not give its approval to the proposal because the jurisdiction conferred by the statute did not extend to a completely new resettlement. Even if did, the proposal went beyond what was necessary in the interests of the beneficiary. The court would, however, approve an alternative proposal deferring the payment of the capital for a further period but which would give her a protected life interest in the meantime. [1963] 3 All E.R. 759.

Re Ball's Settlement Trusts 1968

The plaintiff had a life interest in a trust fund and a testamentary power to appoint, among others, to two of his sons. In default of appointment, the fund was to go to the two sons absolutely. He applied for the court's approval to an arrangement under the **Variation of Trusts Act 1958**, whereby his life interest, the power of appointment and the default provision, were to be replaced by the life interests for the two sons in equal shares. His son's children were to take the fund absolutely on the occurrence of certain events.

Held

❖ (Ch) The court in the exercise of its jurisdiction under Section 1 of the **Variation of Trusts Act 1958** could approve the variation on the behalf of all persons unknown or unascertained who may thereafter be beneficially interested. Although the new trusts were different from the original trust, the substratum of the old trust remained and the arrangement applied for could be described as a variation of the settlement. [1968] 1 W.L.R. 899.

Commentary

The dividing line between a resettlement and a variation giving rise to a new trust but with the substratum of the old trust remaining is a fine one. Although it is clear from *Re Steed's Will Trusts* [1959] 1 All E.R. 609 that the **Variation of Trusts Act 1958** had been drafted in a manner which gives the court flexibility to consider any proposal, the limitation is that it must be a variation and not a resettlement or substitution. In that case the court refused to approve a variation in order to remove a protective trust element as that would have defeated the testatrix's intention. The same approach was taken in *Re Holt's Settlement*, discussed below. This was followed in *Wyndham v Egremont* [2009] EWHC 2076 where the court was asked to approve a variation of trust under s.1 of the **Variation of Trusts Act 1958**, to, inter alia, extend the relevant trust period in order to defer the substantial tax charges which the estate would be subject to if the variation was not approved. The court held that the application amounted to a variation not a resettlement of the trust and hence was approved. The court took account of the fact that the trustees remained the same, the subsisting trust remained largely unaltered and the administrative provisions affecting them were wholly unchanged.

See also *Wright v Gater* [2011] EWHC 2881 where the court found the arrangement there to be a variation although Norris J. was of the view that it was borderline between a resettlement and a variation.

Key Principle

The variation of trust under the **Variation of Trusts Act 1958** must be of benefit to beneficiaries on whose behalf the court is being asked to give consent.

RE REMNANT'S SETTLEMENT TRUSTS 1970

A trust in a will contained a forfeiture clause whereby the testator's grandchildren would forfeit their interest in the testator's estate if they were practicing Roman Catholics at the date of his daughter's death. The testator's two daughters applied to vary the trust including the removal of the forfeiture clause.

Held

❖ (Ch) The court must be satisfied that the variation of the terms of the trust was of benefit to every person on whose behalf the court's consent was being sought. In deciding this, the court was bound to consider not merely their financial benefit but also benefit of any other kind and whether it was a fair and proper arrangement. Here, the proposed variation was fair and proper and was for the benefit of all the beneficiaries on whose behalf the court was asked to give consent. [1970] 1 Ch. 560.

RE WESTON'S SETTLEMENTS 1969

The plaintiff set up two trusts for the benefit of his children. He applied for a variation of the trust to allow the trust to be moved to Jersey for tax purposes.

Held

❖ (CA) The court would not approve a variation of the trust to allow the trusts to be moved to Jersey. Lord Denning suggested that the court should not only consider monetary benefits. [1969] 1 Ch. 223.

WRIGHT V GATER 2011

The beneficiary was a minor whose father died intestate and left a small estate. The father was also the sole beneficiary of his own father's estate ("the grandfather's estate") which at the time of his death had not yet been administered. The minor beneficiary was entitled to over £500,000 under a statutory trust. The reason for the variation was that if the grandfather's estate went to the minor beneficiary, a substantial inheritance tax would be payable. If the minor beneficiary was a direct beneficiary under the grandfather's estate the tax would not be payable. The second reason for the application to vary was that his mother and family members thought it would be better that he would only become absolutely entitled when he became 30 instead of 18 under the statutory trusts.

Held

❖ (Ch) The original proposed variation was close to crossing the line between a variation and resettlement as there would be nothing left of the original statutory trust. More importantly, there was nothing about the minor beneficiary in terms of his character or his setting which would provide evidence that there was a risk that he would not be able to deal with the monies from the grandfather's estate until he attained the age of 30. It would also not be right to have the family members control the purse strings and he should be able to have his autonomy as an adult respected. However the court would be prepared to approve an amended proposal which gave entitlement to the minor beneficiary on attaining the age of 18. [2011] EWHC 2881.

Commentary

Under s.1 of the **Variation of Trusts Act 1958**, where the court is asked to consider whether the variation is one which would benefit the beneficiaries, on whose behalf the court is being asked to give its consent, the benefit need not be financial benefit: *Re Holt's Settlements* [1968] 1 All E.R. 470. It can be a moral or social benefit: *Re C.L.* [1969] 1 Ch. 587.

In contrast to *Re Weston's Settlement,* the court in *Re Windeatt's Will Trusts* [1969] 2 All E.R. 324 approved a variation which resulted in the trust moving to Jersey but in this case it was the beneficiaries' permanent home and they had already resided there for 19 years. Similarly in *Re Seale's Marriage Settlement* [1961] 3 All E.R. 136, the court approved the move of the trust to Canada as the whole family was resident there and had become Canadian nationals.

An example of this is *Ridgwell v Ridgwell* [2007] EWHC 2666 where the court approved a variation under the Act that had the effect of postponing the vesting of the fund in the applicant's children until after the death of her surviving spouse, if she had one. This was beneficial to the children because it would reduce the cost of insuring against inheritance tax, a potential reduction in capital gains tax and provide the trustees with the flexibility to make advancements to the beneficiaries. These benefits outweighed the disadvantage to the children in receiving their interest later. This is similar to the approach in *Re Towler's Settlement Trust*, above, where the court was also prepared to defer the vesting of the gift in favour of the beneficiary until she was more mature and responsible.

In *Wright v Gater,* Norris J. stated that

"...'benefit' need not be financial: and when it is not ... business-like considerations do not provide a sure guide, though the recognition of risk will still have some part to play. In such cases the assessment of benefit and advantage must be approached with caution... lest the process simply becomes a reflection of the perceptions and preferences of the individual judge".

Key Principle

The variation of trust under the **Variation of Trusts Act 1958** must be of benefit to the beneficiaries not merely as a class but also to them as individuals.

RE COHEN'S SETTLEMENT TRUSTS 1965

Under a settlement, the income from the trust fund was to be held on specified trusts until the death of all the settlor's sons. The fund was then to be divided between the settlor's grandchildren and their issue. The settlor's last surviving son applied to the court for approval under the **Variation of Trusts Act 1958** of a scheme which would replace the date of his death with a fixed date as the operative date when the settlor's grandchildren and their issue would take the capital.

Held

❖ (Ch) The court would not approve the arrangement. Although the scheme would benefit the infant beneficiaries who were in existence between now and the fixed date, it was possible (although on the evidence not probable) that the settlor's son would survive the fixed date. This would result in beneficiaries born after the fixed date being deprived of their beneficial interest in the settlement. [1965] 1 W.L.R. 1229.

Commentary

Stamp J. was of the view that the court had to be satisfied that the proposed variation would be of benefit not only to the beneficiaries as a class but also be of benefit to each individual beneficiary on whose behalf consent is being sought under the 1958 Act.

Key Principle

The court can use its power to approve a variation under the **Variation of Trusts Act 1958** to extend the trustees powers of advancement under s.32 of the **Trustee Act 1925**.

CD (A MINOR) V O 2004

The claimant, a minor, was a beneficiary with two others under a trust which was split into three separate funds. The income from the trust had been used to pay part of the claimant's school fees. Monies were also advanced under s.32 of the **Trustee Act 1925** towards her school fees. However, this was insufficient and the claimant applied for a variation of the trust to enable the whole capital from the claimant's fund to be applied to payment of her school fees.

Held

The court could approve a variation under the **Variation of Trusts Act 1958** provided it was satisfied that the variation was for the benefit of the relevant beneficiary. In the present case, the court was satisfied that the variation was for the claimant's benefit. Accordingly it was appropriate to extend the trustees' powers of advancement under s.32 of the **Trustee Act 1925** to advance the whole capital monies from the claimant's fund for the benefit of the claimant. [2004] 3 All E.R. 780.

Commentary

The court was clear that the key criterion for deciding whether to approve a variation was the question of whether the variation was for the benefit of the beneficiary. In the circumstances of the case what was being asked for was the advancement of her whole share in the trust (which was set aside as a separate fund) so that there was sufficient money to pay her school fees. Given that she was solely entitled to her fund the court felt it was appropriate to authorize the variation.

In *Tamlin v Edgar, The Times*, February 23, 2012, the court held that where the court's approval is sought to vary the power of advancement and allow the trustees to make an advancement in excess of the statutory power, the court has to be satisfied from the evidence that the advancement is for the benefit or advancement of the beneficiaries. Such applications are not to be a rubber stamping exercise.

Key Principle

In exercising its discretion under the **Variation of Trusts Act 1958**, there is some uncertainty whether the court can take into account the testator's intention.

GOULDING V JAMES 1996

The testatrix made a will in 1992 in which she directed that her estate was to be given to her daughter, June, and June's husband, Kenneth, in equal shares. The will provided that if June or Kenneth predeceased the testatrix, their interest was to pass to their son, Marcus, when he reached 40. This will was revoked and a new will was drawn up in which June had a life interest in possession of the residuary estate subject to which Marcus was to take absolutely, provided he reached the age of 40. If Marcus died before that, then his children would take the estate absolutely. The testatrix died in December 1994. June and Marcus applied to court for a variation of the trust contained in the will under s.1(1)[c] of the **Variation of Trusts Act 1958**. The variation sought was for 45 per cent of the estate to be held for June, 45 per cent for Marcus and the remaining 10 per cent for Marcus's children. Laddie J.

declined to approve the arrangement as it was contrary to the testa-trix's wishes.

Held

❖ (CA) In deciding whether or not approval should be granted under the 1958 Act, the court's only concern was that the arrangement must be "ben-eficial" to those for whom the court was asked to give consent. The purpose of the section was to enable a *Saunders v Vautier* type of arrangement to occur when it would otherwise be precluded because there were bene-ficiaries who could not give their consent. The variation was approved. [1997] 2 All E.R. 239.

Commentary

Laddie J. at first instance, refused to approve the arrangement because it was contrary to the testatrix's intention. His view was that the court could take into account the testatrix's clear intention in deciding whether to exercise its discretion under the 1958 Act. However, there is nothing in the 1958 Act, which imposes an obligation on the court to take into account the testatrix's intention.

The Court of Appeal reversed Laddie J.'s decision on the basis that the courts' only concern was that any variation was of benefit to those on behalf of whom the court was asked to approve the variation.

In *Wright v Gater* [2011] EWHC 2881 Norris J. was of the view that the application for the approval for a variation should be considered at a hearing where proper argument has been presented, regardless of how straightfor-ward it may be. This is so that the judge can assess the evidence on behalf of those which the judge is asked to give consent.

Key Principle

In deciding whether to give consent under s.1 of the Variation of Trusts Act 1958, the court can take the type of risks which an adult beneficiary would be prepared to take on his own behalf.

RE HOLT'S SETTLEMENT 1969

The plaintiff had a life interest under a settlement and, subject to her interest, was for her children upon attaining the age of 21 in equal shares. The plaintiff wished to surrender half the income in order to benefit her children but to have the trusts varied so that the children's interest would vest only when they attained the age of 30. The income was to be accumulated at the trustees' discretion until the age of 25 or the earlier expiration of 21 years from the date of the court's order. The plaintiff applied for the court's approval to this arrangement on the behalf of persons unborn who may become entitled under the trusts.

Held

❖ (Ch) The court in reaching its decision, can take the type of risk which an adult beneficiary would take on their own behalf when considering whether the arrangement is of benefit to the beneficiaries. Here, as the proposed transaction was for the benefit of the beneficiaries on whose behalf the court was asked to give its consent, the arrangement would be approved. [1969] 1 Ch. 100.

Commentary

The court in reaching its decision can attempt to balance the detriment and benefits to be derived from the proposed arrangement. If this entails a certain amount of risk, this is something that the court is entirely at liberty to do if it is the type of risk that an adult beneficiary would normally take. Contrast this with *Re Cohen's Settlement Trusts*, above.

Key Principle

"Where property ... is held on trusts ... the court may if it thinks fit by order approve on behalf of ... [b] any person (whether ascertained or not) who may become entitled, directly or indirectly, to an interest under the trusts as being at a future date, or on the happening of a future event a person of any specified description or a member of any specified class of persons, so however that this paragraph shall not include any person who would be of that description, or a member of that class, as the case may be, if the said date had fallen or the said event had happened at the date of the application to the court'".

Section 1(1)(b) of the **Variation of Trusts Act 1958**.

RE SUFFERT'S SETTLEMENT 1961

The applicant, who had a life interest under a protective trust in which her children were to take in remainder upon reaching the age of 21, applied to vary the terms of the trust. She had a general power of appointment in the event that she had no children. In default of appointment, the fund was to go to her statutory next of kin, which consisted of three adult cousins. One gave his consent to the application. The applicant was aged 61 and unmarried.

Held

❖ (Ch) The variation sought could not bind the two adult cousins. The court did not have jurisdiction to approve the variation on their behalf under s.1 of the **Variation of Trusts Act 1958** because they fell under the proviso to s.1(1)(b). This was because they would be the statutory next of kin if the applicant had died at the time of the application. [1961] 1 Ch. 1.

Commentary

In *Re Suffert's Settlement*, if the applicant had died at the date of the applicant, the two cousins would have become entitled under the settlement. In contrast, in *Re Moncrieff's Settlement Trusts* [1962] 1 W.L.R. 1344, where the facts were similar, except that the applicant had an adopted son who may have had an interest under settlement, the court was able to give its consent on behalf of the statutory next of kin. This was because they fell outside the proviso to s.1(1)(b) of the 1958 Act. *Knocker v Youle* [1986] 1 W.L.R 934 makes clear that a person with an actual interest, however remote, cannot be a person "who may become entitled" for the purposes of s.1(1)(b) of the 1958 Act.

In *The Canada Trust Co v Browne* 13 I.T.E.L.R. 648 it was made clear that where a variation has been made with the consent of beneficiaries or under an order under the Act if there were minor beneficiaries, the original intention of the settlor is no longer applicable. Once the deed of arrangement was made the original settlement was no longer relevant. The court followed *Re Holmden's Settlement Trusts* [1968] 1 All E.R. 148.

THINK POINT

When does a variation of trust amount to a resettlement and when does it amount to an arrangement?

Is the court order approving the variation of trust made effective by the court order or is the court merely providing consent on behalf of those beneficiaries who are unable to give consent to an arrangement agreed by the beneficiaries? What is the consequence of either approach?

Breach of Trust and Defences

11

INTRODUCTION

The trustee's fiduciary obligations mean that a trustee may be liable for a breach of trust even though there has been no fraud, intent or personal incompetence on his part and may arise from an innocent or a technical breach of trust. A breach of trust arises from an act or omission on the part of the trustee with regard to the administration or the beneficial interests of the trusts.

Where a breach of trust occurs, the trustees' obligations are to make good any loss to the trusts, or, as seen in *Boardman v Phipps* [1967] 2 A.C. 46, to account for any profit made.

The general rule is that a trustee is liable for his own breaches of trust and not that of his co-trustees unless this arises from his own failure by for example, not intervening when he is aware that a breach of trust is being committed or leaving trust property in the hands of a trustee or an agent without supervising or considering the power of intervention (ss.22 and 23 of the **Trustee Act 2000**).

LIABILITY FOR BREACH OF TRUST

Key Principle

A trustee cannot avoid liability for breach of trust by merely leaving the decision-making to his co-trustees.

> BAHIN V HUGHES 1886
>
> One of three trustees to a trust invested trust money in an unauthorised security resulting in loss to the value of the fund. The beneficiary sued the trustees for breach of trust. The other two trustees sought to claim an indemnity from the trustee who wrongfully invested the money.

Held

❖ (CA) Where the management of the trust is left in hands of one of the trustees who commits a breach of trust, the trustees who have remained passive cannot claim an indemnity from the active trustee. [1886] 31 Ch. D. 390.

Commentary

Likewise, in *Townley v Sherborne* (1634) Bridg. J.35 and *Segbedzi v Segbedzi*, Lawtel, May 28, 1999, trustees were held liable for the actions of a co-trustee where they allowed the co-trustees to commit breaches of trust and had remained passive.

Key Principle

Where one trustee has made good the loss arising from a breach of trust, he can claim a contribution from the remaining trustees unless he is also a beneficiary.

CHILLINGWORTH V CHAMBERS 1896

The plaintiff and the defendant were trustees who invested trust funds in unauthorised investments. The plaintiff subsequently became one of the beneficiaries. Some of the unauthorised investments were made before he had become a beneficiary. The plaintiff and defendant were held jointly and severally liable for the loss, which was made good out of the plaintiff's beneficial interest.

Held

❖ (CA) The plaintiff was not entitled to a contribution from the defendant in respect of any part of the loss. [1896] 1 Ch. 685.

Commentary

The general rule in cases where one trustee makes good the loss to the trust as a result of the trustees' breach of trust is that he is entitled to claim a contribution from the other trustees. This is because the trustees are jointly and severally liable for the breach. However, where the trustee who has made good the loss is also a beneficiary, he is not entitled to a contribution from the others. This is because he is treated as having consented or instigated the breach in question.

THE MEASURE OF DAMAGES

Key Principle

Where the trustees commit a breach of trust, they are liable to make good the loss.

BARTLETT V BARCLAYS BANK TRUST CO LTD (No. 1) 1980

A trust owned 99.8 per cent of shares in a private company. The trust was managed by the trustees' department of the bank which later became the defendant trust corporation. In 1960 the defendant needed to raise money in order to pay death duties. It suggested that the private company should go public. The Board of Directors of the company wished to venture into property development. The defendant did not object and the company undertook two property development projects. One project failed whilst the other was a success. However, there was an overall loss. The beneficiaries commenced an action against the defendant.

Held

❖ (Ch) In the case of the professional trustee, the duty of care imposed on such a trustee was higher than the standard of care of the ordinary prudent man of business. The defendant had failed in its duty to the trust and was therefore in breach of trust. Accordingly, the trustee was liable to make good the loss suffered by the trust. [1980] 1 Ch. 515.

Commentary

The measure of damages for breach of trust cases is one of restitution. The trustees must compensate the trust fully for any loss arising from the breach. In *Target Holdings Ltd v Redferns* [1995] 3 All E.R. 785, Lord Browne-Wilkinson stated that (at 793)

> "... the basic rule is that a trustee in breach of trust must restore
> or pay to the trust estate either the assets which have been lost
> ... or compensation for such loss .... [t]hus the common law
> rules of remoteness of damage and causation do not apply".

However, Lord Browne-Wilkinson went on to say that there must be some causal connection between the breach of trust and the loss caused to the estate. This principle of restitution generally applies only in cases of a breach of trust or breach of fiduciary duty but not for other breaches.

The principles used in assessing compensation for loss resulting from a breach of trust depend on the nature of the fiduciary duty which had been breached and whether the trust is a traditional trust or a commercial arrangement.

TARGET HOLDINGS LTD V REDFERNS (A FIRM) 1995
The defendant firm of solicitors acted for the plaintiff mortgagee and the mortgagor. The plaintiff alleged that it was the victim of a mortgage fraud. The mortgagor agreed to purchase a property for £775,000 but it was negligently valued by the second defendant at £2 million. The plaintiff agreed to grant a loan of £1,525,000 secured on the property. The defendant paid over the loan monies, which it held on trust for the mortgagee, prior to the completion of the purchase or the charge. The mortgagor subsequently became insolvent. The plaintiff sold the property for £500,000. The plaintiff sued the first defendant, inter alia, for breach of trust. The defendant argued that there had only been a technical breach and the plaintiff suffered no loss because they had the mortgage to which they were entitled. The plaintiff applied for summary judgment.

Held ....
❖ (HL) A trustee who committed a breach of trust was not liable to compensate a beneficiary for loss suffered if the loss would still have occured regardless of the breach. In the present case, where there was a bare trust arising from a conveyancing transaction, once the transaction was completed, the solicitor's client account could not be reconstituted as a trust fund. Notwithstanding the breach of trust by the defendant, the plaintiff had obtained what they would have obtained if no breach occurred, namely, a valid enforceable mortgage. The plaintiff had therefore suffered no compensatable loss. The defendant was entitled to leave to defend the action. [1995] 3 All E.R. 785.

Commentary ....
The decision makes a clear distinction between the traditional type trust and the trust arising out of a commercial transaction. In the latter, the basis of compensation for breach of trust is by analogy to common law damages i.e. that the plaintiff is to be put in the position he would be in if the breach had not occurred. In the case itself, the plaintiff would have suffered the loss notwithstanding the breach and therefore the defendant was not liable to pay the plaintiff anything more than nominal damages. However, that would be dependent on the evidence in the trial itself. In a breach of trust in the

traditional type trust, the obligation on the trustees is to account for, and restore to, the trust fund that which has been lost. Lord Browne Wilkinson's dictum in *Bartlett v Barclays Bank Trust Co Ltd (No. 1)* (above), applies here.

Key Principle

If the trustees make an unauthorised investment, the trustees will be liable to make good the loss even though the sale was pursuant to a court order and there was a possibility that the investment would not have resulted in a loss if it had been retained.

KNOTT V COTTEE 1852

An executor invested part of the estate in Exchequer Bills in 1846. The court ordered the sale of the investment. The investment was sold that same year but at a loss. In 1848, the court declared that the investment was improper but the price of the Bills had risen by then.

Held

❖ (Ch) The executor was liable for the loss arising from the sale because he had made an improper investment, even though the sale was ordered by the court and the investment would not have resulted in a loss if it had been retained. (1852) 16 Beav. 77.

Key Principle

Where the trustees retain investments improperly, they will be liable for the difference in value between the value when it should have been sold and its present value.

FRY V FRY 1859

A testator directed his executors and trustees to sell his freehold inn as soon as convenient after his death. The testator died in 1834. The trustees received an offer of £900 for the inn in 1836 but they refused to sell. The value of the inn subsequently depreciated in value. The inn remained unsold in 1859 by which time both the trustees had died.

Held

❖ (Ch) The trustees' estates were liable for the difference in value between the £900 and the present value of the inn. (1859) 27 Beav. 144.

Commentary

The principle is clearly one of restitution to the trust. In *Jeffrey v Gretton and Russell* [2011] W.T.L.R. 809 the court held that the trustees were in breach of trust for failing in their duty to keep the trust portfolio under regular review. The trustees kept a dilapidated property for six years whilst they sought to refurbish it. However the beneficiary's claim failed because her share of the proceeds from the eventual sale of the property was more than she would have received had the trustees not kept the property and sold it in 2002.

Key Principle

Where the trustees improperly sell an authorised investment they must replace it or pay the difference between the sale price and the cost of repurchasing the investment.

Phillipson v Gatty 1848

Trustees of a settlement, who had the power to invest trust funds in government stock or real security, sold the stock. The proceeds of sale were improperly invested in a mortgage.

Held

The whole transaction including the sale of the stock must be taken as one unjustifiable transaction and therefore the trustees had to replace the stock. (1848) 7 Hare. 516.

Commentary

In *Re Bell's Indenture* [1980] 1 W.L.R. 1217, the court decided that the loss to the trust should be assessed at the date of the judgment. Thus, where an asset has to be repurchased, this will be as at the date of the judgment and not the date of the breach or the date when the action was commenced.

Key Principle

Where the trustees make a loss on one unauthorised transaction but make a profit on another unauthorised transaction, they cannot set off the profit against the loss, unless they are part of the same transaction.

Bartlett v Barclays Bank Trust Co Ltd (No. 1) 1980

(See above.)

Held

❖ (Ch) The defendant trustee was allowed to set off the profit from one project against the loss from the other project as it could be said to have stemmed from the same policy. [1980] 1 Ch. 515.

Commentary

On the facts of the case, a set off was allowed. In *Dimes v Scott* (1828) 4 Russ. 195, it was decided that trustees would not be entitled to set off the loss made from a breach of trust against the profit arising from another breach of trust. The trust is entitled to keep the profit and be fully compensated for the loss. In *Re Bell's Indenture* (above), the court noted that if the tax liability of the trust has been reduced as a result of a breach of trust, the trustee will not be entitled to the benefit from this. The trustee cannot therefore, set off this reduction in tax against his liability to compensate the trust.

Key Principle

The court has an inherent jurisdiction to award interest in appropriate cases.

WALLERSTEINER V MOIR (NO. 2) 1975

The defendant, a minority shareholder in a company, made allegations against the plaintiff, who was one of the directors. The defendant was sued for libel. The defendant counterclaimed seeking declarations that the plaintiff had been guilty of fraud, misfeasance and breach of trust. Judgment was given for the defendant together with interest. The plaintiff appealed claiming that the court did not have jurisdiction to award interest.

Held

❖ (CA) The court had an inherent jurisdiction to award interest where a fiduciary had benefited from his position. The rate of interest would be fixed at one per cent above the minimum bank lending rate. [1975] Q.B. 373.

Commentary

At common law the court merely had the jurisdiction to award simple interest in specific circumstances—Law Reform (Miscellaneous Provisions) Act 1934 as amended. However, in equity, the court has an inherent jurisdiction to award interest in cases where there has been a breach of trust. However, it is clear that this is not to punish the trustee but to ensure that the trustee has not benefited from the breach of trust. The interest may be either simple or compound interest. In *O'Sullivan v Management Agency and Music Ltd* [1985]

3 All E.R. 351, the court awarded simple interest because the defendant was not involved in an investment business. In some cases, a compound rate of interest may be imposed where the trustee has himself received a higher rate (*Re Emmet's Estate* (1881) 17 Ch. D. 142), where he ought to have received a higher rate of interest (*Jones v Foxall* (1852) 21 L.J. Ch. 725 and *Guardian Ocean Cargoes Ltd v Banco de Brasil* [1992] 2 Lloyd's Rep. 193)—usually where there are commercial factors involved.

In *Westdeutsche Landesbank Girozentrale v Islington LBC* [1996] A.C. 669, the majority of the House of Lords held that equity could only award compound interest where there was fraud or misapplication of funds by a person in a fiduciary position. In the case as there was neither fraud nor receipt of funds as a fiduciary, only simple interest was payable. In dissenting judgments by Lords Goff and Woolf, their Lordships queried why compound interest could not be awarded in a personal claim or at common law where there was a claim for restitution. The House of Lords has now reviewed the position in *Sempra Metals Ltd (formerly Metallgesellschaft Ltd) v IRC* [2007] 4 All E.R. 657 where their Lordships held that compound interest could be ordered in a claim for restitution at common law. The case involved the claim for restitution for advanced corporation tax paid to the IRC which was ruled to be illegal by the European Court of Justice. It is now clear from this case that compound interest can be awarded even though there is no fiduciary relationship.

DEFENCES TO AN ACTION FOR BREACH OF TRUST

[a] Laches and Limitation Act 1980

Key Principle

The limitation period does not apply where the cause of action relates to any fraud or fraudulent breach of trust which the trustee was a party or privy to: Section 21(1)(a) of the Limitation Act 1980.

THORNE V HEARD 1895

The respondent mortgagees sold the mortgaged property under their power of sale in 1878. They used the mortgagor's solicitor to conduct the sale. The solicitor received the proceeds of sale and after payment of the respondents' mortgage kept the balance of the proceeds without paying off the second mortgage. The solicitor continued to pay interest on the second mortgage as if the mortgage was still subsisting. The second mortgagee discovered the fraud in 1892 and brought an action against the respondents for an account and payment of money due.

Held

❖ (HL) The second mortgagee's action was barred by the Statute of Limitations. The respondents were not party or privy to the fraud that was perpetrated by the solicitor, who was independent of the respondents. Further, the proceeds of sale were no longer in their hands. [1895] A.C. 495.

Commentary

The normal limitation period for an action for breach of trust or for the recovery of trust property (apart from infringement of the self dealing rule), must be commenced within six years from the date the cause of action accrued: s.21(3) of the **Limitation Act 1980**. Where fraud is involved, the limitation period does not apply. However, the fraud must be the fraud of or in some way imputable to the person who relies on the Limitation Act and not a third party. In *Gwembe Valley Development Corp v Koshy (No. 3)* [2004] 1 B.C.L.C. 131, the case was found to fall within the ambit of s.21 of the **Limitation Act 1980** as there was a fraudulent breach of trust and thus the defence of laches did not apply. See also *J.J. Harrison (Properties) Ltd v Harrison* [2002] 1 B.C.L.C. 162 and *Central Bank of Nigeria v Williams* [2012] 3 All E.R. 579.

In *Cattley v Pollard* [2007] 2 All E.R. 1086 the court stressed that s.21(1)(a) applied only to express trustees or those who are treated as express trustees, namely persons who assumed the duties of a trustee by a transaction which preceded the breach of trust and occurred before the breach. On the facts of the case, there was no pre-existing trust relationship which had arisen before the relevant transactions and as such the defendant could not be treated as an express trustee. Therefore s.21(1)(a) was not applicable and the limitation period applied.

Key Principle

> "No period of limitation ... shall apply to an action by a beneficiary under a trust to recover from the trustee trust property or the proceeds of trust property in the possession of the trustee...."

Section 21(1)(b) of the **Limitation Act 1980**.

JAMES V WILLIAMS 1999

V died intestate and her estate, which included a house, was held on statutory trusts for her three children. Her son W stayed in the house with T, one of his sisters. No letters of administration were taken out. When W died, he left the house to T and her daughter, the defendant. T later died and left her share of the house to the defendant. The plaintiff, V's other child, commenced an action claiming a one third share of the house. The defendant argued that the action was time barred.

Held

❖ (CA) A constructive trust arose on V's death with W owing a fiduciary duly to his sisters. Consequently, the defendant was a constructive trustee and therefore the plaintiff's claim was not time barred.

Commentary

This case was essentially one in which the plaintiff was seeking to recover trust property from the trustee, the defendant, in this case. In such a case, there is no limitation period. A similar conclusion was reached in *Re Loftus* [2005] 1 W.L.R. 1890.

Key Principle

"... [f]or the purposes of this subsection, the right of action shall not be treated as having accrued to any beneficiary entitled to a future interest in the trust property until the interest fell into possession"

Section 21(3) of the **Limitation Act 1980**.

RE PAULING'S SETTLEMENT TRUSTS 1964
(See Ch.9.)
The trustees pleaded, inter alia, that the limitation period ran from the time the improper advances were made and therefore the beneficiaries were time barred from suing the trustees.

Held

❖ (CA) The beneficiaries had a future interest and therefore the time limit did not start to run until they received their entitlement. The time limit did not run from when the advances were made. [1964] Ch. 303.

Commentary

The proviso to s.21(3) of the **Limitation Act 1980** applied. The limitation period only began to run when they received their full shares under the trust and not before. Therefore, the beneficiaries' action against the trustees was not time barred.

Key Principle

Where the **Limitation Act 1980** does not apply, the defendant may rely on the defence of laches.

> ### NELSON V RYE 1996
>
> The plaintiff retained the defendant to act as his manager between 1980 and 1990. The defendant failed to account to the plaintiff on a regular basis. In 1990, the plaintiff commenced an action against the defendant. The defendant argued that the claim for an account for the period prior to 1985 was time barred under the **Limitation Act 1980** and that the equitable defence of laches and acquiescence applied. The plaintiff replied that as his claim was for breach of fiduciary duty or breach of trust, the Limitation Act did not apply.

Held

❖ (Ch) The defendant was under a fiduciary duty to the plaintiff to account regularly. He had breached this duty and received monies belonging to the plaintiff, which was trust property. Accordingly, the Limitation Act 1980 did not apply. In deciding whether the equitable doctrine of laches and acquiescence applied, the court would take into account the circumstances of the case including the reason and period of delay and the extent of the prejudice to the defendant as a result of the delay. Here, there was an unreasonable delay because the plaintiff had been reluctant to involve himself in financial matters. Consequently, it would be unfair and unjust to allow the plaintiffs' claim pre-1985. [1996] 2 All E.R. 186.

Commentary

The doctrine of laches applies in those cases where the **Limitation Act 1980** does not. This would include cases where there is an allegation that the trustee has been party to or privy to a fraud, or where the claim is against trustees for property or proceeds of sale improperly retained by them or against trustees for the infringement of the self dealing rule. In such cases, depending on the circumstances of the case, the claim may be barred where there has been an unreasonable long period of delay causing prejudice to the defendant. This decision has been followed in *Kershaw v Whelan (No. 2)*, *The Times*, February 10, 1997. However, doubt has been cast on this decision by *Paragon Finance v DB Thakerar & Co* [1999] 1 All E.R. 400 where Millett L.J.

obiter suggested that *Nelson v Rye* was wrongly decided and by the Law Commission (Law Commission No. 270, Limitation of Actions) suggesting that it may be incorrect.

[b] Release, consent and acquiescence

Key Principle
Where the beneficiaries, upon discovering a breach of trust, release or acquiesce to the breach, they cannot thereafter claim against the trustee for that breach of trust.

> RE PAULING'S SETTLEMENT TRUSTS 1964
> (See Ch.9.)
> One of the issues was whether the plaintiff beneficiaries had acquiesced to the breach of trust.

Held
❖ (CA) The plaintiffs could not be said to have acquiesced to the breach of trust unless they knew or ought to have known what their rights were. Here, the plaintiffs were not aware of their rights until they were subsequently advised that the advances may have been improper. Accordingly, the plaintiffs were not debarred from their action by reason of acquiescence. [1964] 1 Ch. 303.

Commentary
Generally, in order for the trustees to be able to establish acquiescence on the part of the beneficiaries, they need to show that the beneficiaries by their conduct impliedly agreed not to enforce their strict legal rights. It should be noted that the beneficiaries could have waived their rights against the trustees. In *Allan v Rea Brothers Trustees Ltd* [2002] 4 I.T.E.L.R. 627 the court held that a beneficiary who had participated or acquiesced in the breach of trust cannot thereafter complain about it even though he had received no benefit from that breach.

Key Principle
Where a beneficiary consents to a breach of trust, he is not entitled to claim compensation from the trustees to the extent of his beneficial interest.

FLETCHER V COLLIS 1905

Property was settled on a husband for life, thereafter to the wife for life and the remainder to the children. In 1885, the whole of the trust property was sold at the wife's request with the husband's consent. The money was handed over to the wife who spent it. The husband was then adjudicated a bankrupt. The trustee replaced the trust property after he was sued by the beneficiaries. The trustee died after this but there was a surplus representing the income. The trustee's personal representative claimed this on the basis that this was partial indemnity from the husband. The husband's trustee in bankruptcy disputed this.

Held

❖ (CA) As the husband had consented to the breach of trust, he could not require the trustee to make good his loss of income resulting from the breach. Accordingly, the trustee in bankruptcy had no claim to the surplus. [1905] 2 Ch. 24.

[c] Impounding the beneficiary's interest

Key Principle

Under s.62 of the **Trustee Act 1925**, where a trustee commits a breach of trust at the instigation, request or consent of a beneficiary, the court may impound the beneficiary's interest.

RE SOMERSET 1894

The tenant for life of a marriage settlement requested the trustees to invest part of the trust funds in a mortgage of a particular property. The trustees followed his request but lent too much on the mortgage. The beneficiaries commenced an action against the trustees for the resulting loss.

Held

❖ (CA) Although the tenant for life had requested that the investment be made, he did not intend to be a party to any breach of trust or to an investment in the mortgage without enquiry. He left it to the trustees to determine whether the investment was a proper investment. Accordingly, the tenant for life's interest would not be impounded. [1894] 1 Ch. 231.

Commentary

The case concerned the predecessor to s.62 of the **Trustee Act 1925**. The rule is that in order for the beneficiary's interest to be impounded, it was necessary to show not only that the beneficiary's request resulted in the breach of trust but must also have been aware that the action would result in such a breach.

[d] Section 61 of the Trustee Act 1925

Key Principle
Under s.61 of the **Trustee Act 1925**, the court may relieve a trustee either wholly or partly, where he is personally liable for a breach of trust, if he has acted honestly and reasonably and ought fairly to be excused.

> PERRINS V BELLAMY 1899
> The trustees of a settlement committed a breach of trust in reliance upon the erroneous advice of their solicitor. The plaintiff commenced an action for breach of trust.

Held
❖ (CA) Although there was a breach of trust, the trustees had acted both honestly and reasonably and therefore the trustees ought to be relieved from personal liability. [1899] 1 Ch. 797.

> NATIONAL TRUSTEES CO OF AUSTRALASIA LTD V GENERAL FINANCE CO OF AUSTRALASIA LTD 1905
> The appellant trustees wrongly paid over two-thirds of the trust fund to the beneficiaries in reliance upon the erroneous advice of their solicitor. The issue arose as to whether the trustees should be relieved from liability.

Held
❖ (PC) A trustee is not entitled to be relieved from liability merely by showing that he acted honestly and reasonably. The trustee must satisfy the court that in all the circumstances of the case, he ought fairly to be excused. Here, the trustee had acted honestly and reasonably but had failed to show why it ought fairly to be excused from liability. [1905] A.C. 373.

Commentary
Both cases concerned the equivalent of s.61 of the **Trustee Act 1925**. In *Perrins v Bellamy*, the court suggested that the trustees ought to be excused if they had shown that they acted honestly and reasonably without showing that the trustees ought fairly to be excused. However, in *National Trustees Co of Australia Ltd v General Finance Co of Australasia Ltd*, the Privy Council insisted that there must be further evidence to show the trustees ought fairly to be excused. It may have been relevant that the trustee in the latter case

was a professional trustee and, therefore, a higher standard of care was imposed. This is reinforced by *Re Pauling's Settlement Trusts* [1964] Ch. 303, below. In *Bartlett v Barclays Bank Trust Co Ltd* (above), the court refused to excuse a trustee's breach of trust under s.61 of the **Trustee Act 1925** because, although the trustee had acted honestly, it had not acted reasonably. The same conclusion was reached in *Lloyds TSB Bank Plc v Markandan & Uddin (a firm)* [2012] 2 All E.R. 884 where the defendant who had acted honestly failed to prove he had acted reasonably and as such the defence under s.61 was not available.

It has been re-emphasised in *Re Evans* [1999] 2 All E.R. 777 that even though the trustee had acted on legal advice, it did not mean that she would automatically be entitled to relief under s.61. The trustee would have to show that in the circumstances of the case that the trustee had acted reasonably and ought fairly to be excused. A recent example is the case of *Re St Andrew's (Cheam) Lawn Tennis Club Trust* [2012] 3 All E.R. 746 where the trustees who had administered the trust had done so on the assumption that the trust deed was valid and on various occasions when legal advice was sought, the issue of the perpetuity period and hence the invalidity of the trust deed, was not identified. It was only subsequently that it was identified as an issue and thereafter at the request of the other parties involved they allowed time to resolve the matter without resort to litigation but this proved unsuccessful. In the circumstances the court decided that the trustees had at all times acted honestly and reasonably and ought fairly to be excused from liability under s.61 of the **Trustee Act 1925**.

A breach of trust giving rise to a contractual liability cannot be excused under s.61: *Segbedzi v Segbedzi*, Lawtel, May 28, 1999.

Key Principle
Where a trustee committed a breach of trust in circumstances where there was a conflict of duty and interest, the court is reluctant to grant the trustee relief under s.61 of the **Trustee Act 1925**.

RE PAULING'S SETTLEMENT TRUSTS 1946
(See Ch.9.)

Held
❖ (CA) Where a bank acted as a paid trustee and had placed itself in a position where its interest as a banker was in conflict with its duty as a trustee, the court would be reluctant to grant it relief under s.61 of the **Trustee Act 1925**. [1964] 1 Ch. 303.

Commentary

The court did not decide that relief was unobtainable but merely that it would be slow to grant a trustee in the position of the bank, relief under s.61. This suggests that if there were exceptional circumstances, the court may be prepared to grant such relief but such occasions would undoubtedly be rare.

Key Principle

The court may relieve the trustee from liability in whole or in part under s.61 of the **Trustee Act 1925**.

> RE KAY 1897
>
> The testator's estate consisted of assets worth £22,000. It was initially thought that there were debts of about £100. The executor paid out a legacy to the widow and provided monies for the maintenance and education of the children. A creditor subsequently claimed £26,000 from the estate.

Held

❖ (Ch) The executor had acted reasonably and honestly. He would be relieved from liability up until the time the creditor's claim was received. Thereafter, he was liable for the payments that were made. [1897] 2 Ch. 518.

Commentary

It is clear from the statutory provision that relief can be given either wholly or in part. This case is an example where it was appropriate to grant partial relief.

[e] Exclusion Clauses

Key Principle

Trustees can rely on an exclusion clause in the trust deed in order to avoid liability for breach of trust.

> ARMITAGE V NURSE 1997
>
> An exclusion clause in a settlement provided that the trustee shall not be liable for any loss or damage occurring to the capital and income unless it was caused by the trustee's own fraud.

Held

❖ (CA) The clause excluded the trustee's liability even though he may have been indolent, imprudent, lacking in diligence, negligent or wilful so long as he has not been dishonest. As the claim against the trustee did not allege dishonesty, the trustee could rely on the clause. [1997] 2 All E.R. 705.

Commentary

Armitage v Nurse makes clear that an exclusion clause is to be restrictively construed and anything that is not clearly within it is deemed as falling outside the ambit of the clause. In *Wight v Olswang*, *The Times*, May 18, 1999, the Court of Appeal stressed that in order to exclude liability for trustees' breaches of trust, the words used in the exclusion clause must be clear and unambiguous. In that case, the words were not clear or unambiguous and therefore the clause could not be used to exclude liability. Ultimately, it is a question of construction of the relevant clause in deciding whether an exclusion clause can exclude a trustee's breach of trust. In *Bonham v Fishwick* [2008] EWCA Civ 373 the court decided that trustees who relied on a legal opinion would not be guilty of any wrongdoing. The trustees were entitled to rely on the exemption clause excluding them from liability. In *Spread Trustee Co Ltd v Hutcheson* [2012] 1 All E.R. 251 the Privy Council suggested obiter that an exemption clause which was worded such that it was clear the parties agreed that the trustees should be liable only in the event of wilful and individual fraud or wrongdoing was valid and could be relied on by the trustees. See also *Bogg v Raper*, *The Times*, April 22, 1998 and *Baker v J.E. Clark & Co (Transport) Ltd* [2006] EWCA Civ 464.

It is also possible that the court will take a stricter approach in cases where the trustees are solicitors. In *Walker v Stone* [2001] Q.B. 902, the Court of Appeal decided that an exclusion clause would not protect the trustees because although they may have genuinely believed that their actions were in the best interests of the trusts, they were not actions that reasonable solicitor-trustees would have taken.

The Law Commission issued its Report on Trustee Exemption Clauses in 2006. The responses to its original consultation report in 2002 highlighted concerns about the way exemption clauses are used widely and that the settler may not be aware of their inclusion or importance. It was advocated that there should be some form of regulation but it noted the concerns on the impact of any regulatory regime on the trustees and their performance. The Law Commission recognised that there are obstacles to statutory intervention in this area as there would be an impact on the trust system as a whole and the possibility that it would have adverse consequences to the trust and its beneficiaries. The Law Commission was of the view that the better approach would be to introduce a rule of practice to be followed by "regulated persons" as the latter would be required to adhere to the rule of practice. It recommended that "any paid trustee who causes a settlor to include a clause in a trust instrument which has the effect of excluding or limiting liability for negligence must before the creation of the trust take such steps as are reasonable to ensure that the settler is aware of the meaning and effect of the clause".

It noted that a number of professional bodies including the Law Society were in the process of developing regulation to give effect to this and recommended that the government should encourage relevant regulatory bodies to adopt a version of the rule of practice appropriate to the circumstances of its memberships and relevant codes of conduct.

THINK POINT

Should the liability of a trustee be fault based?

Is the use of an exemption clause in a trust instrument incompatible with the fiduciary nature of a trustee's obligation?

Tracing

12

INTRODUCTION

The remedies which a claimant may obtain against a defendant are usually personal in nature, for example, the remedy of damages is an order for the defendant to pay a certain sum of money to the defendant. However, there may be some instances where tracing may be more useful, for example, where the defendant has disappeared and tracing may enable the claimant to claim specific property in the defendant's hands, if it is available in the circumstances.

Tracing, which is available at common law and in equity, is a process that allows the property to be followed into the hands of the trustees or a third party who has received the trust property but it is not a right or a remedy. In *Trustee of the Property of FC Jones & Sons (a Firm) v Jones* [1996] 4 All E.R. 721 Millett L.J. suggested that

> "there is no merit in having distinct and differing rules at law and in equity; given that tracing is neither a right nor a remedy but merely a process by which the claimant establishes what has happened to his property. The fact that there are different tracing rules at law and in equity is unfortunate ...".

Lord Millett in *Foskett v McKeown* [2001] 1 A.C. 102, stressed that tracing is neither a claim nor a remedy, but is "merely the process by which a Claimant demonstrates what has happened to his property" as a precursor to the commencement of a legal action.

However, there is still a distinction between common law and equitable tracing in that the latter requires proof of a fiduciary relationship (*Shalson v Russo* [2003] EWHC 1637).

TRACING AT COMMON LAW

For tracing to be available at common law the property which is being traced must be identifiable at every stage but its form can change. However it is not available where the property being traced has been converted into money and that has been paid into a mixed account. Further, common law tracing is not available to a beneficiary under a trust.

Key Principle
Where the property in the asset has not passed, the claimant can trace the asset into the hands of the party holding the property.

TAYLOR V PLUMER 1815
The defendant gave money to his stockbroker for the purchase of exchequer bonds. However, the stockbroker bought American investments and bullion. The defendant pursued the stockbroker and was able to seize the investments. The investments were subsequently sold. The stockbroker was declared bankrupt and his assignees in bankruptcy sought an order that the proceeds of sale belonged to them.

Held
The defendant was entitled to retain the proceeds of sale as the property in them had not passed and was identifiable. (1815) 2 Rose. 415.

Commentary
Tracing at common law is available where the property in the asset has not passed. In *Armstrong DLW GmbH v Winnington Networks Ltd* [2012] EWHC 10, the court stated that

> "...if and where legal title remains with the claimant, a proprietary restitutionary claim at common law is available in respect of receipt by the defendant of a chose in action or other intangible property".

Such a remedy is not available to a beneficiary under a trust or a claim in equity.

Key Principle
The property must be identifiable in order for tracing to be available at common law.

BANQUE BELGE POUR L'ETRANGER V HAMBROUCK 1921
The first defendant fraudulently obtained cheques from his employer drawn on the plaintiff bank. These amounted to about £6,000 and were paid into his bank account. The first defendant then drew cheques on his account and paid them to another defendant, a Ms Spanoghe, with whom he was living. She paid these cheques into her bank account. When the fraud was discovered there was £315 in her bank account. The plaintiff bank sought a declaration that the money was their property and an order that it should be paid to them.

Held

❖ (CA) The money was capable of being traced. The plaintiff bank was therefore entitled to the declaration and the order sought. [1921] 1 K.B. 321.

Commentary

[1] In this case, tracing at common law was available because no other monies were paid into Ms Spanoghe's bank account apart from the proceeds of the fraud. The money was therefore identifiable. Once the monies had been mixed with other property, tracing at common law is not available. If the money had been paid into an overdrawn bank account, the right to trace at common law is lost: *Box v Barclays Bank* [1998] 5 Lloyd's Rep. 185.

[2] It should be noted that the property in the money had not passed to Ms Spanoghe as she had not given any consideration for it.

Key Principle

Tracing at common law is lost where the monies have been mixed in intervening accounts in the bank clearing system.

AGIP (AFRICA) LTD V JACKSON 1992
(See Ch. 6.)
The plaintiff, inter alia, sought to recover the money on the basis of money had and received.

Held

❖ (CA) The common law remedy of tracing was not available. The difficulty was in identifying the origin of money. This could not be done without tracing the money through the New York clearing system where it would have been mixed with other funds. It could not be established at common law that the money with which the Lloyds Bank had been paid was the money from the Tunis Bank. [1991] Ch. 547.

Commentary

[1] The Court of Appeal stated that in determining whether common law tracing was available as a remedy, it did not matter that the money had been transmitted by telegraphic transfer. At first instance, Miller J.'s view was that where the money had been transmitted via telegraphic transfer between banks it was impossible to trace the money at common law. The issue is not the method of payment, but at common law, it is the question of whether it is possible to follow the physical asset from one recipient to another. Where the money has been mixed with other monies, common law tracing is not available.

[2] A similar conclusion was reached in *Bank Tejarat v Hong Kong & Shanghai Banking Corp (CI) Ltd* [1995] I Lloyd's L.R. 239.

Key Principle

Any profit arising from the use of the money or asset that is subject to tracing has to be paid over.

TRUSTEE OF THE PROPERTY OF FC JONES AND SONS (A FIRM) v JONES 1996
The partners of the firm of FC Jones and Sons were adjudicated bankrupt. Before this, the defendant, the wife of one of the partners, paid money to a firm of commodity brokers to invest. Later, she received £50,760 from the brokers. The Official Receiver claimed to be entitled to this money. The defendant argued that she could keep the profits from the investments although the original sum paid to the brokers belonged to the Receiver.

Held

❖ (CA) The Official Receiver's claim to trace the funds was at common law and it was entitled to both the original sum and the profits generated by it. [1996] 4 All E.R. 721.

Commentary

This is a recent example of tracing at common law. Tracing in equity did not apply because the defendant had not received the money as a fiduciary.

TRACING IN EQUITY

[a] A fiduciary relationship must be present

Key Principle

There must be a fiduciary relationship between the parties in order for the remedy of tracing to be available in equity.

> RE HALLETT'S ESTATE 1880
> A solicitor held bonds for his own settlement as well as for a client. He sold the bonds without consent and paid the proceeds of sale into his bank account. Money was deposited and drawn out from the account by the solicitor for his own use. The solicitor then died.

Held

❖ (CA) The right to trace in equity was available in cases where there was a fiduciary relationship between the parties and was not limited to the trustee-beneficiary relationship. The client and the beneficiaries of the settlement were therefore entitled to trace in equity as a fiduciary relationship existed between them. (1880) 13 Ch. D. 696.

> SINCLAIR V BROUGHAM 1914
> A building society carried on an ultra vires banking business. It was ordered to be wound-up and the question arose as to the priority between the shareholders, creditors and customers who had deposited money. It was accepted that the creditors were to be paid first. The issue was whether the shareholders had priority over the customers.

Held

❖ (HL) The customers who deposited money in the bank were not entitled to recover the money on the basis of money had and received. However, they were entitled to trace the funds into the hands of the building society as there was a fiduciary relationship between the building society and the customers but they ranked in pari passu with the shareholders. [1914] A.C. 398.

Commentary

In *AGIP (Africa) Ltd v Jackson* [1990] 1 Ch. 265, Millet J., at first instance, noted that the requirement of a fiduciary relationship before tracing was available in equity had been widely condemned and was dependent on authority rather than principle. He was of the view that this principle should be reconsidered but did not think it was appropriate to do so at first instance. This was also the view of the House of Lords in *Foskett v Mckeown* [2000] 2 W.L.R. 1299 (see below) where Lord Millett was of the view that there was no logical justification for insisting that there is a fiduciary relationship as a precursor to tracing.

Notwithstanding the criticisms, it would seem that the position is now well settled, in that, before tracing in equity is available, the existence of a fiduciary relationship is a necessary prerequisite. The requirement of a fiduciary relationship was accepted by the House of Lords in *Westdeutsche Landesbank Girozentrale v Islington Borough Council* [1996] A.C. 669. In *Shalson v Russo* [2003] EWHC 1637, Rimer J. took the view that the require-ment is still in existence. This case was followed in *Campden Hill Ltd v Chakrani* [2005] EWHC 911 where the court stated that the earlier case of *Foskett v Mckeown* (see below) did not decide that it was not necessary for there to be a fiduciary relationship in order to be able to trace.

Key Principle
The fiduciary relationship necessary for tracing to be available in equity can sometimes arise out of the circumstances of the case.

CHASE MANHATTAN BANK NA v ISRAEL-BRITISH BANK (LONDON) LTD 1981
The plaintiff mistakenly paid a sum of US $2 million to a bank, which in turn paid it to the defendant. The defendant subsequently went into liquidation. The plaintiff sought to trace and recover in equity the sum erroneously paid.

Held
❖ (Ch) Where money was erroneously paid under a mistake of fact, the payer retained an equitable interest in the money. The payee was subject to a fiduciary duty to respect the proprietary interest of the payer. Accordingly, the plaintiff was entitled to trace the money. [1981] 1 Ch. 105.

RE GOLDCORP EXCHANGE LTD (IN RECEIVERSHIP) 1995
A company dealing in gold and other precious metals sold unascer-tained bullion to the first respondents on a "non-allocated basis" for future delivery. The company stored and insured the bullion. The respondents had the right to call for delivery of their portion within seven days. The company encountered financial difficulties and the Bank of New Zealand appointed receivers under the terms of a debenture issued by the company. The receivers applied for directions on the disposal of the bullion. At first instance, the High Court of New

Zealand rejected the first respondents' claims but the Court of Appeal allowed their claim on different grounds.

Held

❖ (PC)

[i] The first respondents had no title in law or in equity to any of the bullion since they had contracted to purchase unascertained goods. No title could pass until the bullion had become ascertained goods.

[ii] The monies paid by the first respondent to the company were not impressed with a trust thereby entitling them to trace into the company's assets. Neither was the company a fiduciary with respect to the monies as these were paid in performance of the contract. [1995] 1 A.C. 74.

Commentary

[1] In *Chase Manhattan Bank NA v Israel-British Bank (London) Ltd*, Goulding J. (at 119) emphasised that the fund to be traced need not have been the subject of fiduciary obligations. It was enough that the payment of the money into the wrong hands gave rise to a fiduciary relationship. In reaching this conclusion, he relied on *Sinclair v Brougham*, above, where there was no intention between the directors of the building society and the customers to create a fiduciary relationship but that nonetheless, a fiduciary relationship arose out of the payment of the money to the Building Society. He also stressed that there was no need for the fiduciary relationship to arise from a consensual transaction.

The fiduciary relationship can also arise from the terms of a contract between the parties. See: *Aluminium Industrie Vaasen BV v Romalpa Aluminium Ltd* [1976] 1 W.L.R. 676. See also *Ultraframe v Fielding*, Lawtel, August 11, 2005 as to fiduciary relationships in the case of shadow company directors. A fiduciary relationship was easily found in *Campden Hill v Chakrani* [2005] EWHC 911 where monies could be traced to a solicitors' account where the solicitor had been party to a fraudulent loan agreement. Similarly in *Clark v Cutland* [2004] 1 W.L.R. 783 monies could be traced where a company director moved company money without authorization into his own pension fund.

[2] The decision in Chase Manhattan was applied by the New Zealand Court of Appeal in *Re Goldcorp Exchange* (at that stage the case was known as *Liggett v Kensington* [1993] 1 N.Z.L.R. 257). It was held there that a fiduciary relationship existed between the company and the respondents because the respondents acquired a proprietary interest in the bullion. However, the Privy Council was of the view that no fiduciary relationship existed between the

company and the respondents. Lord Mustill refused to express any view on whether Chase Manhattan had been decided correctly. However, doubt has been cast on Chase Manhattan by the House of Lords in *Westdeutsche Landeshank Girozentrale v Islington Borough Council* [1996] A.C. 669.

[b] Third parties

Key Principle
Tracing in equity is available against volunteers.

> RE DIPLOCK 1948
> The testator left his residuary estate to be applied for such charitable or benevolent objects as his executors should so decide. The executors distributed the estate amongst a number of charities. It was subsequently declared that the gift was invalid as it was not wholly and exclusively charitable. The next of kin commenced an action, inter alia, to trace the money into the hands of the charities.

Held
❖ (CA) The claim by the next of kin to trace the money into the charities' hands would succeed. This was notwithstanding that the charities had mixed the monies from the estate with their own monies. However, the charities were entitled to assert their own claim to the mixed funds so that the charities and the claimant would share pari passu in the mixed fund. Where the trust monies have not been mixed with the charities' own funds, the charities would hold the monies on trust for the true owner. Further, the application of the remedy must not result in injustice. [1948] 1 Ch. 465.

Commentary
[1] The next of kin succeeded in their claim to trace against the charities by establishing that there was a fiduciary relationship between the parties. The court's view was that it would not be inequitable to trace into the hands of innocent volunteers in this case.

[2] The court also stated that tracing would not succeed against a party who has received the trust monies (or trust property) for value without notice of the claimant's equitable interest in it. The claimant's equitable interest to that extent would be extinguished. In *Independent Trustee Services Ltd v GP Noble Trustees Ltd* [2012] EWCA Civ 195 the Court of Appeal held that a wife who had a an order in her favour in respect of compromised ancillary relief proceedings could be regarded as a bona fide purchaser for value without notice and so could have a valid defence against a tracing claim. However as

she had set aside the order she was no longer entitled to rely on that defence.

[3] The claimant also succeeded in a claim in personam on the basis that there was an equity to recover from a recipient who was wrongly or over paid and such a remedy was available to an unpaid or underpaid creditor, legatee or next of kin.

[4] *Crown Dilmun v Sutton* [2004] EWHC 52 illustrates the classes of persons against whom a remedy can be brought. The first defendant was a company director. Having declined to take up a potential property development scheme on behalf of his employer he set up his own company to take up the very same development scheme. He appointed the second defendant to be the director of the new company. Thus the first defendant was trading for himself against his employer's interests and in breach of his contract of employment. The second defendant should have been aware of the first defendant's breach of fiduciary duty and had acted recklessly as he knew that the first defendant was the claimant's employee. It would be unconscionable for him to retain the benefit of the business deal.

[c] The property must be in a traceable form. See *Barclays Bank PLC v Kalamohan* **[2010] All E.R. (D) 59 (Jun).**

Key Principle
The remedy of tracing in equity is not available where the money has been used to pay off loans or the asset has been dissipated.

> RE DIPLOCK 1948
> (See above.)
> One of the issues was whether it was possible to trace in cases where the money had been used to pay off loans or where the monies have been used to improve properties.

Held
❖ (CA) Where the trust money had been used to pay off loans, the money is regarded as having been lost and therefore it is not possible to use the remedy with regard to this sum of money. Further, where the charities had expended money on the alteration or improvements of their assets or by erecting buildings on the land, the trust money could not be disentangled from the asset or land and therefore an application of the remedy of tracing would result in injustice. [1948] Ch. 465.

Boscawen v Bajwa 1995

The solicitors for the purchaser of the defendant's property also acted for the Abbey National which was providing the loan for the purchase of the property. A sum of £140,000 was transferred to the solicitors to be used to complete the purchase and until then it was to be held for the Abbey National. The solicitors paid £137,405 to the defendant's solicitors to hold for the former's order until completion. Further, a cheque for the balance of £2,595 issued by the purchaser's solicitors was dishonoured. Prior to that, the defendant's solicitors had paid £140,000 to the defendant's mortgagee to discharge the mortgage. However, the sale fell through and the plaintiff, who was a creditor of the defendant, obtained a charging order absolute over the property. The property was later sold and the net proceeds of sale paid into court. The issue arose as to who had a better claim to the money.

Held

❖ (CA) The Abbey National was entitled to the proceeds of sale as it had priority over the plaintiff. The Abbey National was entitled to be subrogated to the defendant's mortgagee legal charge as the money provided by it could be traced into the payment to the defendant's mortgagee. [1995] 4 All E.R. 182.

Commentary

The decision in *Re Diplock* has been followed by Scottish courts in *Style Financial Services Ltd v Bank of Scotland*, *The Times*, May 23, 1995. In *Boscawan v Bajwa*, the court distinguished *Re Diplock*. Millet L.J.'s view was that the favourable treatment given to innocent volunteers who mixed trust monies with his own in *Re Diplock* could not be applied to the facts of the present case. The parties were not wholly innocent volunteers although their conduct did fall short of dishonesty. Unlike *Re Diplock*, in *Boscawen v Bajwa*, although the money was used to pay off what was essentially a loan, it could not be regarded as having been totally dissipated. Accordingly, Abbey National could be subrogated to the position of the defendant's mortgagee and claim the proceeds of sale.

In *Law Society v Haider* [2003] EWHC 2486 the court allowed tracing from a payment discharging a mortgage into the house that was purchased with the mortgage and subsequently to follow the proceeds of sale of that house to a subsequent property that was acquired. In this case the mortgage was used to purchase the home and so could be traced into the house. It would be different if the monies were used to discharge an overdraft or a loan secured on a property that had already been acquired. In that case the monies would have been dissipated and cannot be traced into the property.

Key Principle

The remedy of tracing in equity cannot be used to trace into an overdrawn bank account.

> ### BISHOPSGATE INVESTMENT MANAGEMENT LTD (IN LIQUIDATION) V HOMAN 1994
>
> The plaintiff was the trustee of some pension schemes out of which monies had been improperly withdrawn. These monies were paid into the bank account of one of the Maxwell companies, which became insolvent. The bank account subsequently became overdrawn. The liquidators of the plaintiff sought to trace into this bank account.

Held

❖ (CA) The remedy of tracing in equity did not extend to tracing through an overdrawn bank account whether it had been overdrawn at the time the money was paid in or subsequently. [1994] 3 W.L.R. 1270.

Commentary

Where the money in question has been paid into an overdrawn account, the money is treated as having been lost and therefore tracing cannot be used. This is in line with earlier decisions such as *Re Diplock* (see above).

Key Principle

Where the trustee mixes the funds of two trusts or an innocent volunteer mixes trust funds with his own monies, the rule in *Clayton's Case* may be applied where it does not result in injustice.

> ### CLAYTON'S CASE 1816
>
> D was the senior partner of a firm of bankers where C was a client. After D's death C continued business with the firm until it went bankrupt. C made a claim against D's estate for the amount due to him from the firm at the date of D's death. Although the amounts paid by the firm to C after D's death were enough to pay the amount outstanding at D's death, C argued that these related to the amounts subsequently paid in by him to the account thereby leaving the original amount outstanding.

Held

A presumption that payments in were appropriated to the debts in the order they were incurred would apply in the case of a current account such as bank account. This presumption would not arise where there was an express declaration to the contrary at the time of payment. Since this was absent in this case, the presumption applied and therefore debts outstanding at the date of D's death had been fully discharged. (1816) 1 Mer. 572.

> BARLOW CLOWES INTERNATIONAL LTD (IN LIQUIDATION) V VAUGHAN 1992
> The plaintiff investment company went into liquidation and the issue arose as to whether the investors were entitled to trace into the remaining funds of the company under the rule in *Clayton's Case*.

Held

❖ (CA) The rule in *Clayton's Case* was a convenient method of determining competing claims where several beneficiaries' money had been mixed together in one account. Where injustice would result from its application or be impractical, the rule will not be applied. On the facts of the case, if the rule was to be applied, injustice would result. In the circumstances of the case, there was an alternative method of distribution. It was therefore appropriate to order the investors to share the funds of the company on a pari passu basis in proportion to the amounts due to them. [1992] 4 All E.R. 22.

Commentary

The rule in *Clayton's Case* is often referred to as the "first in first out" rule, i.e. that the money paid in first is deemed to be withdrawn first. This rule only applies in cases where the funds of two trusts are mixed together or where an innocent volunteer mixes his own monies with trust funds. It does not apply where trust monies are mixed with the trustee's own funds. Further, as noted in *Barlow Clowes International Ltd (in Liquidation) v Vaughan,* this is merely a rule of convenience and where it would be impractical or injustice would result from its application, the court need not apply it. The court also took this view in *Commerzbank Aktiengesellschaft v IMB Morgan Plc* [2004] EWHC 2771. Here, the court suggested that

> "where the rule in Clayton's Case does not apply, then (at least where the claimants have an equal right to be paid) it will normally be appropriate for the parties to be entitled to the mixed fund pari passu, i.e. the fund will be shared rateably amongst the beneficiaries according to the amount of their contributions".

Key Principle

Where a trustee mixes trust funds with his own monies, the trustee is presumed to have used his money first before the trust funds are used.

> RE HALLETT'S ESTATE 1880
> (See above.)

Held

❖ (CA) The trustee or fiduciary is deemed to have used his own monies first before using trust monies where the trustee has mixed trust funds with his own. The client and the beneficiaries were therefore entitled to trace into the solicitor's bank account. As there were sufficient funds to meet both claims, it was not necessary to decide which claim had priority. (1880) 13 Ch. D. 696.

> SPACE INVESTMENTS LTD V CANADIAN IMPERIAL BANK OF COMMERCE
> TRUST CO (BAHAMAS) 1986
> A bank trustee that had the express authority to deposit trust funds with itself did so and subsequently went into liquidation.

Held

❖ (PC) As the mixing of trust funds with the trustee's own monies had in this case been entirely lawful and proper, the beneficiaries retained no proprietary interest in the monies deposited with the bank trustee. Accordingly, tracing was not available against the assets of the Bank. [1986] 1 W.L.R. 1072.

Commentary

[1] In *Re Hallett's Estate*, Jessel M.R. decided that the solicitor must be presumed to have used his own money before using trust monies. Thus, the money left in the account must be trust monies, to which the client and the beneficiaries of the settlement were entitled.

[2] The decision of the Privy Council in *Space Investments Ltd v Canadian Imperial Bank of Commerce Trust Co (Bahamas)* should be restricted to situation where the bank is also a trustee. This was a suggestion by Lord Mustill in *Re Goldcorp Exchange* (above). It is also necessary for the bank trustee to have received express authorisation to deposit the trust monies with it.

[3] In *Sinclair Investments (UK) Ltd v Versailles Trade Finance Ltd (in administrative receivership)* [2011] EWCA Civ 347 the Court of Appeal was of the view that where a fiduciary in breach of trust had mixed funds held on trust with his own funds, the beneficiary could trace against the fiduciary still

holding the monies. However the onus of proof is on the fiduciary to establish on the balance of probabilities as to the part of the mixed fund which was his own monies.

Key Principle

The rule in *Re Hallett's Estate* is subject to the principle that until all the trust monies are restored, the beneficiary has a first charge over all the assets purchased with money from the bank account.

RE OATWAY 1903

The testator and M were co-trustees under a will. Trust monies were later paid into the testator's own bank account which contained some of his own money. He used some money from the account to purchase shares and subsequently dissipated the rest of the monies in the account. The testator died insolvent and the shares were subsequently sold. The question arose as to whether the beneficiaries were entitled to trace into the proceeds of sale of the shares.

Held

❖ (Ch) The trust had a first charge over the proceeds of sale of the shares. The beneficiaries' claim had to be satisfied before that of the creditors. [1903] 2 Ch. 356.

Commentary

Joyce J. stated (at 360) that

> "... when any money drawn out has been invested, and the investment remains in the name or under the control of the trustee, the rest of the balance having been dissipated by him, he cannot maintain that the investment which remains represent his own money alone, and that what has been spent and can no longer be traced and recovered was money belonging to the trust".

Joyce J. went on to say that in these circumstances, the order of priority of payments and withdrawals from the account is immaterial. This represents an exception to *Re Hallett's Estate*, above.

Key Principle

Where the trustee has mixed trust monies with his own monies and subsequently draws out more than his own money therefore spending some of the trust monies, any subsequent monies paid in will not be subject to tracing.

JAMES ROSCOE (BOLTON) LTD v WINDER 1915

W purchased the business of a company and one of the terms of the agreement was that W would collect some of the debts of the business and pay them over to the company. The debts amounting to £623 were collected by W. He paid £455 of this into his bank account. He then withdrew all the monies standing to his credit from the account but left £25 in the account. The money was used by W for his own purposes. Later, he paid some money into the account and when he died, there was a credit balance of £358 in the account. The company claimed a charge over this money.

Held

❖ (Ch) The company was only entitled to a charge over the £25 that had not been withdrawn. [1915] 1 Ch. 62.

Commentary

It was decided that where a trustee or fiduciary pays money into his own bank account and withdraws money from it but subsequently pays in more money, it cannot be presumed that the money paid in later was intended to replace the trust monies. Where the trust monies have been spent, tracing is only available against the trust monies that remained ("the lower intermediate balance" rule).

Key Principle

Where trust money has been mixed with the trustee's or the volunteer's own monies, the beneficiary can claim any profit arising from the investment to the extent to which the trust monies were used in the acquisition of the investment.

RE TILLEY'S WILL TRUSTS 1967

A testator appointed his wife as one of the executors, giving her a life interest in his estate with remainder to his son and daughter in equal shares. After his death in 1932, his widow redeemed the mortgage on some of the testator's property using £513 of her own money. By 1952, £2,237 was accumulated as trust capital and over this period of time she had mixed her own money with monies belonging to the trust. In 1945, she had an overdraft of £23,536. The daughter died in 1955 and the plaintiff was her personal representative. The widow died in 1959. The plaintiff applied for an order that the daughter's estate should, by virtue of her half interest in the testator's estate, have half the proportion of the profits of the purchases made by the widow. This was to the extent that the defendants, who were the widow's personal representatives, could not establish that these were bought with her own money. The defendants claimed that the plaintiff was only entitled to a charge on the widow's bank account for half the trust monies plus interest.

Held
❖ (Ch) As the trust monies were not used to purchase assets but to reduce her overdraft at the bank, tracing could not be used. [1967] Ch. 1179.

Commentary
Ungoed Thomas J. suggested obiter, that where there are profits arising from the use of trust monies in breach of trust, the beneficiary could adopt the investment and retain the profits arising from it to the extent to which the investment had been acquired through the use of trust monies.

Key Principle
Where trust monies had been used to partly pay the premiums of an insurance policy, the beneficiaries were entitled to claim restitution of the premiums plus a pro rata share of the profits or increase in value from the innocent third party insurance company.

FOSKETT V MCKEOWN 2000
M misappropriated money entrusted to him for the purchase of land in Portugal. He used part of the money to pay two of the premiums on his life assurance policy. Prior to the payment being made he had divested the beneficial interest in the policy to his three children. M committed suicide. The claimant, one of the prospective purchasers, claimed to be entitled to the proceeds of the policy. The Court of Appeal decided that the purchasers were only entitled to the return of the premiums with interest.

Held
❖ (HL) The purchasers' claim was an assertion of an equitable proprietary

interest arising out of the mixing of the premiums with the value of the policy. As such the purchasers were entitled to a pro rata share of the monies from the policy. [2000] 2 W.L.R. 1299.

Commentary
The House of Lords allowed the appeal by the claimants on the basis that they were claiming a proprietary interest in the policy monies arising from the fact that the money used to pay for some of the premiums belonged to them. Their Lordships recognised that as such, there was no discretion for the court to exercise. The Court in *Shalson v Russo* [2003] EWHC 1637 followed this case but stressed that the ruling in *Foskett v McKeown* did not remove the distinction between common law and equitable tracing. Equity still required that there must be some fiduciary duty in existence.

THINK POINT

Does the decision in *Re Hallett's Estate* contradict *Re Oatway*? How could the cases be reconciled?

Do you consider that there should be a difference between tracing at common law and in equity?

Equitable Remedies

....

13

INTRODUCTION

At common law the only remedy available is the remedy of damages. As this was sometimes not an adequate remedy, equity developed a range of remedies to be applied in cases where damages were to prove inadequate. The equitable remedies are discretionary in nature but at the same time are exercised in accordance with established principles especially the equitable maxims. The court will also not grant an equitable remedy unless it is satisfied that the defendant is able to comply with the order as "equity will do nothing in vain" – *Jones v Lipman* [1962] 1 All E.R. 442. The equitable remedies include:

- account;
- rescission;
- rectification;
- restitution;
- specific performance; and
- injunction.

This chapter will focus on the two remedies of specific performance and injunction.

....

SPECIFIC PERFORMANCE

The remedy of specific performance is essentially a court order compelling the defendant to comply with the terms of the contract between the parties. The Chancery Amendment Act 1858 (Lord Cairns' Act) which gives the court jurisdiction to award damages in lieu of or in addition to the remedy of specific performance is still available even though the Act has been repealed.

Key Principle ....
The court will be prepared to grant the remedy of specific performance where the plaintiff has performed his or her part of the bargain.

HART v HART 1881

The plaintiff, Mrs Hart, sought an order for the specific performance of an agreement for a separation deed, which formed part of the compromise between the parties in earlier divorce proceedings. As a result of the compromise, the plaintiff did not pursue further litigation in respect of the divorce.

Held

❖ (Ch) The court had power to enforce specific performance of an agreement to enter into a separation agreement. This agreement was not too vague to be enforced by the court. [1881] 18 Ch.D. 670.

Key Principle

The lack of mutual availability of the remedy of specific performance in a contract will be one of the factors that the court will take into account.

PRICE v STRANGE 1978

The plaintiff, who continued to occupy his maisonette after his underlease had expired, reached an oral agreement with the defendant. It was agreed that in return for remedial works to the property, the defendant would grant the plaintiff a new underlease at an increased rent. The defendant subsequently repudiated the agreement and refused to allow the plaintiff to continue with the remedial work. However, the defendant continued to accept rent for the next five months. The plaintiff applied for an order of specific performance.

Held

❖ (CA) Although the plaintiff had not carried out all the remedial work, specific performance was the appropriate remedy. In any case, the defendant had waived her right to claim lack of mutuality by allowing the plaintiff to do some of the remedial work and accepting the increased rent. [1978] Ch. 337.

Commentary

Traditionally, the lack of mutual availability of the remedy of specific performance to the parties in the case, was detrimental to an application for the remedy of specific performance: *Flight v Boland* (1882) 4 Russ. 298. However, it is now regarded as one of the factors the court will take into account in deciding whether to exercise its discretion together with the circumstances prevailing at the date of the hearing.

Key Principle

Where there is a contract for the sale of ascertained goods, the court has the power to grant specific performance.

> ### BEHNKE V BEDE SHIPPING CO 1927
> The plaintiff, a ship owner, brought an action against the defendant owners of the steamship "City", inter alia, for an order for specific performance of a contract. The defendants argued that it was not a case in which specific performance ought to be decreed.

Held

❖ (KB) Under s.52 of the Sale of Goods Act 1893 the court may, if it thinks fit, order specific performance of a contract for the sale of a ship. Accordingly, specific performance of the contract would be ordered. [1927] 1 K.B. 649.

Commentary

Section 52 (now of the Sale of Goods Act 1979) gives the court a power to order specific performance in any action for breach of contract to deliver specific or ascertained goods. However, specific performance of a contract for ascertained or specific goods will be granted only in cases where they are unique, because otherwise, damages will be an adequate remedy. In *Cohen v Roche* [1927] 1 K.B. 169, the court refused to order specific performance of a contract for the sale of eight Hepplewhite chairs. See also *Falcke v Gray* (1859) 4 Drew. 651.

In *Sharif v Sadiq*, Lawtel, May 18, 2004 in relation to the sale of land it was held that the formalities required under the Law of Property (Miscellaneous Provisions) Act 1989 had to be satisfied for specific performance to become available. An agreement to exchange contracts was not sufficient for these purposes.

Key Principle

In contracts for the sale of unascertained goods, the court may enforce the contract where the circumstances justify it.

> ### SKY PETROLEUM LTD V VIP PETROLEUM LTD 1974
> The plaintiff had an agreement with the defendant for the supply of petrol and diesel at a fixed price. At a time when supplies were restricted, and where it was unlikely that the plaintiff could find an alternative supplier, the defendant terminated the contract. The

plaintiff sought an injunction to restrain the defendant from with-holding supplies.

Held

❖ (Ch) To grant the injunction in this case would in effect be to grant an order for the specific performance of the contract to sell unascertained goods. Such an order would not normally be granted, as damages would be an adequate remedy. However, it was clear that damages would not be an adequate remedy. Accordingly, the injunction would be granted. [1974] 1 W.L.R. 576.

Commentary

The court acknowledged that this amounted to granting specific performance of a contract for the sale of unascertained goods. However, the court was of the view that it had jurisdiction to grant specific performance in cases where the circumstances justified it. In *Howard E Perry & Co Ltd v British Railways Board* [1980] 1 W.L.R. 1375, the court granted an order for the delivery of 500 tons of steel, as the steel was not readily available on the open market at the time, and damages would not adequately compensate the plaintiff. A different view was taken in *Societe Des Industries Metallurgiques SA v The Bronx Engineering Co Ltd* [1975] 1 Lloyd's Rep. 465, where an injunction was refused to prevent the removal of a piece of machinery which was readily available in the open market.

Key Principle

The court is reluctant to grant specific performance of a contract to pay money but may do so in appropriate cases.

BESWICK V BESWICK 1968

An uncle agreed in writing to transfer his business to his nephew in consideration of the nephew paying his aunt an annuity for life. After the uncle's death, the nephew made one payment to the aunt but refused further payments. The aunt commenced an action against the nephew in her capacity as the administratrix of her husband's estate and in her own capacity.

Held

❖ (HL) The aunt, in her capacity as administratrix of her husband's estate, was entitled to an order for specific performance of the contract entered into between her husband and the nephew. She could not succeed in her own capacity, as she was not a party to the contract. [1968] A.C. 58.

Commentary

The court granted the remedy of specific performance because damages would have been an inadequate remedy. If damages were awarded, the estate would only be granted nominal damages, as it had suffered no loss. The **Contracts (Rights of Third Parties) Act 1999** has now changed this. This Act allows third parties to the contract to sue the parties to the contract so long as the contract is for their benefit and the application of the Act has not been excluded. Hence, *Beswick v Beswick* would now be decided differently. Section 1(5) makes clear that the third party has all the remedies as a party to the contract including specific performance and injunctions.

Key Principle

The court is reluctant to grant an order for the specific performance of a contract requiring constant supervision.

> CO-OPERATIVE INSURANCE SOCIETY LTD V ARGYLL STORES (HOLDINGS) LTD 1997
>
> The defendant had a 35-year lease of premises and carried on the business of a supermarket. One of the covenants in the lease provided that the defendant would keep the supermarket open for the duration of the lease. The defendant sold the supermarket and stripped out the premises, despite a written notice by the plaintiff to keep it open as a supermarket. The Court of Appeal granted an order for specific performance. The defendants appealed to the House of Lords.

Held

❖ (HL) The appeal would be allowed because the practice of not granting orders which compelled a business to continue was based on sound sense and should not be departed from. One of the reasons for this was that the court was reluctant to grant an order for specific performance of a contract that required constant supervision. Further, the obligation contained in the clause could not be regarded as sufficiently precise to be capable of specific performance. [1997] 3 All E.R. 297.

Commentary

[1] This case was followed in *Spectrum Telecom Ltd v MCI Worldcom International Inc*, Lawtel, November 22, 1999 where the court granted a limited specific performance order in order to allow the claimant to find an alternative supplier.

[2] In appropriate cases, the court may be willing to grant an order for specific performance even though the contract requires constant supervision. For example, where the contract is clear as to what has to be done. In *Posner v Scott-Lewis* [1987] Ch. 25, the court ordered a landlord to appoint a resident porter in accordance with the covenants entered into by the landlord, as what had to be done was sufficiently defined.

Key Principle

In cases of contracts of employment, the court may grant an order of specific performance or equivalent remedy against an employer to continue the employment of the employee, where the employer retains full confidence in the employee's ability.

POWELL V LONDON BOROUGH OF BRENT 1987

The plaintiff was promoted to the post of Principal Benefits Officer after an interview. A few days after she reported for work, the defendant informed her that her appointment was defective, as there was a possible breach of the equal opportunity code. The plaintiff sought an injunction to restrain the defendant from advertising the post and requiring them to treat her as if she was properly appointed.

Held

❖ (CA) The plaintiff was entitled to an injunction until the trial of the action. Although as a general rule there can be no specific performance of a contract of service, the present case was an exception to it. The evidence showed that the defendant had full confidence in her ability to do the job. [1987] I.R.L.R. 446.

Commentary

[1] *De Francesco v Barnum* (1890) 45 Ch. D. 430 represents the equitable approach to such contracts where the court was reluctant to grant specific performance of contracts of employment as to do so might be to convert such contracts into contracts of slavery. Note also *Subaru Tecnica International Inc v Burns*, Lawtel, December 17, 2001.

[2] In cases where an order is sought against the employer, as a general rule, the courts are reluctant to grant such an order. However, where the employer retains full confidence in the ability of the employee and where it is just to do so, an order compelling the continued employment of the employee may be granted. See *Hill v C.A. Parsons & Co Ltd* [1972] Ch. 305.

Key Principle

In building contracts, where the work to be carried out is clear a court may grant a specific performance order.

> **MAYOR, ALDERMEN AND BURGESSES OF WOLVERHAMPTON V EMMONS 1901**
>
> The plaintiffs sold a plot of land abutting a street to the defendant. The defendant covenanted to erect buildings on it within a specified time. Subsequently, it was agreed that the defendant was to erect eight houses in accordance with specified plans. The defendant failed to perform the agreement.

Held

❖ (CA) The facts of the case fell within the exception to the general rule that specific performance of a building contract will not be ordered. An order would be made for the specific performance of the contract to build the eight houses in accordance with the specified plans. [1901] K.B. 514.

Commentary

Romer J. suggested that a building contract would be specifically enforced where three conditions are satisfied. They are: the work is sufficiently defined; the plaintiff has a substantial interest in the contract being performed such that damages would be an inadequate compensation; the defendant is in occupation of the plaintiff's land in accordance with the contract. Building contracts not satisfying these criteria may not be specifically enforced because of the need for constant supervision. In *North East Lincolnshire Borough Council v Millennium Park (Grimsby) Ltd*, *The Times*, October 31, 2002, the Court of Appeal stated, obiter, that specific performance would only be granted in exceptional circumstances where the defendant does not have possession of the land.

Key Principle

Although the court is reluctant to grant an order for specific performance of a repairing covenant against a tenant, it would do so in appropriate cases.

> **RAINBOW ESTATES LTD V TOKENHOLD LTD 1998**
>
> The issue was whether the court would grant an order for specific performance of a tenant's repairing covenant.

Held

❖ (Ch) Damages were an inadequate remedy as there was no proviso for re-entry on breach of covenant in the lease in order to allow the landlord to forfeit the lease. There was also no covenant giving the landlord the right to enter onto the premises in order to carry out the repairs and recoup the costs from the tenant. [1998] 2 All E.R. 860.

Commentary

Normally, the court would not grant an order for specific performance of a tenant's repairing covenant in a lease because of the issue of constant supervision. However, the facts of the case were sufficiently unique to justify the court's departure from the general rule. The court stressed that it was prepared to grant such an order so long as there was no injustice or oppression on the tenant and provided it was not seen as a way of avoiding the effect of the Leasehold Property (Repairs) Act 1938. However, the court has granted specific performance of a landlord's obligation to repair: *Jeune v Queen's Cross Properties Ltd* [1974] Ch. 97. In *Bluestorm v Portvale Holdings*, Lawtel, February 13, 2004 the tenant was not permitted the equitable remedy to set off service charges against the landlord's non-performance of a repairing obligation. This was because the non-performance by the landlord was itself caused by the tenant's failure to pay service charges.

Key Principle

In deciding whether to grant specific performance, the court will take into account the application of the equitable maxims.

QUADRANT VISUAL COMMUNICATIONS LTD V HUTCHISON TELEPHONE (UK) LTD 1993
The defendant agreed to purchase the plaintiff's portable and car telephone business. The consideration was partly calculated on the number of subscribers signing up after the sale. The plaintiff failed to disclose that it had entered into an agreement with a third party for the provision of free portable phones in return for vouchers. The plaintiff sought an order for specific performance.

Held

❖ (CA) After taking into account the plaintiff's conduct, the court would refuse to grant an order for the specific performance of the defendant's contractual obligations. The plaintiff did not come with clean hands as they failed to disclose the existence of the other agreement. The court's discretion in granting an order for specific performance could not be fettered by a term in the agreement. [1993] B.C.L.C. 442.

> PATEL V ALI 1984
> The defendant husband and wife contracted to sell their house to the plaintiffs. The husband became bankrupt thereby delaying the sale. In the meantime, the wife became ill and whilst pregnant with her second child, had one leg amputated. The husband ended up in prison and the wife later gave birth to a third child. As a result of this, she was dependent on relatives and friends living nearby.

Held

❖ (Ch) The court was justified in refusing specific performance of the contract on the grounds of hardship arising after the contract. Accordingly, it would be just to discharge the order for specific performance. [1984] Ch. 283.

Commentary

In deciding whether to grant specific performance, the court will have regard to the equitable maxims and therefore where the claimant's conduct is reprehensible, or where there is hardship, the court can refuse to grant the order. In *Patel v Ali*, the court took into account circumstances arising after the contract had been entered into. This has been followed in *Matila Ltd v Lisheen Properties Ltd* [2010] EWHC 1832 where the claimants sought specific performance of a number of contracts for the grant of leasehold interests over a number of residential apartments and commercial units in Southport. One of the issues the court had to consider was whether the claimants could succeed in an application for specific performance and, if so, whether nonetheless specific performance should be refused in the exercise of the discretion of the court. The court decided that as a matter of principle, the impossibility to complete the contract due to financial hardship could be a valid ground for not granting specific performance. However, on the facts of the case, the defendant had not been open about its position and hence it did not have sufficient information to conclude that completion of the contract was in fact impossible.

Other relevant factors include the doctrine of laches or delay (see *Mills v Haywood* (1877) 6 Ch. D. 196; *Hazard Brothers & Co Ltd v Fairfield Properties Co (Mayfair) Ltd* [1977] 121 S.J. 793, *Eagleview Ltd v Worthgate Ltd*, Lawtel, October 7, 1998 and *Sharma v Farlam Ltd* [2009] EWHC 1622) and questions of public policy. It was stated in *Fisher v Brooker* [2009] 4 All E.R. 789 that "laches is an equitable doctrine, under which delay can bar a claim to equitable relief".

Key Principle

The court can grant damages in equity in lieu of specific performance. This may be useful where for some reason common law damages are not available.

> ### WROTH V TYLER 1974
> The plaintiff was the purchaser of a house from the defendant. The purchase could not be completed because the defendant's wife registered a right of occupation under the Matrimonial Homes Act 1967. The house was worth £7,500 at the time but its value rose to £11,500 by the time of the trial.

Held

❖ (Ch) It was inappropriate to grant specific performance in this case. However, damages would be awarded in lieu thereof under Lord Cairns' Act. Damages awarded in equity must be a true substitute for specific performance. Therefore, the damages will be based on the difference in value between the date of the contract and the date of trial. [1973] 1 Ch. 30.

> ### JOHNSON V AGNEW 1978
> The defendant contracted to buy a piece of land from the plaintiffs but failed to complete the purchase. The plaintiffs obtained an order for specific performance. Before the order was enforced, the mortgagees of the property took possession and sold the property for a lower price. The plaintiffs then claimed for an order that the defendant should pay the balance of the purchase price less the amount from the sale or alternatively, a declaration that the contract had been repudiated and damages at common law.

Held

❖ (HL) As the order for specific performance could not be complied with, the plaintiff was entitled to apply to the court to end the contract and obtain damages appropriate to the breach of contract. The court could use its power under Lord Cairns' Act to award damages in lieu of specific performance. [1978] Ch. 176.

Commentary

The House of Lords in *Johnson v Agnew* stated that although Lord Cairns' Act allowed for damages to be awarded in some cases where damages were not recoverable at common law, the assessment of damages should be on the same basis. The Act did not warrant the assessment of damages otherwise than on a common law basis. Therefore, if *Wroth v Tyler* is taken as authority that the quantum of damages at common law and equity can be different, that is to be doubted. There is also some doubt whether the damages awarded in *Wroth v Tyler* could not have been awarded at common law. In the case of a breach of contract, the damages should normally be awarded at the date of the breach of contract. In *Johnson v Agnew*, this was the date when specific performance was no longer possible. Where the facts of the case warrant it, a departure from the normal rule is permitted, if, it not doing so would cause injustice.

INJUNCTIONS

The terminology and criteria for the grant of injunctions has been changed by the Civil Procedure Rules 1998. Under r.l, the court is directed to have regard to the overriding objective to ensure that the cases are dealt with justly. This includes ensuring that the parties are on equal footing, saving expense, dealing with the case in ways that are proportionate to the amount of the claim, the importance and complexity of the case and the financial position of the parties. More importantly, the courts are directed to ensure that the case is dealt with expeditiously and fairly.

[a] Interim prohibitory injunction (previously known as interlocutory injunction)

The High Court's jurisdiction to grant interim injunctions is found in s.37 of the Supreme Court Act 1981 and the County Court's jurisdiction is from s.38 of the County Courts Act 1984. The remedy of injunction is a remedy in personam i.e. that it acts against the person. Hence, the remedy is available where the defendant can be served with the order even though he may be outside the jurisdiction—s.37(3) of the **Supreme Court Act 1981**. Where the defendant fails to comply with the order this amounts to a contempt of court punishable by imprisonment, fine or in the case of a company, the sequestration of property. For example, in *Crystalmews Ltd (in Liquidation) v Metterick* [2006] EWHC 2653, the defendant was held in contempt of court for failing to comply with a freezing order which had not yet been served on her but she had become aware of it.

There are a number of defences to the remedy of an injunction. These include:

- delay—in the case of an interim injunction there is a need to show urgency otherwise the injunction can be decided at trial (*E.E. & Brian*

Smith (1928) Ltd v Hodson [2007] EWCA Civ 1210). In the case of a final injunction, delay is not fatal (*Kelsen v Imperial Tobacco Co Ltd* [1957] 2 All E.R. 343);

- acquiescence by the claimant (*Sayers v Collyer* [1884] Ch. D. 103);
- hardship; and
- the conduct of the plaintiff on the basis of the equitable maxim "he who comes to equity must come with clean hands".

Key Principle

In deciding whether to grant an interim injunction, the court takes into account various factors.

AMERICAN CYANAMID CO V ETHICON LTD 1978

The plaintiff patented a synthetic absorbable surgical suture. The defendant also produced synthetic absorbable sutures but with a different chemical composition. The plaintiff applied for an interlocutory injunction to restrain the defendant from selling the sutures.

Held

❖ (HL) The court should consider the balance of convenience in deciding whether to grant an interlocutory injunction. If there was any doubt as to whether damages would compensate the parties, it was prudent to preserve the status quo. In the circumstances of the case, the injunction should be granted. [1975] A.C. 396.

ARACI V FALLON 2011

The claimant applied for an interim prohibitory injunction where the claimant sought to restrain the defendant from riding any horse other than a horse named "Native Khan" at the Epsom Derby in June 2011. The claimant argued that it was a breach of the Retainer Agreement between the claimant and the defendant where the defendant agreed to ride the claimant's horse "Native Khan". The defendant had given notice that he would not be able to ride that horse and was planning to ride the horse "Recital". The court refused to grant the injunction on the basis that damages were an adequate remedy.

Held

❖ (CA) The appeal would be allowed and an interim injunction would be granted. Although the agreement provided for the assessment of damages for less serious breaches of contract this does not imply that damages would be an adequate remedy in every case. The clause in respect of the payment of damages was focussed on the defendant refusing to ride his horse but it did not provide for the consequences of the defendant acting in breach of a negative obligation. The balance of convenience test did not apply as the defendant was close to breaking his contract. In addition damages would not be easy to calculate in this case and it was also not clear if the defendant could pay them. [2011] EWCA Civ 668.

Commentary

The House of Lords in *American Cyanamid Co v Ethicon Ltd* suggested that in deciding whether to grant an interlocutory injunction, the court should take into account the following matters: whether there is a serious question to be tried; the adequacy of damages to the plaintiff and the defendant; the balance of convenience—this would include the maintenance of the status quo and any special factors; and the relative strength of the parties' case, where all the other factors are evenly balanced. In *Wake Forest University Health Services v Smith and Nephew Plc* (2009) F.S.R. 11, the court stressed that in deciding the balance of convenience, one of the important factors was the duration which the injunction would last. In that case, the court granted the injunction as it would only last for a relatively short period of time and hence it was appropriate to maintain the status quo.

In view of the **Civil Procedure Rules 1998**, the court will have to bear in mind the overriding objective when deciding whether to grant an interim or other injunction. The question still remains as to what criteria the court will then follow. On the one hand, there are cases such as *Biguzzi v Rank Leisure Plc* [1999] 1 W.L.R. 1926, where Lord Woolf stated that the Civil Procedure Rules are a self contained code and that the "earlier authorities are no longer generally of relevance". On the other hand, in *PG Mavros (Private) Ltd v Pouter*, Lawtel, July 23, 1999 and *United Pan-Europe Communications NV v Deutsche Bank AG*, Lawtel, May 19, 2000, the court applied *American Cyanamid Co v Ethicon Ltd* without real consideration of how they related to the Rules.

In *National Commercial Bank Jamaica Ltd v Olint Corp Ltd* [2009] UKPC 16, a decision of the Privy Council, Lord Hoffman stated that

" ... the purpose of an interlocutory injunction is to preserve the status quo ... [t]he court may order a defendant to do something or not to do something else, but such restrictions on the defendant's freedom of action will have consequences ... which a court has to take into account. The purpose of such an injunction is to improve the chances of the court being able to do justice after a determination of the merits at the trial. At the interlocutory stage, the court must therefore assess whether granting or withholding an injunction is more likely to produce a just result".

His Lordship went on to state that

" ... in practice, however, it is often hard to tell whether either damages or the cross-undertaking will be an adequate remedy and the court has to engage in trying to predict whether granting or withholding an injunction is more or less likely to cause irremediable prejudice (and to what extent) if it turns out that the injunction should not have been granted or withheld, as the case may be. The basic principle is that the court should take whichever course seems likely to cause the least irremediable prejudice to one party or the other".

This provides some authoritative guidance as to the basis for which the court should consider in deciding whether to grant an interlocutory injunction or not.

Key Principle

In applying the American Cyanamid guidelines, the court should avoid having to resolve difficult issues of fact and law. Any view as to the relative strength of the parties' case should be reached only where it is apparent from the affidavit evidence.

SERIES 5 SOFTWARE LTD V CLARKE 1996

The plaintiffs were the owners of a software package called QC 2000. The defendants, who were the plaintiff's employees, removed the software, client lists, the accounts and equipment. They resigned from the company claiming that their salaries had not been paid. The plaintiff applied for an interlocutory order to restrain the defendants from disclosing their trade secrets to third parties or from contacting any of its clients.

Held

❖ (Ch) The court should avoid having to resolve difficult issues of fact and law when deciding whether to grant an interlocutory order. Any view as to the relative strength of the parties' case should be reached only where it is apparent from the affidavit evidence. On the facts, having regard to the adequacy or inadequacy of damages and the balance of convenience, it was inappropriate to grant the order. [1996] 1 All E.R. 853.

Commentary

Laddie J. stated (at 865) that

> "... [i]n my view Lord Diplock did not intend ... to exclude consideration of the strength of the parties' case in most applications for interlocutory relief. It appears to me that what is intended is that the court should not attempt to resolve difficult issues of fact or law on an application for interlocutory relief. If, on the other hand, the court is able to come to a view as to the strength of the parties' case on the credible evidence, then it can do so".

The consideration of the relative strength of the parties' case is not therefore as a last resort. It is difficult to reconcile this with *American Cyanamid Co v Ethicon Ltd.*

Key Principle

The American Cyanamid guidelines are applied with a degree of flexibility.

OFFICE OVERLOAD V GUNN 1977

The plaintiff applied for an interlocutory injunction against the defendant, who was his employee, restraining the defendant from competing with the plaintiff in accordance with the restraint of trade covenant in the contract of employment.

Held

❖ (CA) The merits of the case had to be considered as the interlocutory injunction would effectively dispose of the matter since the trial was unlikely to take place until several years after. [1977] F.S.R. 3.

Commentary

There are a number of situations where the American Cyanamid guidelines are inapplicable. They include:

(a) where the defendant has no arguable defence (*Patel v W H Smith (Eziot) Ltd* [1987] 1 W.L.R. 853);

(b) where there is a likelihood of a defence under s.221 of the Trade Union and Labour Relations (Consolidation) Act 1992; cases involving public rights (*Secretary of State for the Home Department v Central Broad-casting Ltd, The Times,* January 28, 1993);

(c) where it would finally dispose of the matter (*Cayne v Global Natural Resources Plc* [1984] 1 All K.R. 225); and

(d) applications for interim mandatory injunctions (*Shephard Homes Ltd v Sandham* [1971] 1 Ch. 340).

It was stressed by the Privy Council in *National Commercial Bank Jamaica Ltd v Olint Corp Ltd* [2009] UKPC 16 that the decision whether to grant an interlocutory or interim injunction was not a tick box exercise as that failed to do justice in the context of the complexity of a decision as to whether or not to grant such an injunction.

Key Principle

The court has to have regard to the Human Rights Act 1998 including the freedom of expression and right of privacy in appropriate cases.

IMUTRAN LTD V UNCAGED CAMPAIGNS LTD 2001

The claimant applied for the continuations of various injunctions against the defendants restraining the misuse of confidential information and infringement of copyright in respect of the claimant's research into xenotransplantation. The defendants argued that in considering whether to continue with the injunctions, the court should consider the right of freedom of expression contained in art.10 of the European Convention on Human Rights and the provisions of s.12(4) of the **Human Rights Act 1998**.

Held

❖ (Ch D) On the facts of the case, although the **Human Rights Act 1998** required the court to pay particular attention to the right of the freedom of expression, there was nothing in this case that would lead the court to the conclusion that the injunction ought to be refused. The requirement in the Act for the claimant to be in a position where it could be shown that its case had a likelihood of succeeding was slightly more onerous than the real prospect of success requirement as found in *American Cyanamid Co v Ethicon Ltd* but that the difference is so minimal as to make no real difference. The injunctions would therefore be continued. (2001) H.R.L.R. 31.

The defendant appealed against the first instance decision where an injunction was granted to prevent it from publishing or further publishing the wedding photographs of Michael Douglas and Catherine Zeta-Jones. The third claimant was the owner of OK! Magazine with whom the first and second claimant had granted exclusive rights for the publication of those photographs.

Held

❖ (CA) Although English law recognised the right of privacy as provided for in art.8 of the European Convention on Human Rights, there are different degrees of privacy and this had an impact on the interaction between the right to privacy and the freedom of expression. The wedding in question was not a private affair and the first and second claimant had sold part of the privacy to the third claimant in return for a substantial amount of money. The balance of convenience was in the defendant's favour because the claimant's loss could be quantified if the injunction was refused. Accordingly the injunction would be discharged. [2001] 2 W.L.R. 992.

TSE v Newsgroup Newspapers Ltd 2011

The first claimant, who was a married footballer with children, had an adulterous relationship with the second claimant. A journalist contacted the first claimant's representative in respect of a story that was due to be published about their relationship. The claimants obtained an interim injunction prohibiting the publication of anything that would identify the claimants as the applicants or information about their relationship.

Held

❖ (QBD) In considering the effect of the European Convention on Human Rights and s.12(4) of the **Human Rights Act 1998** the information referred to which was private information was no longer secret and as such one of the purposes of the injunction was no longer relevant. However, the extent and the tone of publications showed that the evidence originally submitted was correct. There was a need to grant the injunction to prevent harassment and intrusion into the lives of the claimants as well as the first claimant's family. Accordingly the injunction should continue. [2011] EWHC 1308.

Commentary

These cases reflect the continuing importance and impact of the **Human Rights Act 1998** in English jurisprudence and the approach the courts are adopting in the application of the Act in its decisions.

The approach the courts have taken in respect of dealing with injunctions in respect of private information is a two stage process with the court undertaking a balancing act: *Murray v Express Newspapers Plc* [2009] Ch. 481. The first stage is to decide if there is a reasonable expectation of privacy assessed as an objective question i.e. what the reasonable expectation is of a person affected by the publicity. Only if the first stage is answered in the affirmative does the court consider the second stage which is

> "...whether in all the circumstances the interest of the owner of the information must yield to the right to freedom of expression conferred on the publisher by Article 10".

In some instances the fact that the private information is already widely known may negate the grant of an injunction. In *LNS v Persons Unknown* [2010] EWHC 119, the court refused to grant an interim injunction preventing the publication of information in respect of a footballer's personal relationship as well as reporting on the application itself. The judge initially granted an interim injunction but refused to renew it as it was clear that the information was already widely circulated by word of mouth so the injunction would not serve any purpose. Tugendhat J. (at para.130) stated that

> "I accept that the information sought to be protected is no[w] in the public domain in the sense that there is nothing left to be protected. But the evidence is that there has been wide circulation amongst those involved in the sport in question, including agents and others, and not just amongst those directly engaged in the sport. If the injunction ought otherwise be granted, I would not refuse it on this basis. But the fact that the information has become as widely available to so many people, means that an injunction is less necessary or proportionate than would otherwise be the case".

See also *Doncaster MBC v BBC* [2010] EWHC 53 where the court refused to grant an injunction on the basis that there was no evidence to show that the BBC was planning to release the confidential information and *Donald v Ntuli* [2010] EWCA Civ 1276. The latter has been followed in *MNB v News Group Newspapers Ltd* [2011] EWHC 528 and *XJA v News Group Newspapers Ltd* [2010] EWHC 3174.

In *KGM v Newsgroup Newspapers Ltd* [2011] All E.R. (D) 281 the court was reluctant to grant unlimited protection against publication of private information. The court decided it was unable to say that it would have been necessary or proportionate, either in the interests of the administration of justice or for the protection of the Claimant under Article 8, to restrict the freedom of expression under Article 10 of any of these Respondents. In *Goodwin v NGN Ltd* [2011] EWHC 1437 the applicant who was the former chief executive of the Royal Bank of Scotland sought to restrain the disclosure of a sexual relationship between himself and a female work colleague. NGN applied to vary the grant of an injunction claiming that there was public interest in its disclosure. The court decided that it would be appropriate to allow disclosure of the work colleague's job description but not her name. Although the publication would be an intrusion into her privacy it was not such as to warrant the denial of the newspapers right of the freedom of expression under Article 10 of the ECHR. Tugendhat J. stated obita that

> " ... it is in the public interest that there should be public dis-
> cussion of the circumstances in which it is proper for a chief
> executive (or other person holding public office or exercising
> official functions) should be able to carry on a sexual relationship
> with an employee in the same organisation. It is in the public
> interest that newspapers should be able to report upon cases
> which raise a question as to what should or should not be a
> standard in public life".

Key Principle
The court can award damages in lieu of an injunction.

JAGGARD V SAWYER 1995
The defendant, in breach of covenant, built a house. This also resulted in trespass as access to the house was by way of a private road. The plaintiff commenced proceedings for an injunction to restrain use of this private road.

Held
❖ (CA) An injunction would not be granted, as this would cause the house to be landlocked. The injury to the plaintiff was small and it was possible to estimate its value in monetary terms. Further, having regard to the plaintiff's failure to apply for an injunction early, and the defendant's conduct, it would be oppressive to grant such an injunction. In assessing damages, the court would value the plaintiff's rights at a price that is reasonable for the release or relaxation of the covenant and the grant of a right of way. [1995] 1 W.L.R. 269.

REGAL V PAUL PROPERTIES LTD 2007

The claimant claimed that the defendants who were developing two properties across from his property had infringed his right to light and sought a mandatory injunction compelling the destruction of part of the building. At first instance the court decided that there was a nuisance but granted damages in lieu of an injunction.

Held

❖ (CA) The court was wrong to impose the burden on the claimant to prove why damages should not be awarded. Once there was an actionable nuisance, the claimant was entitled to the injunction to prevent the infringement of his rights. Hence, the appeal would be allowed and injunction granted. [2007] Ch. 135.

Commentary

In *Jaggard v Sawyer* [1995] 1 W.L.R. 269, damages were awarded in equity, which otherwise would not be available at common law. There is no inconsistency with *Johnson v Agnew*, which, although is authority for the proposition that the assessment of damages at common law and equity should be the same, their Lordships recognised that one exception to this was where damages were not available at common law. In the latter situation the court did not have to follow the common law rules.

In *Mortimer v Bailey* [2004] All E.R. 436, the court declined to award damages in lieu of an injunction. An injunction to pull down building works erected in breach of a restrictive covenant was granted. It was said to be clear that the defendant had wilfully broken the covenant taking the calculated risk that damages would be granted. The decision in *Regan v Paul Properties Ltd* [2007] Ch. 135 follows this approach but also makes it clear that the burden to prove why damages should not be awarded is not on the claimant but on the defendant.

A useful guide as to the award of damages in lieu of injunction is found in the dicta of Smith L.J. in *Shelfer v City of London Lighting Co* [1895] 1 Ch. 287. It was suggested that damages would be awarded where:

(a) the injury to the plaintiff was small;
(b) the injury can be valued in monetary terms;
(c) the injury could be compensated adequately by a small payment; and
(d) it would be oppressive to grant the injunction.

It must be emphasised that these are merely guidelines and they have not always been universally applied. However, they were applied by the Court of Appeal in *Jaggard v Sawyer*, above. See also *Horsford v Bird* [2006] U.K.P.C. 3.

[b] Freezing injunctions (previously known as Mareva injunctions)

Key Principle
Where it is likely that the defendant may dispose of or remove his assets from the jurisdiction, the court has the jurisdiction to grant an injunction to restrain him from doing so.

> MAREVA COMPANIA NAVIERA SA V INTERNATIONAL BULKCARRIERS SA 1975
> The defendants chartered the plaintiff's ship, the Mareva, which it sub-chartered to a third party. After having paid two instalments, the defendant defaulted in its payment to the plaintiffs. The plaintiffs obtained an injunction preventing the defendant from disposing or removing any of its monies.

Held
❖ (CA) Where it appeared that a debt was due and owing and there was a danger that the defendant may dispose of its assets so as to defeat the plaintiff's claim, the court had jurisdiction to grant an injunction to prevent this. This was a proper case for such an injunction to be granted. [1975] 2 Lloyd's Rep. 509.

Commentary
Lord Diplock in *The Siskina* [1979] A.C. 210, stated that the purpose of this type of injunction was to ensure that a fund was available within the jurisdiction if the court found in the plaintiff's favour. Therefore it would not be appropriate to grant a freezing order merely because the defendant was short of money as this did not necessarily prove that he intended or would intend to dissipate his assets: *Midas Merchant Bank Plc v Bello*, Lawtel, October 14, 2002. See also *Lawson v Mizzi* [2010] EWHC 55 where an order was granted as the evidence was such that there was a risk of the defendant dissipating her assets and fleeing the jurisdiction.

The approach was reemphasised in *JSC BTA Bank v Solodchenko* [2010] EWCA Civ 1436 where Longmore L.J. stated that the freezing injunction

> " ... can only be granted when the claimant has a good arguable case and there are reasonable grounds to suppose that a defendant may dissipate his assets before judgment is pronounced. The purpose of the injunction is to preserve a defendant's assets, subject to dealings in the ordinary course of business so that, if and when a judgment is pronounced, the defendant still has assets to meet that judgment. The injunction

provides no security; if, after judgment, the defendant's assets, as preserved, are less than his liabilities, a judgment creditor has no greater call on those assets than any other unsecured creditor".

Exceptionally, the court may be prepared to indicate in principle and in advance of the cause of action arising whether it would be prepared to grant an injunction in event that the cause of action does arise: *Re Q's Estate* (1999) 1 Lloyd's Rep. 931. However the court stressed that the discretion was to be exercised carefully and was not to be abused.

The courts can grant a freezing injunction as an aid to the execution of a judgment in order to prevent the judgment debtor from disposing his assets: *Masri v Consolidated Contractors Co SAL* [2008] EWCA Civ 303.

Key Principle
The freezing injunction is not intended to pressurise the defendant into settling the case.

CAMDEX INTERNATIONAL LTD V BANK OF ZAMBIA (NO. 2) 1997
The plaintiff obtained a Mareva injunction against the defendant, which prevented the release of unissued Zambian bank notes to the defendant.

Held
❖ (CA) The purpose of such an injunction was to prevent the removal or dissipation of assets from the jurisdiction. It was not intended to pressurise the defendant into settling the case. The Zambian bank notes had no value on the open market until they were issued. As such the notes were not assets to which the injunction could attach. [1997] 1 All E.R. 728.

Commentary
This was a case where public policy was relevant. If the court prevented the defendant, the Central Bank of Zambia, from getting the bank notes, it would have caused substantial national hardship. However, the principle from the case is clear—the purpose of the injunction is to preserve assets until trial, not pressurise the defendant into settling the case.

The application for a freezing injunction should be ancillary to an existing cause of action.

The plaintiff advanced a large sum of money to the defendant for use in a business in Russia. The defendant misappropriated the money. The defendant was detained by a Monaco court and ordered that the defendant's assets in Monaco be frozen. The plaintiff made an ex parte application in Hong Kong for a worldwide Mareva injunction. The issue arose as to whether the Hong Kong court had jurisdiction to grant such an injunction against a defendant who was out of jurisdiction in support of an action in a foreign jurisdiction.

Held

❖ (PC) A Mareva injunction could not stand independently of a substantive claim for relief within the court's jurisdiction. [1996] 1 A.C. 284.

Commentary

[1] The rule used to be that the court had no jurisdiction to grant a freezing (Mareva) injunction where it is not ancillary to a cause of action within the jurisdiction of the court. Under s.25 of the Civil Jurisdictions and Judgments Act 1982, a High Court has jurisdiction to grant a Mareva injunction in England before the trial or after judgment, even though there is no cause of action in England, so long as a court in one of the contracting states has jurisdiction. An example of the application of this provision is the case of *Credit Suisse Fides Trust SA v Cuoghi* [1997] 3 W.L.R. 871. The Court of Appeal refused to discharge a worldwide Mareva injunction against a defendant to proceedings in Switzerland, but who was resident and domiciled in the UK. Since Switzerland was a Lugano Convention contracting state, and the subject matter of the proceedings was within the Brussels Convention, the court had jurisdiction under s.25 to grant relief. The court noted that nothing in the section prevented it from granting a worldwide Mareva injunction.

In *Ryan v Friction Dynamics Ltd*, Lawtel, June 5, 2000, the court stressed that the court must use particular caution in exercise of the jurisdiction under s.25 as the English court may not be apprised of all the facts of the case. Further, the court stated that under s.25, where there was no cause of action within jurisdiction, it was desirable that the injunction contained the same terms as the order of the foreign court and should indicate which court has the primary role for enforcing the orders. In *Banco Nacional de Comercio Exterior SNC v Empresa de Telecomunicationes de Cuba SA* [2007] 2 All E.R. 1093, a worldwide freezing order was refused because it was inexpedient to do so. This was because there was a domestic order protecting assets in the UK and as there were other enforcement proceedings in other jurisdictions, confusion and disharmony may result from the order being granted.

[2] Section 25 has been extended by the **Civil Jurisdiction and Judgments Act 1982** (Interim Relief) Order 1997, to cover proceedings commenced or about to be commenced in a non-contracting state. If the situation in *Mercedes Benz AG v Leiduck* were to arise in the UK, the court can now grant interim relief.

[3] In *Fourie v Le Roux*, *The Times*, October 8, 2004 it was held that the lower court did not have jurisdiction to grant a freezing injunction unless the applicant had already or was immediately or almost immediately issuing proceedings after the grant of the order. In *Raja v van Hoogstraten* (2004) 4 All E.R. 793 the Court of Appeal found that the lower court was wrong to proceed with the hearing to commit in the absence of the contemnor where matters beyond his control prevented him from attending.

Key Principle

Specific criteria have to be satisfied before a freezing injunction is granted.

THIRD CHANDRIS SHIPPING CORPORATION V UNIMARINE SA 1979
The plaintiffs, who were the respective owners of three ships, had substantial claims against the defendant who had chartered their vessels. They obtained three separate Mareva injunctions restraining the defendant from removing assets, including monies in its bank account in London.

Held

❖ (CA) As there were assets within the jurisdiction and there was a real risk that the defendant would dissipate or dispose of its assets before trial, the defendant's application to discharge the injunctions would be dismissed. [1979] 1 Q.B. 645.

Commentary

Lord Denning (at 668–669) suggested that certain guidelines must be complied with. The plaintiff should:

(a) make full and frank disclosure of all material facts which he has knowledge of;
(b) give particulars of his claim against the defendant;

(c) give reasons for believing that the defendant has assets within the jurisdiction;

(d) give grounds for believing that there is a real risk of the assets being disposed of or dissipated before the judgment is satisfied; and

(e) give an undertaking in damages.

Failure to make full and frank disclosure of all material facts could result in the court discharging the injunction in appropriate cases. In *Gulf Interstate Oil Co LLC v Ant Trade and Transport Ltd of Malta* [1999] 1 Lloyd's Rep. 867, the court discharged the freezing injunction as the non-disclosures were serious and would have affected the court's decision. A similar conclusion was reached in *Itsalat International Co Ltd v Allied TC Plc* [2009] EWHC 1265.

In addition, general equitable principles would be applicable and if there is an inordinate delay in applying for a freezing injunction without any valid explanation, then the court may refuse an application for such an order. In *Cherney v Neuman* [2009] EWHC 1743 the court refused an application for a worldwide freezing injunction where the application was only made eight months after the commencement of the main proceedings. The court was of the view that such injunctions are normally requested because there is a serious risk of dissipation of assets and given that the application was only made eight months after the action had commenced there was clearly no risk of dissipation or secretion of the defendants' assets.

Key Principle

The court has jurisdiction to grant a freezing injunction covering worldwide assets.

REPUBLIC OF HAITI V DUVALIER 1990

The plaintiffs commenced action in France against the defendant to recover US $120 million alleged to have been embezzled by the defendants. The plaintiffs issued a writ in England, claiming orders restraining the defendants from disposing certain assets and requiring disclosure of their oilier assets.

Held

❖ (CA) The court had jurisdiction to grant a Mareva injunction covering worldwide assets pending trial of the action. However, cases where such orders are granted will be rare. [1990] 1 Q.B. 202.

Commentary

In *Motorola Credit Corp v Uzan* [2004] 1 W.L.R. 113 the Court of Appeal ruled on a case which involved applications for worldwide freezing orders in relation to litigation in another jurisdiction where the defendants were not domiciled or resident in the jurisdiction. In such a case it was said that there were five considerations to bear in mind:

i)   would the order interfere with the management of the case in the leading jurisdiction;

ii)   would the law of the leading jurisdiction allow for such an order;

iii) would the orders be a cause of disharmony;

iv) would there be a conflict as to jurisdiction; and

v)   would the court be making an order which it could not in practice enforce.

This was applied in *Mobil Cerro Negro Ltd v Petroleos de Venezuela SA* (2008) 1 Lloyd's Rep. 684 where the court stressed that the defendant or the dispute should have a sufficiently close link with the jurisdiction of the court or there must be some other compelling fact to support the proceedings in the absence of such a close link.

Key Principle

In granting a freezing injunction covering worldwide assets, the court imposes strict safeguards.

DERBY & CO LTD V WELDON 1989
The plaintiffs sued the defendants, inter alia, for breach of contract, negligence, breach of fiduciary duty, deceit and conspiracy to defraud, by having dealt in cocoa and cocoa futures for their own benefit. The plaintiffs applied for a Mareva injunction covering the first two defendants' assets both within and outside the jurisdiction. The plaintiffs appealed against the decision not to grant the worldwide Mareva injunction.

Held

❖ (CA) In addition to satisfying the normal criteria for the grant of a Mareva injunction, it was also necessary for the plaintiff to show that any English assets available were insufficient, that there were foreign assets and that there was a real risk of disposal or dissipation of these assets. The court must also be satisfied by undertaking or proviso that the defendant would not be oppressed by exposure to multiplicity of proceedings, be protected against misuse of the information obtained from the disclosure order and that third parties would be adequately protected. In the circumstances of the case, it must be just and convenient to grant a worldwide Mareva. Accordingly, the Mareva injunction covering the defendants' assets outside the jurisdiction would be granted. [1989] 2 W.L.R. 276.

> **DERBY & CO LTD V WELDON (NOS 3 AND 4) 1990**
> (See above.)
> The plaintiffs sought a worldwide Mareva injunction against the third and fourth defendants. Neither of them appeared to have assets within the jurisdiction.

Held

❖ (CA) In suitable cases, the court has jurisdiction to grant a Mareva injunction covering foreign assets. The existence of assets within the jurisdiction was not a precondition for the grant of such an injunction. It was an adequate sanction against the defendant that failure to comply with the injunction would result in him being barred from defending the action. Further, as the injunction operated in personam, it did not offend the principle that courts should not make orders infringing the exclusive jurisdiction of other countries. Accordingly, there was jurisdiction to grant a Mareva injunction. [1990] 1 Ch. 65.

Commentary

It is clear that the courts would require that these safeguards be complied with before the court will be prepared to grant a freezing injunction covering worldwide assets. The sanction for non-compliance was re-emphasised in *Canada Trust Co v Stolzenberg (Mareva injunction)*, *The Times*, November 10, 1997.

Key Principle

In deciding whether to grant permission to enforce a worldwide freezing injunction in a foreign jurisdiction, the court has to be satisfied that it is just and convenient to do so.

> **DADOURIAN GROUP INTERNATIONAL INC V SIMMS 2006**
> This was an action in respect of an arbitration award of US $4.5 million in Switzerland. The claimant obtained a worldwide freezing injunction which contained an undertaking not to enforce the order abroad

without permission. The claimant sought permission to enforce the injunction.

Held

❖ (CA) The court at first instance had failed to take account of the possible oppression of a third party in Switzerland which the claimant would be including in the action. The court also failed to properly consider the law and practice in Switzerland. However, it was prepared to exercise its discretion and allowed the permission to enforce the injunction in Switzerland to stand as it had been proved that there was a real prospect that there were assets in that country and it was reasonable and proportionate for the claimant to seek to enforce the injunction there. [2006] 1 W.L.R. 2499.

Commentary

Arden L.J. noted that this was the first time that the issue of the exercise of the discretion to grant permission to enforce a worldwide freezing injunction had come before it on appeal. The Court of Appeal set out guidelines, which are referred to as the Dadourian guidelines, which governs the grant of permission to enforce a worldwide freezing injunction in a foreign jurisdiction. These are as follows:

[1]   The principle ... is that the grant of that permission should be just and convenient for the purpose of ensuring the effectiveness of the worldwide Freezing Order, and ... that it is not oppressive to the parties to the English proceedings or to third parties who may be joined to the foreign proceedings.

[2]   All the relevant circumstances and options need to be considered. ... Consideration should also be given to the proportionality of the steps proposed to be taken abroad ...

[3]   The interests of the applicant should be balanced against the interests of the other parties to the proceedings and any new party likely to be joined to the foreign proceedings.

[4]   Permission should not normally be given in terms that would enable the [Claimant] to obtain relief in the foreign proceedings which is superior to the relief given by the worldwide Freezing Order.

[5]   The evidence in support of the application for permission should contain all the information ... necessary to make the judge reach an informed decision, including evidence as to the applicable law and practice in the foreign court, evidence as to the nature of the proposed proceedings to be commenced and evidence as to the assets believed to be located in the jurisdiction of the foreign court and the names of the parties by whom such assets are held.

[6]   The standard of proof as to the existence of assets that are both within

the worldwide Freezing Order and within the jurisdiction of the foreign court is a ... real prospect that such assets are located within the jurisdiction of the foreign court ...

[7] There must be .... a risk of dissipation of the assets ....

[8] Normally the application should be made on notice to the Respondent, but in cases of urgency, where it is just to do so, the permission may be given without notice ....

Key Principle

Although a freezing injunction is an equitable remedy, it also operates in rem and can bind third parties.

Z Ltd v A-Z and AA-LL 1982

The plaintiffs had been defrauded of large sums of money that had been, allegedly, paid into accounts at various London banks. Prior to the issue of the writ, the judge granted Mareva injunctions against 36 defendants, which included six clearing banks. A question arose as to the position of third parties that were served with a Mareva injunction.

Held

❖ (CA) A Mareva injunction also acted in rem and therefore everyone with knowledge of the injunction had to comply with the order and was guilty of contempt of court if he assisted in the disposal of the subject matter of the injunction. [1982] 1 Q.B. 558.

Commentary

Unlike normal equitable remedies a freezing injunction acts both in rem and in personam (see *Derby & Co Ltd v Weldon*, above) and can bind third parties who had been served with notice of the injunction. However, as a safeguard, a claimant may be required to undertake to indemnify any third party affected by the order against all reasonably incurred expenses in complying with the order, and all liabilities flowing from this compliance. The House of Lords in *Customs & Excise Commissioners v Barclays Bank* [2006] 3 W.L.R. 1 held that a third party affected by the terms of a freezing order was responsible to the court to comply. This, however, did not place a duty of care on the third party to the claimant. Thus the bank in the case was not under a duty of care towards the Commissioners to take reasonable care to prevent assets leaving the customer's account.

[c] Search orders (previously known as Anton Piller Orders)

Key Principle
The court has jurisdiction to grant an order allowing for the claimant to enter upon the defendant's premises to inspect and remove documents relevant to the case.

> **ANTON PILLER KG V MANUFACTURING PROCESSES LTD 1976**
> The plaintiff alleged that the defendant, who was its agent in England, had been passing confidential information to a rival company. The plaintiff applied for an interim injunction to restrain the defendants from infringing their copyrights and disclosing confidential information and for an order to enter upon the defendant's premises to inspect and remove relevant documentation.

Held
❖ (CA) Where the plaintiff had a strong prima facie case of actual or potential serious damage, and there was clear evidence that the defendants possessed documents that they might destroy or dispose of, the court had an inherent jurisdiction to grant an order for the entry, inspection and removal of relevant material from the defendants' premises. [1976] 1 Ch. 55.

Commentary
Ormrod L.J. identified three criteria which have to be satisfied before the court can exercise its discretion to grant a Search Order on a without notice application. They are that:
(a) there must be a strong prima facie case;
(b) there is serious potential or actual harm to the interests of the plaintiff as a result of the defendant's actions; and
(c) there is clear evidence that the defendant has in his possession incriminating evidence or things and there is a real possibility that this may be destroyed before any with notice hearing application can be made.

Such orders are also available in matrimonial disputes although in practice this appears rare. In *Imerman v Tchenguiz* [2010] EWCA Civ 908, Lord Neuberger stated

" ... there is the availability in the Family Division, just as in the other divisions of the High Court, of Mareva (freezing) and more particularly Anton Piller (search) orders. What is surprising,.., is the extreme rarity in the Family Division of any application for an Anton Piller order".

Key Principle

In cases not involving infringement of intellectual property rights or passing off, the defendant can claim the privilege against self-incrimination and refuse to provide the information or documents.

> TATE ACCESS FLOORS V BOSWELL 1991
>
> The plaintiffs alleged that the defendants had defrauded them of large sums of money and obtained an Anton Piller order against them. The defendants applied to set aside the Anton Piller order relying on the privilege against self-incrimination.

Held

❖ (Ch) The Anton Piller order would be set aside against the first three defendants. Where the privilege against self incrimination applies, it protects the defendant from having to produce and verify documents or information, and would prevent the plaintiff from entering onto premises to search for and seize the documents. [1991] C.L.R. 512.

Commentary

[1] This problem can be avoided if the claimant is able to remove the risk that the information obtained will be used in subsequent criminal proceedings. This is by securing the written agreement of the Crown Prosecution Service (CPS) that they do not wish to make use of this information. As suggested in *AT&T Istel Ltd v Tally* [1993] A.C. 45, a suitable clause to this effect must be included in the order. However, such a clause can only be included if the CPS has given its prior written consent: *United Norwest Co-operative Ltd v Johnstone*, *The Times*, February 24, 1994.

[2] Where the search order may reveal evidence likely to expose the defendant to criminal proceedings, the order must contain a proviso which adequately protects the defendant's right to claim the privilege against self-incrimination: *IBM United Kingdom Ltd v Prime Data International Ltd* [1994] 4 All E.R. 748.

[3] The privilege against self-incrimination is now found in s.7(7) of the Civil Procedure Act 1997.

Key Principle

In cases involving passing off and/or infringement of intellectual property rights, s.72 of the **Supreme Court Act 1981** prevents the defendant from relying on the privilege against self-incrimination.

> COCA COLA CO V GILBEY 1995
> P, one of the defendants, applied to discharge an Anton Piller allowing his premises to be searched in connection with an alleged infringement of the plaintiff's intellectual property rights. P alleged that he would be incriminating himself and exposing himself to the risk of violence.

Held

❖ (Ch) P's application would be dismissed. P could not rely on the privilege against self-incrimination in cases involving infringement of intellectual property rights. Likewise, the risk of violence to P was not a ground upon which such an order could be discharged. [1995] 4 All E.R. 711.

Commentary

Section 72 of the **Supreme Court Act 1981** removes the privilege of non self-incrimination where there is an action based on passing off or infringement of intellectual property rights.

Key Principle

The courts have imposed strict guidelines for the execution or enforcement of the Search Order.

> COLUMBIA PICTURE INDUSTRIES INC V ROBINSON 1987
> The plaintiffs obtained an Anton Piller against the defendant. It was alleged that the defendant had infringed the plaintiff's copyright in films. In the execution of the order, some documents and material were taken which did not form part of the order. Other items were lost whilst in the plaintiff solicitors' custody. The defendant applied to set aside the Anton Piller order and for damages.

Held

❖ (Ch) The purpose of the order was to preserve evidence, where there was a risk of destruction or disposal of such evidence prior to the trial. The plaintiffs and their solicitors had acted oppressively and abused their powers in the execution of the order by seizing and retaining material not covered by the order and subsequently losing it. It was also inappropriate for the solicitors to retain material where there is a dispute as to its ownership. The originals should be returned, once copies have been made, and a detailed record of material taken must be made prior to its removal from the premises. Consequently, the plaintiffs were liable to the defendants in damages, assessed to include aggravated damages. [1987] Ch. 38.

Commentary

Clause 7 of the Practice Direction [Practice Direction (CPR PD25A) (Interim Injunctions) 1999] makes provision for the preservation of evidence and property. It states that:

(a) the supervising solicitor must be experienced on the operation of search orders and independent of the applicant or its solicitors;

(b) the solicitor must explain the terms and effect of the order to the respondent and where the solicitor is a man and the respondent is likely to be an unaccompanied woman, another woman must accompany the solicitor;

(c) the order must be served between office hours, Monday to Friday;

(d) only materials covered by the order can be removed and the search must be in the presence of the respondent or his employee;

(e) the solicitor must compile a list of items taken, checked by the respondent and a report must be provided to the applicant's solicitors who shall serve a copy on the respondents and file a copy in court; and

(f) the search order must not be carried out at the same time as a police search warrant.

These requirements reflect former case law criteria. See *Universal Thermosensors Ltd v Hibben* [1992] 1 W.L.R. 840.

THINK POINT

Is there a distinction between when damages should be awarded in lieu of an order for specific performance and in lieu of an injunction?

Do you think it is appropriate for the courts to extend the grant of a freezing injunction to cover worldwide assets and do you consider that the remedy is effective?

EQUITABLE REMEDIES

Index